SIMPLIFIED APPROACH TO REAL TIME SYSTEM

SIMPLIFIED APPROACH TO REAL TIME SYSTEM

By

Yogyata Jain

Assistant Professor (CSE)

IET Bhaddal, Ropar

(Formerly in Chitkara University Punjab)

UNIVERSITY SCIENCE PRESS

(An Imprint of Laxmi Publications (P) Ltd.)

BANGALORE • CHENNAI • COCHIN • GUWAHATI • HYDERABAD

JALANDHAR • KOLKATA • LUCKNOW • MUMBAI • RANCHI

INDIA • USA • GHANA • KENYA

SIMPLIFIED APPROACH TO REAL TIME SYSTEM

Printed and bound in India
Typeset at Excellent Graphics
First Edition: 2015
USA-9740-150-SIMP APP REAL TIME SYS-JAI
ISBN 978-93-83828-36-4

Published in India by

UNIVERSITY SCIENCE PRESS
(An Imprint of Laxmi Publications Pvt.Ltd.)
113, GOLDEN HOUSE, DARYAGANJ,
NEW DELHI - 110002, INDIA
Telephone : 91-11-4353 2500, 4353 2501
Fax : 91-11-2325 2572, 4353 2528
www.laxmipublications.com info@laxmipublications.com

Branches

©	Bangalore	080-26 75 69 30	
©	Chennai	044-24 34 47 26,	24 35 95 07
©	Cochin	0484-237 70 04,	405 13 03
©	Guwahati	0361-254 36 69,	251 38 81
©	Hyderabad	040-27 55 53 83,	27 55 53 93
©	Jalandhar	0181-222 12 72	
©	Kolkata	033-22 27 43 84	
©	Lucknow	0522-220 99 16	
©	Mumbai	022-24 91 54 15,	24 92 78 69
©	Ranchi	0651-220 44 64	

C—
Printed at:

For my Loving Son

Hirdey Jain

&

Caring Husband

Deepak Jain

Contents

PREFACE

The book is in very simple language. I have tried to ensure that the book clear whole concepts related to real time system. Book is according to PTU syllabus and I have specially made it for PTU students. Daily life and practical examples used in book to clear the concepts more clearly. To achieve this I have made six chapters of this book.

I felt a need to write a book on the subject that was simple and easy to understand. A book can solve general facing problems and provide a comprehensive view of real time system. This thought provided me to write a book on real time system.

Since this book provides comprehensive coverage of basic concepts of real time system avoids complicated mathematical formula and makes minimal assumptions, it will benefit a wide spectrum of audience. This includes students studying RTS for the first time or doing research on RTS; engineers engaged in real time protocol design and marketing people. All will find this book extremely readable and very informative.

Your comments are valuable to me. I will appreciate if you will notify me of any error or admissions in the book. So, please send your comments and valuable suggestions for improvement I will be glad to incorporate your comments for next edition of the book.

— Author

ACKNOWLEDGEMENT

Writing and publishing of this book could not attain successfully without the support of number of people associated with it and sincere efforts made by an author.

Firstly, I would like to thanks worthy chairperson Er. Kulwinder Gurcharan Singh, Director General R. Jha and Associate Director J.S. Kanwar for their valuable direction.

I would also like to thanks Mrs. Jyoti Snehi Assistant Professor CSE Department in Chitkara University Punjab for her valuable guidance.

I would also like to express my sincere gratitude to Dr. Sanjay Singla, HOD CSE Department of IET Bhaddal, Ropar for inspiration and Mrs. Aarti Mahajan, CSE Department Assistant Professor in IET Bhaddal for guiding me.

I would also deeply appreciate the assistance provided by my husband Deepak Jain, my mother in law Rukmani Jain and father in law Arihant Jain for their invaluable help and support for completion of this book.

— Author

OM SAI NATH

SYLLABUS

PUNJAB TECHNICAL UNIVERSITY

JALANDHAR

BOOK IS ACCORDING TO PTU SYLLABUS

CS – 324 REAL TIME SYSTEMS (ELECTIVE I)

Introduction: Definition, Issues in Real Time Computing, Structure of a Real Time System. Task Classes.

Characterizing Real Time Systems and Tasks: Introduction, Performance measures for real time systems: Traditional performance measures, Performability, Cost functions and hard deadlines.

Task Assignment and Scheduling: Introduction, Classical uniprocessor scheduling algorithms: Rate Monotonic, EDF algorithm, Task assignment, Fault tolerant scheduling.

Real Time Databases: Basic definitions, Real time Vs. General purpose databases, Main memory databases, Concurrency control issues, Databases for hard real time systems.

Real Time Communication: Introduction, Architectural issues, Protocols: Contention based protocols, Token based protocols, Deadlines based protocols, Stop and Go Multihop protocol, The polled bus protocol, Hierarchical round robin protocol.

U.A. TECHNICAL UNIVERSITY, DEHRADUN

MCA 5.5 (2) Real Time Systems

Unit-I: Introduction to Real Time Systems, Prioritites, Embedded Systems, Task, Classification & Requirements, Deadlines, Soft, Hard.

Unit-II: Firm Real Time Systems, Introduction to Real Time Operating Systems, Task Management, Inter Process Communication, Case Studies of Maruti II, HART OS, VRTX etc.

Unit-III: Characterizing Real Time Systems and Task, Task Assignment & Scheduling Theory, Fixed and Dynamic Priority Scheduling Uniprocessor (RM and EDF), Multiprocessor (Utilization Balancing, Next-fit for RM & Bin-Packing Assignment for EDF) Scheduling.

Unit-IV: Programming Languages and Tools, Real Time Databases. Real Time Communication, FDDI, Specification and Verification using Duration Calculus, Flow Control, Protocols for Real Time (VTCSMA, Window, IEEE 802.3, IEEE 802.4, IEEE 802.5, Stop and Go Protocol, Media Access Protocol).

Unit-V: Fault, Fault Classes, Fault Tolerant Real Time System, Clocks, Clock Synchronization, Issues in Real Time Software Design.

ANNA UNIVERSITY SYLLABUS

B.Tech CSE – 7th Sem

UNIT I: INTRODUCTION

Introduction-Issues in Real Time Computing, Structure of a Real Time System. Task Classes, Performance Measures for Real Time Systems, Estimating Program Run times. Task Assignment and Scheduling—Classical Uniprocessor Scheduling Algorithms, Uniprocessor Scheduling of IRIS Tasks, Task Assignment, Mode Changes, and Fault Tolerant Scheduling.

UNIT II: PROGRAMMING LANGUAGES AND TOOLS

Programming Language and Tools–Desired Language Characteristics, Data Typing, Control Structures, Facilitating Hierarchical Decomposition, Packages, Run-time (Exception) Error Handling, Overloading and Generics, Multitasking, Low Level Programming, Task Scheduling, Timing Specifications, Programming Environments, Run-time Support.

UNIT III: REAL TIME DATABASES

Real Time Databases—Basic Definition, Real Time Vs. General Purpose Databases, Main Memory Databases, Transaction Priorities, Transaction Aborts, Concurrency Control Issues, Disk Scheduling Algorithms, Two-phase Approach to Improve Predictability, Maintaining Serialization Consistency, Databases for Hard Real Time Systems.

UNIT IV: COMMUNICATION

Real Time Communication—Communications Media, Network Topologies Protocols, Fault Tolerant Routing. Fault Tolerance Techniques—Fault Types, Fault Detection. Fault Error Containment Redundancy, Data Diversity, Reversal Checks, Integrated Failure Handling.

UNIT V: EVALUATION TECHNIQUES

Reliability Evaluation Techniques—Obtaining Parameter Values, Reliability Models for Hardware Redundancy, Software Error Models. Clock Synchronization—Clock, A Nonfault-Tolerant Synchronization Algorithm, Impact of Faults, Fault Tolerant Synchronization in Hardware, Fault Tolerant Synchronization in Software.

GAUTAM BUDDH TECHNICAL UNIVERSITY, LUCKNOW

(TCS 041) REAL TIME SYSTEMS

UNIT-I: INTRODUCTION

Definition, Typical Real Time Applications: Digital Control, High Level Controls, Signal Processing etc., Release Times, Deadlines, and Timing Constraints, Hard Real Time Systems and Soft Real Time Systems, Reference Models for Real Time Systems: Processors and Resources, Temporal Parameters of Real Time Workload, Periodic Task Model, Precedence Constraints and Data Dependency.

UNIT-II: REAL TIME SCHEDULING

Common Approaches to Real Time Scheduling: Clock Driven Approach, Weighted Round Robin Approach, Priority Driven Approach, Dynamic Versus Static Systems, Optimality of Effective-Deadline-First (EDF) and Least-Slack-Time-First (LST) Algorithms, Offline Versus Online Scheduling, Scheduling Aperiodic and Sporadic jobs in Priority Driven and Clock Driven Systems.

UNIT-III: RESOURCES ACCESS CONTROL

Effect of Resource Contention and Resource Access Control (RAC), Nonpreemptive Critical Sections, Basic Priority-Inheritance and Priority-Ceiling Protocols, Stack Based Priority-Ceiling Protocol, Use of Priority-Ceiling Protocol in Dynamic Priority Systems, Preemption Ceiling Protocol, Access Control in Multiple-Unit Resources, Controlling Concurrent Accesses to Data Objects.

UNIT-IV: MULTIPROCESSOR SYSTEM ENVIRONMENT

Multiprocessor and Distributed System Model, Multiprocessor Priority-Ceiling Protocol, Schedulability of Fixed-Priority End-to-End Periodic Tasks, Scheduling Algorithms for End-to-End Periodic Tasks, End-to-End Tasks in Heterogeneous Systems, Predictability and Validation of Dynamic Multiprocessor Systems, Scheduling of Tasks with Temporal Distance Constraints.

UNIT-V: REAL TIME COMMUNICATION

Model of Real Time Communication, Priority-Based Service and Weighted Round-Robin Service Disciplines for Switched Networks, Medium Access Control Protocols for Broadcast Networks, Internet and Resource Reservation Protocols, Real Time Protocols, Communication in Multicomputer System, An Overview of Real Time Operating Systems.

1

Real Time Systems

1.1 INTRODUCTION

Real time systems respond to the input immediately. They follow timing constraints. They have to give their outputs in time. Producing the output, after precise time degrade system performance, leads to catastrophic failure and sometimes output is useless for both systems and users. They have to the response in the order of milliseconds or in a microsecond. Deadlines are necessary and must be fulfilled for the proper functioning (output) of the system. A failing system is not able to achieve its tasks with definite deadlines. Deadlines of all the tasks must meet, regardless of system load. Example is a printer, phone and fax machines, driving a vehicle such as cars and others. Non real time system does not follow these conditions; they do not have any timing constraints.

Characteristics of Real Time System:

There are certain features of real time system as shown in Fig. 1.1:

1. Real time systems respond to the input immediately.
2. They follow timing constraints.
3. Real time systems deliver output on time. As output produced after the time constraints do not have any affect.
4. Failure to respond is as bad as the wrong response.
5. They produce outputs within specific deadlines.

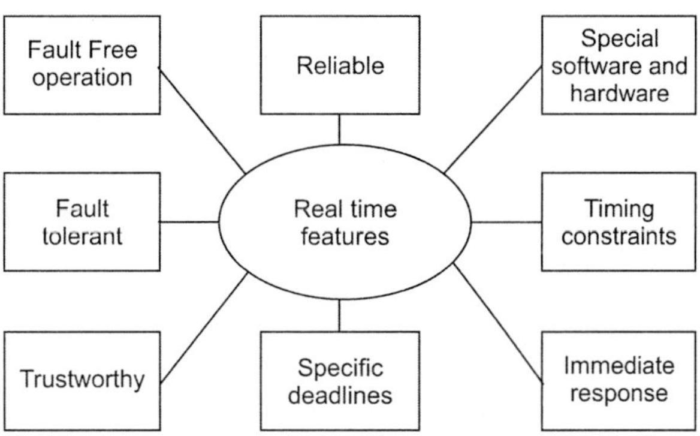

Fig. 1.1. Real time features.

6. Real time systems are trustworthy.
7. Real time systems are more reliable than a Non-real time system.
8. Real time systems fault tolerant.
9. Real time systems have certain hardware and software requirements to complete their tasks within a specific time.

1.2 ARCHITECTURE OF REAL TIME SYSTEM

The architecture of a real time system also knows as block diagram, structure, or components of a real time system. To understand the Architecture of Real Time System, consider an example of an aircraft control system. Controlled process is that by which functioning of the aircraft will be controlled by using brakes, accelerators and others as shown in Fig. 1.2.

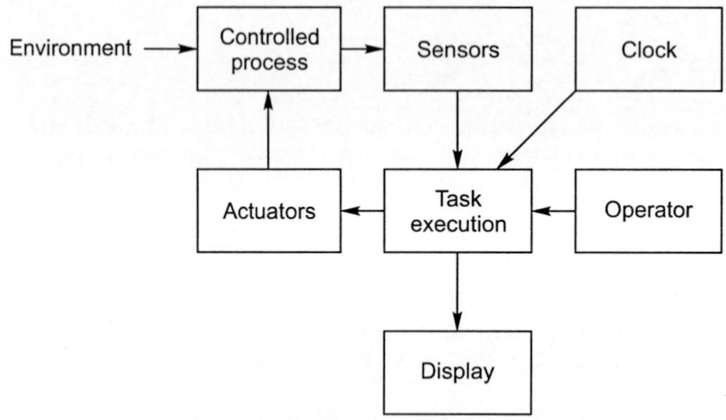

Fig. 1.2. Real time architecture.

Sensors sensed the data and maintained the proper flow of aircraft. As the system has numbered of tasks to perform, the system, which is having the highest priority will execute first and the other will be later. Sensor checked the proper flow of execution. Task execution takes the help of the operator to operate or execute the task. Monitors or Actuators get the final output. Actuators will pass the output to control process for the feedback. Given tasks should be completed in a specific time, and this will be maintained by a clock.

Rates: Includes sensors and actuators, peripheral and control program.

Phases: Includes takeoff, cruise, and landing, etc.

1.3 REAL TIME SYSTEM TASKS

Real time system tasks value functions because they produce their output in time, these tasks understand the value of time. Output should be finite or within a specified period. Example of value functions or types of real time system tasks are:

1. Hard Real Time System (HRTS)
2. Soft Real Time System (SRTS)
3. Firm Real Time System (FRTS)

Hard Real Time Systems (HRTS): The systems in which task must be completed within a specific time or deadline. It is mandatory to produce the output within a specific time or deadlines as shown in Fig. 1.3. For example, flight control systems, Aircraft and Nuclear Power Plant system.

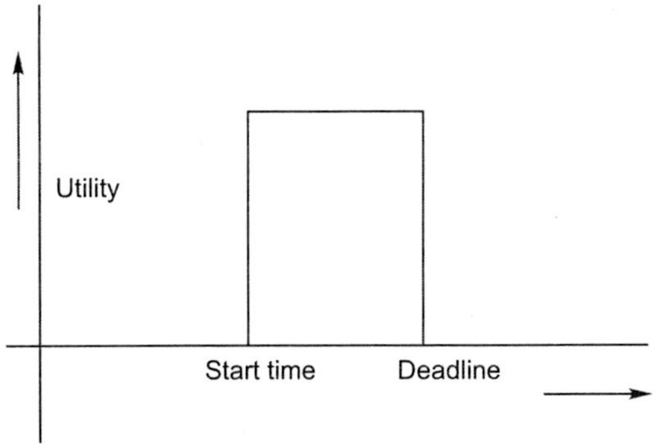

Fig. 1.3. Hard real time systems.

The characteristics of such systems are:

(*a*) Hard real time systems are safety critical, these systems consider the safe side of the user (user can be a patient, a pilot, etc.)

(*b*) Hard real time systems are mission critical; these systems achieve the goal of the system with-in specified deadlines.

(*c*) Producing the output after the specific deadline may lead to chance of occurring life loss or big financial damage.

Consider an example of aircraft:

Aircraft system must respond to the input immediate, if it does not do so then it will cause:

- A hole in the ground
- Catastrophic failure
- Life loss
- Big financial damage
- Aircraft will not be controllable.

Soft Real Time Systems (SRTS): Soft real time system also responds to input immediately within a specific time, but sometimes systems will still function correctly although some of its deadlines are missing as shown in Fig. 1.4. Missing deadlines degrade the system performance. For example, online transaction systems, airline reservation systems, etc.

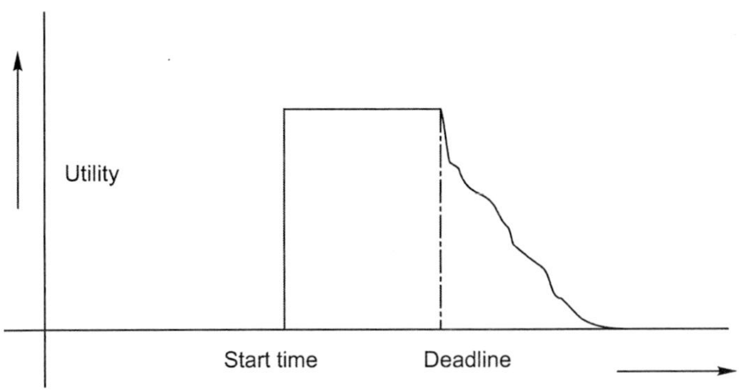

Fig. 1.4. Soft real time systems.

The characteristics of such systems are:

- The deadline can miss occasionally.
- No catastrophic failure occurs.
- These systems are less expensive.
- Produce output in terms of Quality-of-Service (QoS).

Firm Real Time Systems (FRTS): These systems are like soft real time system but late delivery of service is not tolerable as shown in Fig. 1.5. Its examples are Audio and Video Conferencing.

The characteristics of such systems are:

- Missing deadlines leads to financial loss.
- Recovery is possible, but not easily.
- Produces outdated output, if a task does not follow a deadline.
- Examples are forecasted systems.

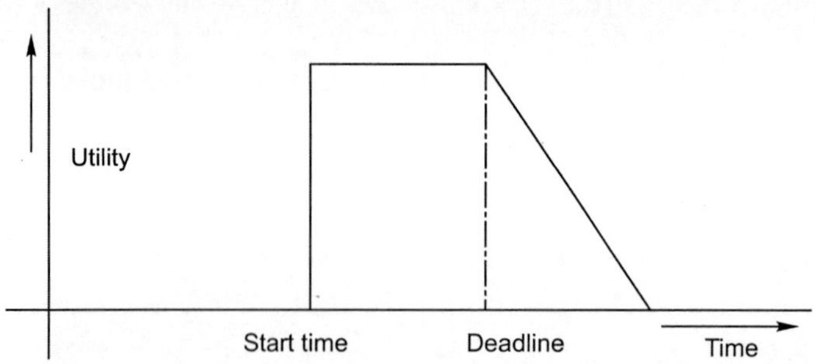

Fig. 1.5. Firm real time systems.

1.3.1 Task Classes

The task could classify in two ways: By the predictability of their arrival and by the consequences of they are not executing on time as shown in Fig. 1.6. Timing Constraints are of three types:

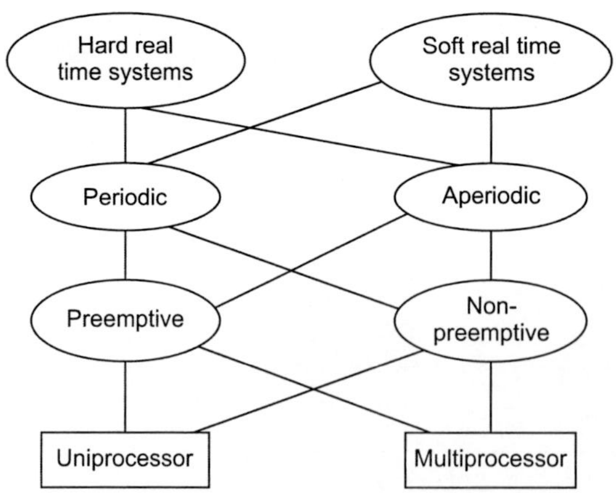

Fig. 1.6. Real time system tasks.

1. Periodic and Aperiodic Tasks

- **Periodic tasks:** These tasks occur at regular intervals of time. These tasks follow hard deadlines and their period occurred in the worst-case execution.
- **Aperiodic tasks:** These tasks are event-driven and generated randomly. Aperiodic tasks tend to have soft deadlines.
- **Sporadic tasks:** These tasks are as aperiodic tasks with minimum inter-arrival time. Sporadic tasks are aperiodic in nature, but they have hard deadlines.
- These tasks handle emergency conditions and exceptional situations.

2. Critical and Non-critical Tasks

(*a*) **Critical tasks:** These tasks cannot miss their deadlines and completed in specific time *e.g.* Aircraft Control System.

(*b*) **Non-critical tasks:** These are like soft real time system in which deadline can be missing, but it leads to performance degradation.

3. Preemptive and Non-preemptive Tasks

(*a*) **Preemptive tasks:** A task preempted by other tasks. The task having the shortest deadline assigned a highest-priority and another one assigned a lower priority task. Only a higher-priority task can preempt a lower priority task. High priority tasks will execute first and the other will be later.

(*b*) **Non-preemptive tasks:** A task cannot preempt by any other tasks. A higher priority task cannot preempt lower priority tasks, although higher priority tasks miss its deadlines.

Comparison between tasks and functions:

Tasks and functions are sometimes similar but there are some important differences.

Table 1.1. Tasks vs. functions.

S. No.	Functions	Task
1.	Functions can return a value.	A Task cannot return a value.
2.	A function can only enable other functions.	A task can enable a function or other tasks.
3.	Execution of a function involves at least one argument passing.	A task can have zero or more arguments.
4.	Function execution does not follow any deadline.	Task execution must follow specific deadlines.
5.	A function can perform its function in zero simulation time.	Tasks can execute both in zero simulations and in non-zero simulation time.

1.3.2 Comparison between HRTS and SRTS

Comparison between hard real time systems and soft real time system with their characteristics listed below:

Table 1.2. HRTS vs. SRTS.

S.No.	Characteristics	HRTS	SRTS
1.	Response time	Hard required	Soft desired
2.	Peak load performance	Predictable	Degraded
3.	Control of pace	Environment	Computer
4.	Safety	Often Critical	Non critical
5.	Size of data files	Small/Medium	Large
6.	Data Integrity	Short term	Long Term

1.4 REAL TIME COMPUTING ISSUES

A real time system must be more reliable than a non-real time system. These systems should be able to run in any environment. Real time computing systems differ from other systems in two ways:

- Real time systems are more specific in nature.
- Missing deadlines sometimes lead to severe damage.

Its examples are, CPU Scheduling or task scheduling. Scheduling of real time systems discussed in the next chapters.

Example:

Task Scheduling: Real time system does not use Round- Robin scheduling. Task-Execution time should be predictable in a real time system.

1.5 REAL TIME WORLD

Real time applications are everywhere; it has many applications starting from tiny to very large and these applications cover the whole world as shown in Fig. 1.7.

Fig. 1.7. Real time system world.

Soft Deadlines Example

Kitchen applications: Fridge, microwave cooker, and bread maker are examples of soft deadlines. These applications are very tiny, and their working is similar. These applications execute with some events, follow timing constraints in order of milliseconds or microseconds. These applications have user interface, and these interfaces are buttons and digital display.

Entertainment products: VCR, MP3, DVD player and TV are examples of soft deadlines. These applications execute with some events, follow timing constraints in order of milliseconds or microseconds. These applications have user interface, and these interfaces can be internal or external to the product.

Health goods: Syringe pump, blood pressure meter and blood-glucose meter are examples of soft deadlines. These applications are very small, and their working is similar. These applications execute with some events, follow time constraints in order of milliseconds or microseconds and measure with real-world guidelines. These applications have user interface, and these interfaces are buttons and digital display. In these, the delivery devices have hard deadlines, and the monitoring devices have soft deadlines.

Hard Deadline Example

Workplace goods: Printer, phone and fax machines are examples of hard deadlines. They must respond to the input immediate within a specific time. These applications handle real time data. These applications execute with some external events, follow timing constraints in order of milliseconds or microseconds. These applications are a mixture of soft and hard deadlines. These applications have a user interface, and these interfaces are buttons and digital display.

Other Applications

1. **Multimedia:** Real time system is widely used in multimedia applications such as audio and video conferencing and Tele's seminars. It accesses locally and remotely by different users. In an example of four people are interacting with each other through the internet as shown in Fig. 1.8.
2. **Medical care system:** Diagnose and monitor the patient disease within a specific time. Data accessed from a clinical database as shown in Fig. 1.9. Monitoring alarms indicate the serious disease; it starts to vibrate when a problem appears in the patient. Doctor can access the real data from the internet and can talk or chat with their friends by informing them patient disease. This system is widely used in rural areas in which doctor facility is not fully available.

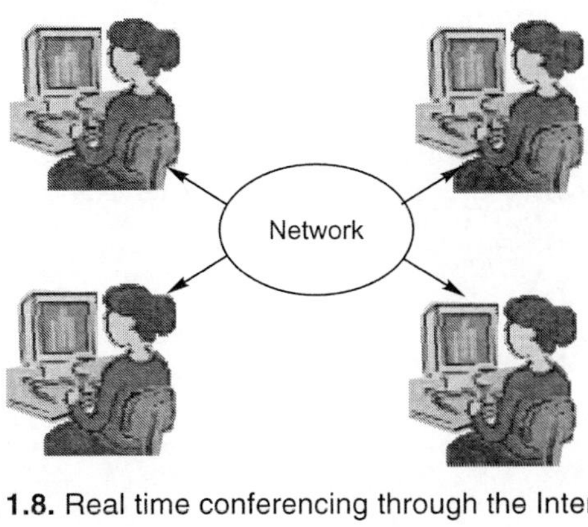

Fig. 1.8. Real time conferencing through the Internet.

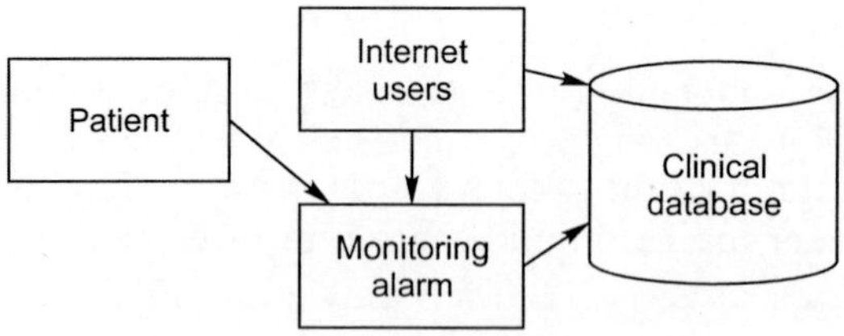

Fig. 1.9. Real time system in medical.

3. **Flight control system:** These systems mainly consider the safety of a pilot. Controlled process controls the complete process as shown in Fig. 1.10.

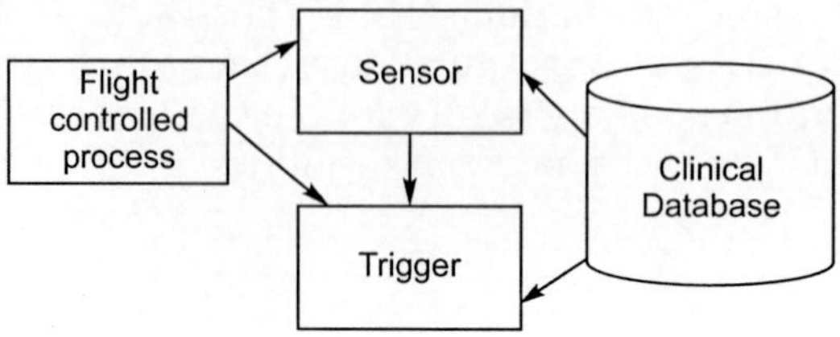

Fig. 1.10. Real time system in flights.

The clinical database contains the total data. Sensors sense the input data and trigger execute the task a user wants to perform.

4. **A nuclear power plant system:** Sensor senses the data and trigger execute the task and produced output as shown in Fig. 1.11. The database contains the whole data. Sensors sense the input data and controlled process controls the entire operation. Trigger executes the task a user wants to perform.

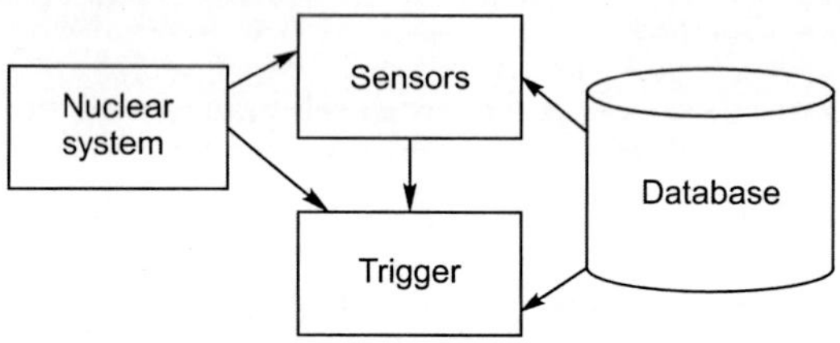

Fig. 1.11. Nuclear plants.

1.6 REAL TIME OPERATING SYSTEM

Real Time Operating Systems specially used for real time applications. They produce the result in specific time following the timing constraints. An embedded system there is no operating system as shown in Fig. 1.12.

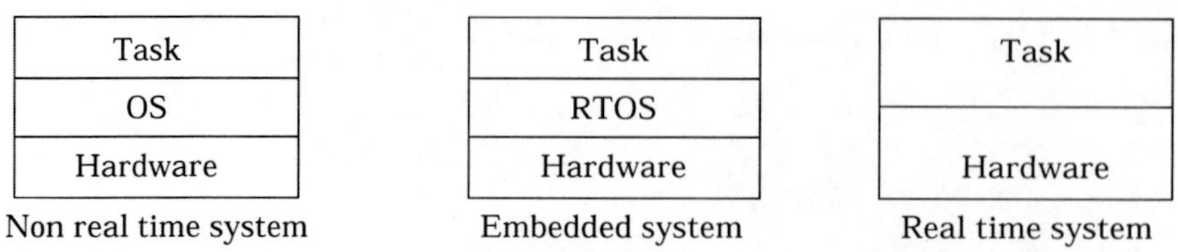

Fig. 1.12. RTOS.

1.7 REAL TIME SYSTEM COMPONENTS

It has mainly three components as shown in Fig. 1.13.

These are:

1. Controlled process
2. Sensors
3. Output.

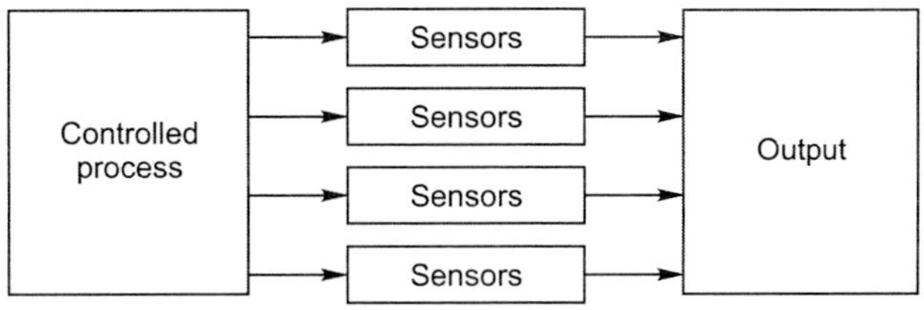

Fig. 1.13. Real time components.

1.8 PROGRAMMING STYLES

It follows five programming styles as shown in Fig. 1.14. These are:

- **Imperative Language:** It is sequential language and its example is Ada.
- **Functional Language:** It is recursive language and its example is Lisp.
- **Declarative Language:** It is logic language and its example is Prolog.
- **Data Flow Machines:** Its example is Luster.
- **Finite States Machine:** Its example is synchronous language.

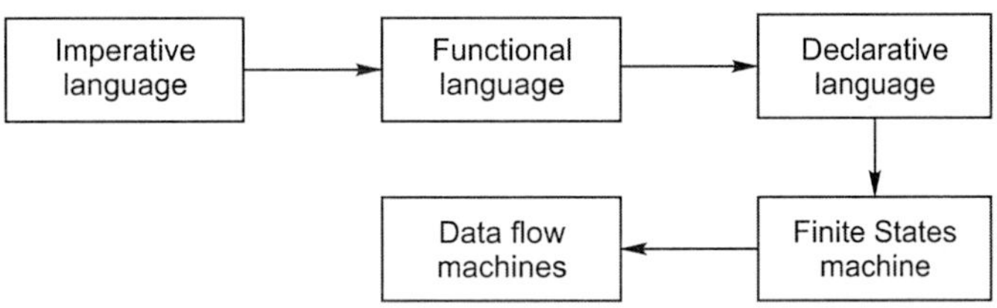

Fig. 1.14. Real time languages style.

1.9 COMMUNICATION BASED MODEL

Processors and resources interact with each other as shown in Fig. 1.15.

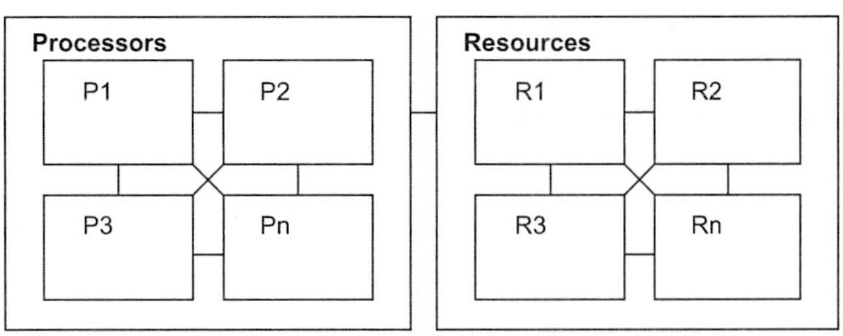

Fig. 1.15. RTS model.

SUMMARY

- Real time systems respond to the input immediately.
- They follow timing constraints.
- Output produced, after specific time leads to catastrophic failure.
- They have to respond in order of milliseconds or in microseconds.
- All tasks must meet deadlines, regardless of system load.
- A system said to failing, when a system is not able to achieve its tasks with specific deadlines.
- Real time systems are trustworthy and fault tolerant.
- Real time system uses various task classes such as critical, non-critical, preemptive and non-preemptive tasks and others.
- Real time systems have certain hardware and software requirements to complete their tasks within a specific time.

EXERCISES

1. What is virtual memory?
2. What is throughput, turnaround time, waiting time and response time?
3. What is the state of the processor, when a process is waiting for some event to occur?
4. What is the important aspect of a real time system or mission critical systems?
5. What is the difference between hard and soft real time systems?
6. What is hard disk and what is its purpose?
7. What is CPU scheduler?
8. What is context switch?
9. What is cache memory?
10. What is a real time system?
11. List the important considerations when selecting a processor.
12. List out the uses of RTC
13. Define a system.
14. What are the two essential units of a processor on an embedded system?
15. Give examples for the general-purpose processor.
16. Define Real Time Clock (RTC).
17. Name the important terms of the RTOS
18. Define processes.
19. What meant by PCB?
20. Define tasks and Task state.
21. Define Task Control Block (TCB).
22. Draw the process state transitions.
23. What are the goals of RTOS?
24. What is RTOS?
25. List the functions of a kernel. What are the two methods by which a running requests resources?
26. What are the functions of device manager?

27. What is the difference between real time sharing and time-sharing?
28. Define the effect of missing deadline.
29. Define catastrophic failure.
30. Give examples of hard, soft and firm real time system.
31. Give the applications of real time systems.

Fill in the Blanks

1. Real time system responds in the order of ______ seconds.
2. Deadlines of all the tasks must meet, regardless of system ______ .
3. ______ further pass the output to controlled process for the feedback.
4. Hard real time systems are ______ and ______ critical.
5. Producing the output after the specific deadline may lead to chances of occurring ______ or ______ damage.
6. ______ Deadlines degrade the system performance.
7. In Firm real time system, late delivery of service is not ______ .
8. In preemptive task, a task can be ______ by other tasks.
9. A task can have ______ or ______ arguments.
10. Round Robin scheduling is ______ used in real time system.

True/False

1. Deadlines of all the tasks must meet, regardless of system load. (T/F)
2. Fridge, microwave and cooker are an example of hard deadlines. (T/F)
3. Syringe pump, blood pressure meter and blood glucose meter are examples of soft deadlines. (T/F)
4. Printer, phone and fax machines are examples of hard deadlines. (T/F)
5. Real time system is widely used in multimedia applications. (T/F)
6. Real time operating systems not used for real time applications. (T/F)
7. A real time system is more reliable than non-real time system. (T/F)
8. Real time systems are trustworthy. (T/F)
9. Real time systems are not fault tolerant. (T/F)
10. Actuator used for feedback in real time system. (T/F)

MULTIPLE CHOICE QUESTIONS

1. HRTS stands for
   (*a*) Hard rare time system (*b*) Human resource transaction system
   (*c*) Hard real time system (*d*) All of the above
2. In real time system, actuator is used for:
   (*a*) Feedback (*b*) Producing noise
   (*c*) Introducing interference (*d*) Sensing the data
3. The trigger is used to
   (*a*) Input the data (*b*) Output the data
   (*c*) Executing task (*d*) None of the above

4. Missing a deadline may lead to:
(*a*) Catastrophic failure (*b*) Financial loss
(*c*) Human loss (*d*) All of the above

5. Which system produces QoS?
(*a*) HRTS (*b*) SRTS
(*c*) FRTS (*d*) All of the above

6. Audio and video conferencing is used in
(*a*) HRTS (*b*) SRTS
(*c*) FRTS (*d*) All of the above

7. Which scheduling is not used in real time system?
(*a*) RM (*b*) DM
(*c*) Round Robin (*d*) None of the above

8. Workplace goods are examples of:
(*a*) HRTS (*b*) SRTS
(*c*) FRTS (*d*) All of the above

9. Kitchen appliances are examples of:
(*a*) HRTS (*b*) SRTS
(*c*) FRTS (*d*) All of the above

10. Health goods are examples of:
(*a*) HRTS (*b*) SRTS
(*c*) FRTS (*d*) All of the above.

QUESTIONNAIRES

1. What is real time system?

Ans. Real time systems respond to the input immediately. They have some specific time called timing constraints in which they have to give their outputs. Producing the output, after specific time degrade system performance, leads to catastrophic failure and sometimes output is useless for both system and user. They have to respond in order of milliseconds or in microseconds.

A CAR-AND-DRIVE EXAMPLE

The driver is the real time controller, the car is the controlled process, and the other cars together with the road conditions and weather make up the operating environment.

2. Explain all types of system
(*i*) Soft real time system
(*ii*) Hard real time system

Ans. (*i*) **Soft real time system:** missing deadlines leads to system performance degradation. Its examples are online transaction systems and electronic games etc.

(*ii*) **Hard real time system:** The systems in which task must be completed within a specific time or deadline. It is compulsory to produce the output within specified time or deadlines.

3. What are the issues in real time system?

Ans. A real time computer must be very reliable than its individual hardware and software component. It must be capable of working in harsh environments.

For example, task scheduling. Real time computer is important in two ways. Firstly, they are much more specific in their applications, and second, the consequence of failure leads to catastrophic failure.

4. Define real time database.

Ans. Real time database is used to store refers to a spectrum of information systems, ranging from stock price quotation systems, to track records databases, to real time file systems. A real time database contains image objects that represent a real world object. For example, air traffic controls database contains image objects represent aircraft in the courage area.

5. Explain release time, deadlines and timing constraints.

Ans. Release time: The release time of job is the time at which the job becomes available for execution. The job can be scheduled and executed at any time on or after its release time whenever its data and control dependency conditions met.

6. Describe Trigger Generator.

Ans. The "Trigger generator" is the mechanism used to trigger the execution of individual jobs. It is not a separate hardware while it is part of the executive software. Its jobs are periodic in nature, *i.e.*, they execute regularly. The Schedule for these jobs obtained offline and obtained from a scheduler.

7. Explain all types of tasks classes in real time system

Or

Explain the concept of periodic and a periodic task with the help of suitable example.

Ans. There are five types of task classes:

(*i*) Periodic and aperiodic tasks

(*ii*) Sporadic task

(*iii*) Critical task

(*iv*) Non-critical task

(1) **Periodic task:** There are many tasks in real time systems done repetitively. For example, one may wish to monitor the speed altitude and attitude of an aircraft every 100 ms.

(2) **Aperiodic task:** These tasks occur only occasionally. For example, it is used when the pilot wishes to execute a large number of subtasks of a task.

(3) **Sporadic task:** These tasks bounded with imperative time called sporadic tasks.

(4) **Critical tasks:** Critical tasks are those whose timely executions are critical; if deadlines missed, catastrophic failure can occur. Critical tasks often executed at a higher frequency than other tasks.

(5) **Noncritical tasks:** these tasks are not critical to the application. Sometimes they become useless if not completed within a deadline. The goal of these tasks is to maximize the percentage of jobs successfully executed within their deadlines.

8. Explain issues in real time system.

Ans. Architecture Issues:

(*a*) **Processor architecture:** because of the cost factor, off-the-shelf processors are generally used, real time designs seldom design their own processor, for this reason, the processor architecture is not treated by real time system designer.

(*b*) **Network architecture:** To make systems reliable provides sufficient processing capacity, most real time systems are multiple processor machine.

(*c*) **Architecture for clock synchronization:** In order to facilitate the interaction between the multiple units of a real time system, clocks synchronized and preferably used.

(*d*) **Fault-tolerance and reliability evaluation:** Real time system must be reliable and fault-tolerant.

Operating System Issues:

(*a*) **Task assignment and scheduling:** The scheduling of tasks done to meet the time deadlines which is the goal of a real time operating system.

(*b*) **Communication protocols:** have inter-processor communication that has the predictable delays and is controllable.

(*c*) **Failure management and recovery:** when a processor or software module fails, the system must limit such failure and recover from it.

(*d*) **Clock synchronization algorithm:** uses locked locks for hardware synchronization.

Other Issues:

(*a*) **Programming languages:** real times engineers need much greater control our timing and used to interface to the special purpose device.

(*b*) **Databases:** Real time database applications are stock market, airline, reservations and artificial, Intelligence.

(*c*) **Performance measures:** Commonly used performance measures such as conventional reliability and throughput are useless for real time systems.

2 Characterizing Real Time Systems

2.1 REAL TIME SYSTEM PERFORMANCE MEASURE

Real time systems are everywhere. They appear both in small and large applications. They can start from video gasmes to control and monitoring system of a nuclear power plant. The behaviours of these systems are such that they have to respond to input immediately. Often these systems response times are in the order of milliseconds or in microseconds.

If the nuclear control and monitoring system does not respond to meltdown conditions quickly, subsequently there may be a sequence or catastrophic failure. In video games, if the system does not respond quickly then life will damage or loss in the virtual world. Time is an essential part of a real time computer system. Real time systems have unique challenges to the description, growth and testing of software.

Real time systems used for critical applications. Thus, the system must be carefully:

- Designed
- Validated before operation.

Validated implies

1. The system design checked using formal and informal methods.
2. The system must be able to describe performance and reliability.

It is the first choice of performance measures. Performance refers to the response time or throughput (when systems respond to the user), and this is checked by the users each time. Performance measures must be brief. Performance measure takes actual requirement of the system and leaves the others.

Example 1: Sometimes performance depends on the system, the way a system response. Suppose a typewriter is typing on a terminal. He sees the response to the terminal. If the typing speed and seeing on the display is not noticeable, then it is perfect and otherwise performance will be degraded. User is typing continuously, but output is not showing on the screen then it become useless for the user.

Example 2: Another example is of pacemaker. Performance metrics of pacemaker is:

- Response time
- Battery power.

A pacemaker does not need to be very fast, but it should be so fast that it gives the guarantees of patient health and safety. A failing system is not able to achieve its tasks with required deadlines. Deadlines of all the tasks must meet, regardless of system load. A pacemaker will fail if it does not respond to a change in pulse rate of the patient within a specific time so that discomfort or cardiac damage cannot occur.

Pacemaker performance criterion determines the success if there will be healthy patient, and the pacemaker will be failed if there will be injured patient and, which may lead to death of the patient.

Example 3: An example of a flight control system, where the system must pass flight control information from the pilot to the flight controls in a timely manner in order to control the aircraft in flight. This performance criterion is critical. The performance of the flight control system ensures the safety of the aircraft and pilot. In this example, the environments in which this system operates and the rates at which they interact are all important.

Example 4: An example is an industrial robot, which has to produce various products to meet production margins of the month in an Industry. This is a very critical task, because a single product manufactured by following various steps and environment interaction. System designer needs to work hard.

2.2 PROPERTIES OF PERFORMANCE MEASURE

Performance depends on many factors, because it relates to various different things. Some performances are measurable and others are not. The performance of real time system divided into three groups:

1. **Qualitative Binary Criteria:** This criteria measure the quality of real time system. It is not in terms of quantity, but includes timing constraints, behaviour and correct functional correctness of the system. All these terms related to one another, without this system, quality could not measure as shown in Fig. 2.1.
2. **Qualitative Regular Criteria:** This is not relates to quantity. It relates to the safety of the both systems and user. This criteria deal with Reliability and flexibility of the system. The system should fault tolerant. The system should be able to work in any environment, in the worst-case condition regardless of the system load.
3. **Quantitative Criteria:** This criterion measures the quantity of the real time system using various metrics.

A good performance measure must:

- Represent an efficient encoding of relevant information
- Provide an objective basis for the ranking of candidate controllers for a given application

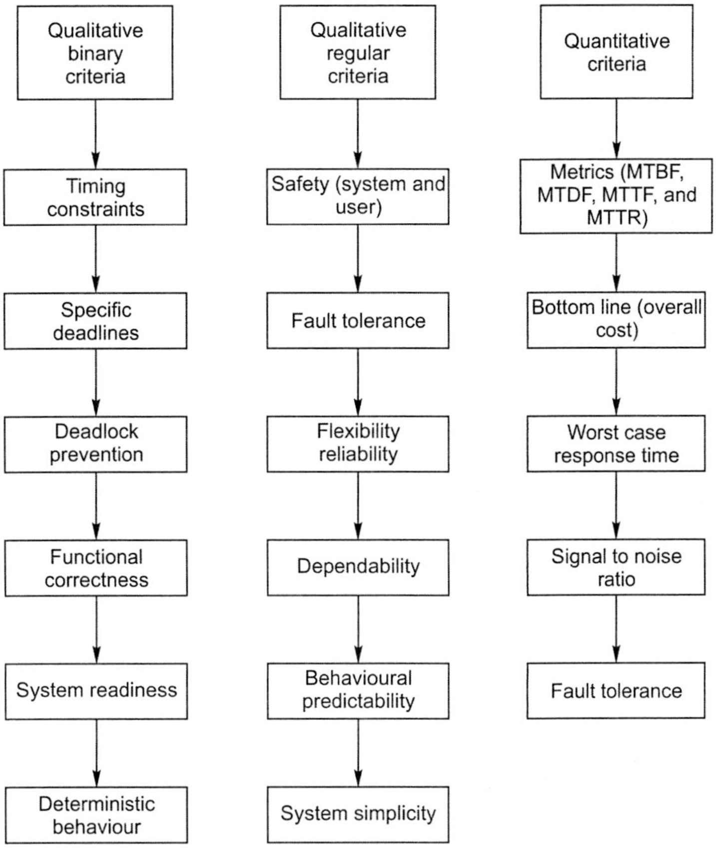

Fig. 2.1. Performance measures of real time system.

- Provide objective optimization criteria for design
- Represent verifiable facts.

This is showing in Fig. 2.2.

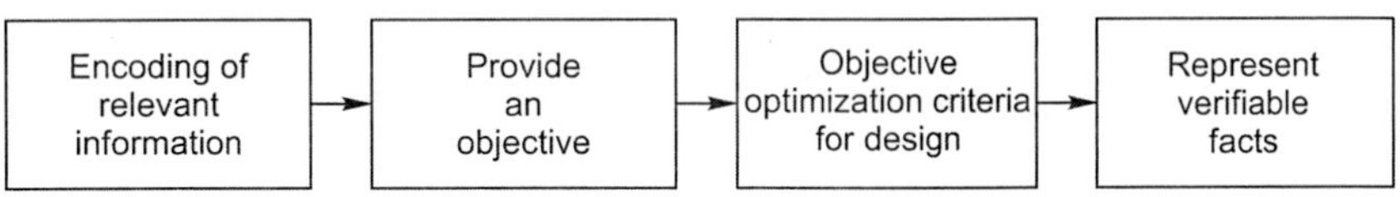

Fig. 2.2. Good performance measure.

Encoding of relevant information: Real time system provides accurate and actual information according to the requirements of the user within specific deadlines. It must full fill the requirement of the user. It has the ability to meet all deadlines.

Provide an objective a given application: Real time system must provide output in specified time. Time is an essential part for a real time computer system.

Provide objective optimization criteria for design: Optimization technique followed while designing a real time system.

Represent verifiable facts: Real time system must provide accurate and actual information a user needs with in specific deadlines.

2.2.1 Traditional Performance Measure

There are certain various traditional methods of measuring real time system performance as shown in Fig. 2.3. These are:

- Reliability is the probability the system will not fail in an interval.
- Availability is the portion of time for a system will be available.
- Throughput is the average number of instructions per unit time that a system can process.
- Capacity Reliability (CR): Capacity of the system, even work in high load conditions called the worst case.
- Expected capacity survival time is the expected time for CR will work in continuity.
- Computational availability: This is the expected value of the system computation capacity at any given time.
- Cost Functions (CF) for hard deadlines: Cost vs. Response times, response time—the time take for the system to generate output from any associated input.
- Mean computation before failure.
- Computational reliability.
- Per formability.
- Accomplishment Levels (AL).

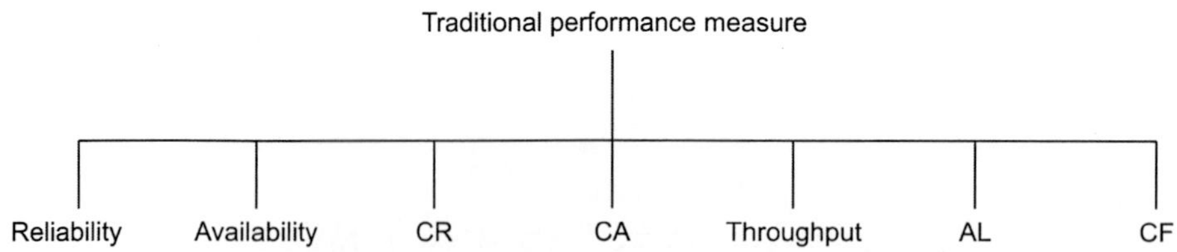

Fig. 2.3. Traditional performance measure.

The correctness of a real time system depends not only on the logical result of the computation, but also on the time at which the results produced.

Drawbacks of traditional performance measure:

- Reliability depends on either the hardware or software, independent of each other
- Availability cannot achieve practically because it cannot meet execution deadlines.
- Throughput does not measure response time.
- Hardware, software and the application software do not relate with each other.

2.3 PERFORMABILITY

Performability means a system should be able to perform even in the presence of faults. It is the combination of performance and reliability. It is the trustworthiness of a system, which means that fault appearance put less impact on the system performance. Performability tests to check system performance applied to all kinds of hardware, software components and fault tolerant systems. Reliability checks whether the system is reliable or not. Actually, reliability is the probability of failure-free operation in a specific time in a finite environment. Real world systems do not only fail; they can also be degraded. A degradable system is that which gives the output after the specific time. To measure the performability, various metrics are used. This metric called performance metrics. This metric can be in terms of quality or quantity. Some performance metrics related to timing, *e.g.*, the response time or execution time, while others related to quality, *e.g.*, precision, or efficiency of an operation. The quality of a system measured, if a system is present at that time. Performance metric measures fault free operation because they do not depend on faults and failures, so they only measure a quality of failure-free operation. Reliability and performance measured independently. Reliability measures an occurrence of failures, and performance is only measurable during failure-free operation. It used in systems in which they have just two states called binary up and down.

As shown in Fig. 2.4, performability analysis can have different scopes.

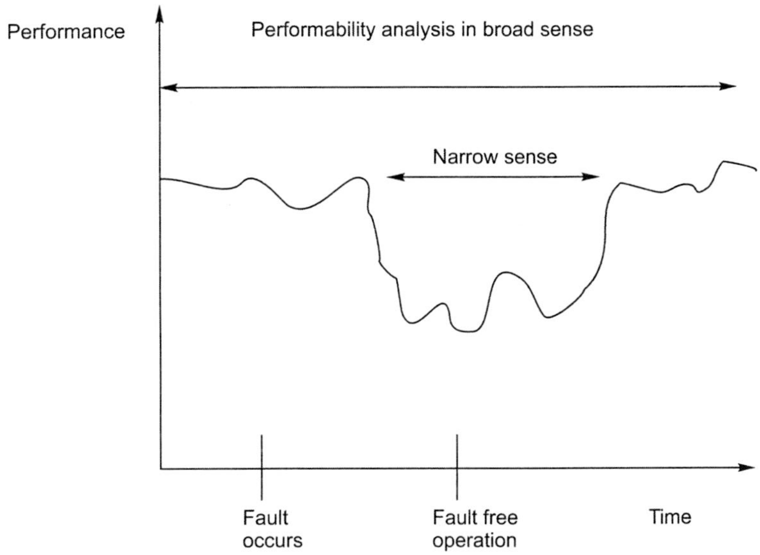

Fig. 2.4. Scope of performability.

Performability analysis in the narrow sense informs the quality of a service only between fault occurrence and fault-free operation. Performability analysis in the wide sense quantifies the quality of a service over the complete operation. Consequently, the performability analysis in the extended sense overlaps in some way with normal performance analysis.

Performability improves traditional performance measures by:

- Explicitly
- Formally accounting for the fact that the performance of a real time computer should be tied to the consequent performance of the process that it controls.

The controlled process is having several accomplishment levels, the levels a user has to achieve. Every level is associated with the execution of a certain set of control tasks. To accomplish each control task requires the real time computer to run a set of control algorithms. Performability defined as the probability that the computer system will allow each accomplishment level to meet.

More formally, if there are n accomplishment levels:

$$A_1, A_2, A_3, A_4 \ldots\ldots, A_n,$$

The Performability of the real time system is given by

$$P(A_1), P(A_2), \ldots\ldots, P(A_n)$$

where, $P(A_i)$ is the probability of achieving the desired task.

2.3.1 Performability Hierarchy

As shown in Fig. 2.5, in performability hierarchy, there are 4 views. Each view is more detailed than the one above it. Each view driven by the requirements of the one above it and receives input from the one below it. By defining the accomplishment levels, traditional performance measures will reduce.

Throughput = Accomplishment level – number of jobs processed per unit time.

View 0: specifies the variables of the controlled process, what actually a user wants to achieve (Accomplishment Levels). For example, in case of the car driving case, the user has to run the car smoothly by following controlled process instructions.

View 1: is more detailed in specifying the controlled process tasks that must be run. It specifies that the task will complete in a specific time or deadlines. The controlled process task is to run car smoothly by controlling brakes, accelerators and others.

View 2: is more detail in that it specifies which algorithms run to meet each of the controlled-process tasks in View 1.

View 3: considers the hardware structure, the OS and the application software attributes to run the real time system smoothly.

Example: Landing portion of a flight.

The aircraft has an automatic landing system, which allows it to land even in zero-visibility weather. If the automatic-landing feature on the airport is not working when the landing phase begins, and if the destination airport has low-visibility weather, the aircraft diverted to another airport. If the automatic landing feature fails during the automatic landing, there is a crash.

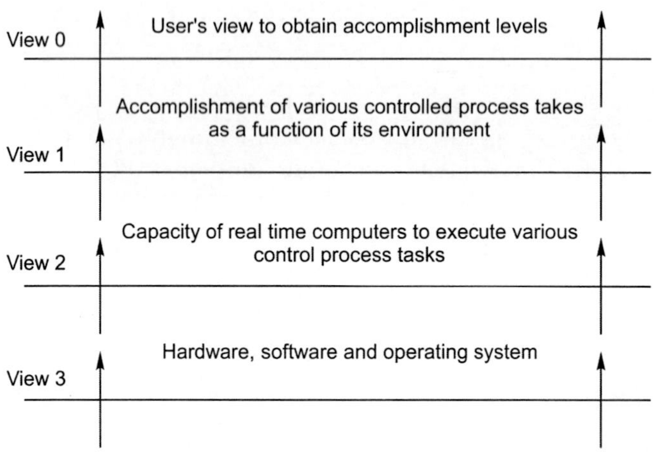

Fig. 2.5. Performability hierarchy.

Therefore, Accomplishment levels are:

A_0 : Safe arrival at the designated destination

A_1 : Diversion to another airport, but safe landing there

A_2 : Crash

This can be translated into 2-tuple state description at View 0: (a_0, b_0)

$$a_0 = \begin{cases} 0 & \text{if the aircraft is not diverted} \\ 1 & \text{if the aircraft is diverted} \end{cases}$$

$$b_0 = \begin{cases} 0 & \text{if the aircraft does not crash} \\ 1 & \text{if the aircraft crashes} \end{cases}$$

$$a_1 = \begin{cases} 0 & \text{if the visibility of the airport is good at designate airports} \\ 1 & \text{if the visibility of the airport is poor at designated airports} \end{cases}$$

$$b_1 = \begin{cases} 0 & \text{if the AL feature is functional during the landing phase} \\ 1 & \text{if the AL feature fails before the landing phase begins} \\ 2 & \text{if the AL feature fails during the landing phase begins} \end{cases}$$

$$c_1 = \begin{cases} 0 & \text{if all the flight-critical mechanical parts work correctly} \\ 1 & \text{if there is a flight-critical mechanical failure} \end{cases}$$

View 1: Operating environment is the weather at the airport. The control task that needs to run is the automatic-landing (AL) feature. The view-1 is represented in a 3-tuple (a_1, b_1, c_1).

The probability of being in each of these states depends on the weather, on the state of the mechanical components, and on the state of the computer systems.

Table 2.1. Mapping of view-0 states to accomplishment levels.

Accomplishment Level	Corresponding View States
A_0	(0,0)
A_1	(1,0)
A_2	(0, 1) (1, 1)

Table 2.2. Mapping of view-1 states to view-0 states.

Accomplishment Level	Corresponding View States
(0, 0)	(0, 0, 0), (0, 1, 0), (0, 2, 0), (1, 0, 0)
(0, 1)	(0, 0, 1), (0, 1, 1), (0, 2, 1), (1, 0, 1), (1, 2, 0), (1, 2, 1)
(1, 0)	(1, 1, 0)
(1, 1)	(1, 1, 1)

Similarly, other views might create and their mapping will perform.

2.3.2 Qualities of Performability

Table 2.3 lists the various qualities of performability.

Table 2.3. Performability qualities.

Information Hiding	Each view is more detailed than the previous one and functions of the one view is hidden from the other one.
View 0 (User)	For the users to get accomplishment levels.
View 1 (Control Engineer)	List the set of environmental conditions, controlled process performance and computer performance that maps into each accomplishment level of view 0.
View 2	Concern with the capacity of the computers to meet each demands in view 1.
View 3	Focuses on hardware, software and operating system (scheduling).

2.4 COST FUNCTIONS AND HARD DEADLINES

Hard deadlines imply a given task must be complete in specific deadlines. On completion of the task may lead to sequence failure or catastrophic failure. For the reliability of the system, all tasks should be complete in time. Hard real time systems are safety and mission critical. Safety critical means for the safe side of the user (user can be a patient, a pilot etc.) output must be produced within specific time and mission critical means purpose is to achieve the goal of the system and it must be achieved within specified deadlines. Producing the output after the specific deadline may lead to chances of occurring life loss or big financial loss.

Hard real time system tasks designed as a set of cooperating sequential process. A process consists of operation that executed in a prescribed order. In the hard real time, there are two types of processes: periodic processes and asynchronous processes. A periodic process consists of a computation that executed repeatedly, once in each fixed period. A typical use of processes is to read the sensor data and update the current state internal variables and outputs. An asynchronous process consists of a computation that responds to internal and external events.

2.4.1 Cost Functions for Tasks

As the hard deadline related to cost, so hard deadline must be achieve in time. Otherwise financial loss can occur, which can be too big to control. Therefore, for that purpose, the cost of each task measured. If in a task set, a task missed its deadline, then it advances, it should be measurable that how much cost impact it has on the overall cost of the system. So cost of each hard task fined. Cost functions of the response time are obtained by comparing the performability of a real time system with zero response time to a system with the given positive response time. The cost function of a particular task execution is given by $P(\mu) - P(0)$. Where $P(\mu)$ is the performability associated with a response time t.

As Controlled process controls the whole task of the system, so it should be designed effectively in terms of hard deadlines and cost functions. This design includes hardware and software design and many other factors. Software design related to controlling algorithm implementation, task assignment and scheduling, redundancy management, error detection and recovery. Hard deadline related to the fault tolerance of the system. A system must be able to work even in the presence of fault or regardless the load of the system. All the tasks in a system must meet its deadlines in the specific time even in the presence of faults. Other factors include topology of the network in which system is used, number of processors, synchronization of processors and types of interconnection network used.

Cost function in terms of total completion time and average response time calculated as:

average response time	$\frac{1}{n}\sum_{i=1}^{n}\left(f_i - a_i\right)$
total completion time	$\max_i \left(f_i\right) - \min_i \left(a_i\right)$
maximum lateness	$\max_i \left(f_i - d_i\right)$

While considering the cost function, five types of systems exist in reality, these are:

1. **Non-real time system:** these systems do not follow time constraints; output produce any time. In these systems, deadline does not matter.

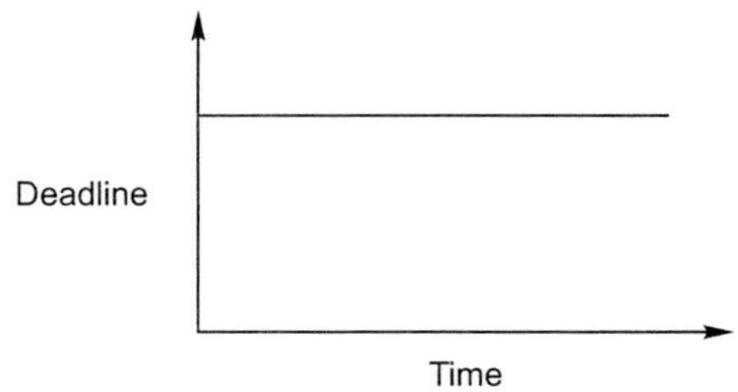

2. **Hard real time system:** must produce output in specific time. All tasks must meet their deadlines.

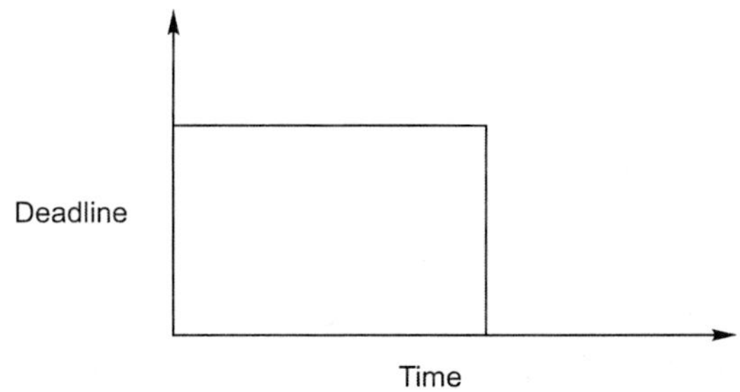

3. **Soft real time system:** Soft real time system also responds to input immediately within a specific time, but sometimes tasks missed their deadlines. Missing deadlines degrade the system performance.

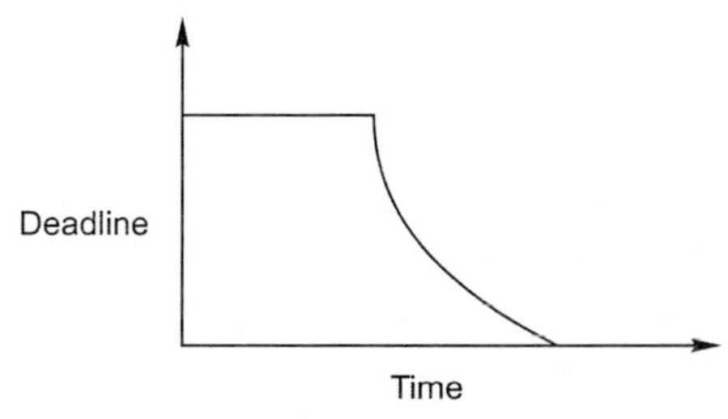

4. **Firm real time system:** The systems are like soft real time system but late delivery of service is not tolerable.

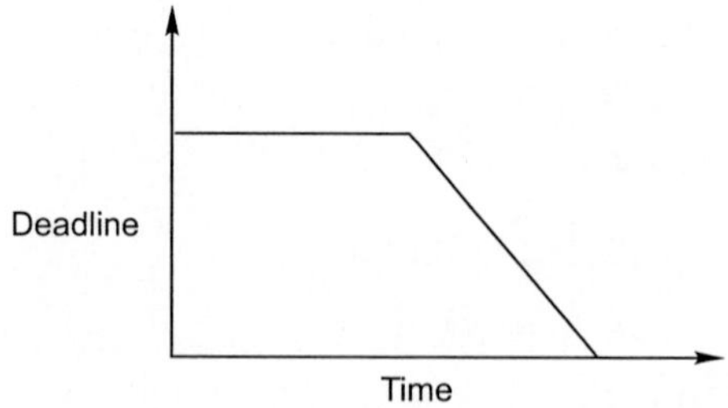

5. **On-time real time system:** is as hard real time system produces their output in specific time without missing their deadlines.

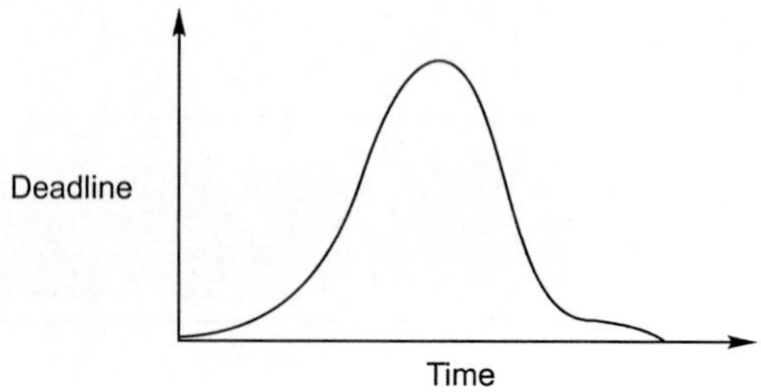

Example 1: Activities of a car control system. Let

1. WCET = Worst Case Execution Time
2. T = Time Period
3. D = Deadline

Speed measurement: WCET = 14 ms, T = 30 ms, D = 10 ms

Processor speed:

30 ms = execution time + sleep (X)

Main desirable properties of real time system in terms of cost functions and hard deadlines:

- *Timeliness:* system gives output on time.
- *Predictability:* system behaviour should be able to predict, before it is put into operation. So that cost and deadline of the system decided in advance. E.g., response and completion time of system.
- *Testability:* system should be easy to test, whether the system can meet all the hard Deadlines and budget of the organization.
- *Cost optimality:* cost of the system in terms of hardware and software design. E.g., energy consumption, memory blocks, etc.
- *Maintainability:* must easily modify from modular structure to ease system.
- *Robustness:* system must be able to work regardless of the workload.
- *Fault tolerance:* system must be able to work even in the presence of fault.

Example 2: A computer system partitioned between hard real time system and non real time system. Front end of the computer system is made hard real time and back end is made non-real time. It is the best configuration but sometimes this configuration limits the speed, efficiency and performance of the front end computing. As front end is restricted to timeline constraints but the back end is not, it also limits the system's flexibility and adaptability.

SUMMARY

- This chapter explains the traditional and modern performance metric methods. Various methods used to explain the concept. The system design checked using formal and informal methods.
- The system must be able to describe performance and reliability.
- There are various qualitative binary criteria, qualitative regular criteria and quantitative criteria.
- Various good performance exists such as represent an efficient encoding of relevant information, provide an objective basis for the ranking of candidate controllers for a given application, provide objective optimization criteria for design and represent verifiable facts
- Various drawback exist in traditional approach such as reliability depends on either the hardware or software, independently of each other, availability can't be achieved practically because it can't meet execution deadlines, throughput does not measure response time, hardware, software and the application software does not relate with each other and these drawbacks are removed by using modern methods.
- Users view achieved by using various accomplishment levels. Many views exist such as view 0, view 1, view 2 and view 3. Each view is more detail than the previous one and functions of the one view hidden from the other one.
- Hard real time system tasks designed as a set of cooperating sequential process. A process consists of operation that executed in a prescribed order. In hard real time system, there are two types of processes: periodic processes and asynchronous processes. A periodic process consists of a computation that executed repeatedly, once in each fixed period. A typical use of processes is to read the sensor data and update the current state internal variables and outputs. An asynchronous process consists of a computation that responds to internal and external events.
- As Controlled process controls the whole task of the system, so it should be designed effectively in terms of hard deadlines and cost functions. This design includes hardware and software design and many other factors. Software design related to control algorithms implementation, task assignment and scheduling, redundancy management, error detection and recovery. Hard deadline related to the fault tolerance of the system. A system must be able to work even in the presence of fault or regardless the load of the system.
- A computer system partitioned in to both hard real time system and non real time system. Frond end of the computer system is made hard real-time and back end is made non-real time. It is the good configuration but sometimes this configuration limits the speed, efficiency and performance of the front end computing. As front end is restricted to time line constraints but back end is not, it also limits the system's flexibility and adaptability.

EXERCISES

1. Explain traditional performance measure of real time system.
2. Explain modern performance measure of real time system.
3. Give an example to measure performance measure.
4. Give comparison between traditional performance measure and modern method. Explain which approach is the best and why?
5. What does mean software reliability and software validation?

6. Explain characteristics of performance measure.
7. Give drawbacks of traditional performance measure.
8. Explain performability with an example in detail.
9. Explain hard deadlines and cost function.
10. Explain qualities of performability.
11. Is hard deadline and cost function are related with each other? If yes then explain with an example.
12. Why cost function not used for soft real time applications?
13. Define response time.
14. Define deadline.
15. Define availability.
16. Define reliability.
17. Define computation time.
18. Define throughput.
19. Define worst-case condition.
20. Define performance measure.
21. Define latency time, seek time and rotation time.
22. Explain deadlock prevention methods.
23. What do you mean by fault tolerance?
24. Explain procedure of measuring the fault.
25. What do you mean by worst-case response time?
26. Explain signal to noise ratio.
27. Explain with example, which method mostly used in terms of quantity and quality.
28. Is firm real time system relates with cost, if no explaining it?
29. What do you mean by simplicity of the system?
30. Define bottom line, which also called budget or total cost of the system.

Fill in the Blanks

1. System design checked using ______ and ______ methods.
2. System must be able to describe ______ and ______ .
3. Time is an essential part for ______ computer system.
4. Real time system must provide ______ and ______ information a user needs with in specific deadlines.
5. Reliability is the probability the system ______ in an interval.
6. Availability could not be achieved practically because it cannot meet ______ deadlines.
7. Throughput does not measure ______ time.
8. Performance metrics measures ______ free operation.
9. Hard real time system tasks designed as a set of ______ process.
10. An asynchronous process consists of a computation that responds to ______ and ______ events.

True/False

1. Real time system provides accurate and actual information a user needs. (T/F)
2. Time is not an essential part for a real time computer system. (T/F)

3. Reliability is the probability the system will not fail in an interval. (T/F)
4. Availability is not the portion of time for a system will be available. (T/F)
5. Throughput is the average number of instructions per unit time. (T/F)
6. Capacity of the system, even work in high load conditions called worst case. (T/F)
7. Throughput can measure response time. (T/F)
8. Hardware, software and the application software relate with each other. (T/F)
9. Reliability is the probability of failure-free operation in a specific time in a specific environment. (T/F)
10. The controlled process does not have accomplishment levels. (T/F)

MULTIPLE CHOICE QUESTIONS

1. CR stands for
   (*a*) Capacity reliability (*b*) Capability reliability
   (*c*) Capacitance reliability (*d*) None of the above
2. To measure the performability, which metrics are used
   (*a*) Performance metrics (*b*) Simple metrics
   (*c*) Normal metrics (*d*) General metrics
3. Performability analysis have scopes
   (*a*) Narrow scope (*b*) Broad scope
   (*c*) Both (*a*) and (*b*) (*d*) None of the above
4. Qualitative binary criteria use
   (*a*) Timing constraints (*b*) specific deadlines
   (*c*) Deadlock prevention (*d*) All of the above
5. Qualitative regular criteria has
   (*a*) Safety (*b*) Fault tolerance
   (*c*) Dependability (*d*) All of the above
6. Quantitative Criteria has
   (*a*) Fault tolerance (*b*) Bottom line
   (*c*) Signal to noise ratio (*d*) All of the above
7. Traditional performance are
   (*a*) Computational reliability (*b*) DM
   (*c*) Round Robin (*d*) None of the above
8. Hardware, software and operating system appears in:
   (*a*) view 0 (*b*) view 2
   (*c*) view 1 (*d*) view 3
9. User obtain accomplishment levels in:
   (*a*) view 0 (*b*) view 2
   (*c*) view 1 (*d*) view 3
10. Control engineers appears in:
   (*a*) view 0 (*b*) view 2
   (*c*) view 1 (*d*) view 3.

QUESTIONNAIRES

1. Define reliability.

Ans. A system should be reliable. It must be able to work even in the presence of worst-case overload and fault. It defined as the probability in which system will not fail in that time.

2. Define availability.

Ans. Availability is the portion/fraction of time for which system is available.

Other is the computational availability. This is the expected value of the system computation capability at any given time.

3. Define virtual memory.

Ans. With virtual memory, a task can take more time in execution. Therefore, it is good to avoid using virtual memory. It takes very long time to handle page faults.

4. Define compiler.

Ans. The Compiler converts the source code into machine code.

5. Define operating system.

Ans. Operating system is the interface between system and user. It handles task scheduling and memory management.

6. Explain the factor which estimating program run times.

Ans. These factors are:

1. **Source code:** code written by user. This code needs to be interpret or compiler for final execution.
2. **Compiler:** The compiler converts the source code into machine code.
3. **Processors:** processors, memory devices and I/O devices execute the machine code.
4. **Operating system:** The operating system handles task scheduling and memory management.

3 Task Assignment and Scheduling

3.1 INTRODUCTION

Computer systems are present everywhere. Examples of computer usage vary from playing computer games to diagnosing a shuttle in space. Real time systems respond to the input immediately. They have some specific time called timing constraints in which they have to give their outputs. Producing the output, after specific time degrade system performance, leads to catastrophic failure and sometimes output is useless for both system and user. They have to respond in order of milliseconds or in microseconds. Deadlines are necessary and must fulfilled for the proper functioning (output) of the system.

Hard real time systems strictly follow the time constraints and meet the deadline of various tasks. If the timing constraints of hard real time systems are not meeting, then it may lead to catastrophic failure, like financial or human loss. Therefore, once the system is in use, it is very important for designers to ensure that all deadlines of all the tasks met.

When a fault occurs in the system, then the hard real time system does not produce output on specific time. Output comes after the specific time, does not produce any significant effect, output should be at the time. For example, in the stock market, if the stock trading halted for sometimes then it has no usage. Hard real time systems must satisfy all the timing constraints and should be fault tolerant in the presence of faults. The timing constraints of the real time applications achieved by using task scheduling and reliability achieved by means of fault-tolerance.

3.1.1 Task Characteristics

A task is a program or a code block, which after execution gives same result. Task is the basic component of scheduling. Examples of task are reading sensor data, data processing and transmission of sensor data etc. Characteristics of various tasks are shown in Fig. 3.1.

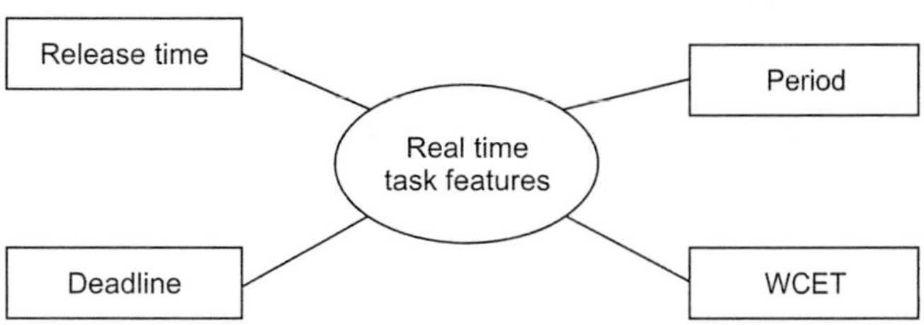

Fig. 3.1. Real time task features.

Period: These tasks occur at regular intervals of time. These tasks follow hard deadlines and their periods occur in the worst-case execution.

Release Time: In each period, a task released, that task is ready to execute at the beginning of each period. This period called the release time of the task.

Deadline: Each task must complete its execution before its completion time. In this, there are two types of deadline. A relative deadline is the time in which a task must finish its execution relative to its released time. The absolute deadline of a task is the time equal to released time plus the relative deadline.

WCET: WCET (Worst-case Execution Time) is the maximum time that a task can take to complete the execution of the task. WCET is the most important for schedulability analysis in hard real time systems. It is a software development metrics.

3.1.2 Precedence Graph

Sometimes the tasks of a real time system are dependent on one another. This dependency exists because of resource sharing or precedence constraints. In resource sharing, all the tasks shared a single resource; some tasks blocked from execution until the shared resource is the free. In precedence constraints, one task may need to wait until another task finishes its execution. In precedence constraints, waiting occurs while in resource sharing blocking occurs.

Process synchronization: A computer system could have *concurrent* processes because:

- Multiprogramming or Multitasking-one task started before another task finishes.
- Multiprocessing- in this there are more than one (central) processor and I/O devices.

A *precedence graph* is the graph in which tasks execute on an order. A precedence graph is a directed *acyclic* graph whose nodes correspond to individual statements. Precedence graph actually shows the dependency of different tasks. One task output used by the second task as input, so until first task is not complete second task cannot start. An edge from P_i to P_j means that P_i must execute before P_j. *Pi* is a predecessor of P_j. P_j is a successor of P_i. For example, P_2 and P_3 can execute only after P_1 complete its execution. P_4 executed after P_2 complete its execution and so on. It is shown in Fig 3.2.

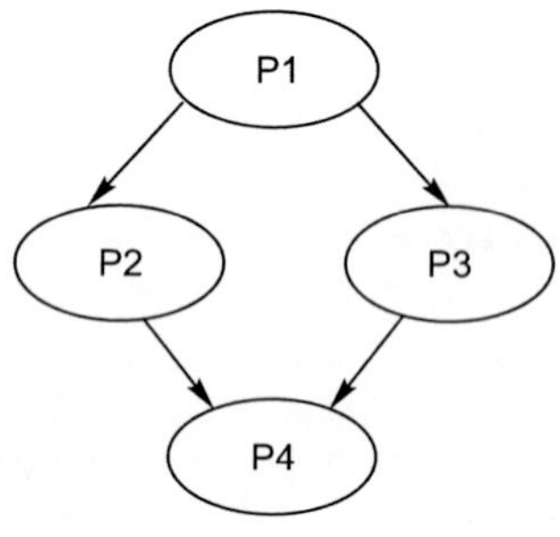

Fig. 3.2. A precedence graph.

A precedence graph shows precedence relation.

Two processes are independent, means they do not depend on each other (the output of one task is not need to another task).

3.1.3 Ready Tasks

These tasks are ready to execute. These tasks have not completed their execution until because some reason and they placed in the queue (waiting queue) of ready tasks.

3.1.4 Static and Dynamic Priority Task

When two or more ready tasks exist in the waiting queue, then priorities assigned to these tasks before their execution. These priorities assigned based on the shortest deadline. This priority can be *static* or *dynamic*.

Static Priority or Fixed Priority: as the name implies, this priority when assigned to a task never changes during run time. In a task set, all the tasks will have the same priority relative to any other task set. For example, the RM scheduling algorithm assigns static priorities to tasks such that shorter the period of the task higher is the priority.

Dynamic Priority: as the name implies, priority of the task changes during run time. In dynamic priority, different jobs of a task may have different priorities relative to other tasks in the system. For example, Earliest-Deadline-First (EDF) scheduling algorithm assigns dynamic priorities to tasks such that a task whose absolute deadline is the nearest has the highest priority.

3.1.5 Preemptive and Nonpreemptive Scheduling

There are two three types of scheduling. First is, preemptive and non-preemptive scheduling and second is conserving and non-work conserving scheduling and the third is an online and offline scheduling. A scheduling algorithm is preemptive; a task can preempt the other task. Only a high priority task can preempt lower priority tasks. Priorities assigned based on their deadlines. Shorter or nearer the deadline, the higher is the priority. Means a higher priority task executed first and the other later on. A non-preemptive scheduling cannot preempt any task, although the task is missing its deadline. A higher priority task is also in waiting queue. A currently executing task always completes its execution before another ready task starts execution. This will result in worse schedulability performance than in the preemptive case.

3.1.6 Work and Non-work Conserving Scheduling

Work conserving scheduling implies that a processor cannot be idle, if tasks are waiting for the processor in waiting queue. A processor is in a busy state. A ready task in waiting queue executed first and if there is, no any ready task then processor becomes idle. RM and EDF algorithms are work-conserving algorithms. While in case of non-work-conserving algorithm, although there are a number of tasks in ready queue but processor do not care for that, and get idle. Scheduling types are shown in Fig. 3.3.

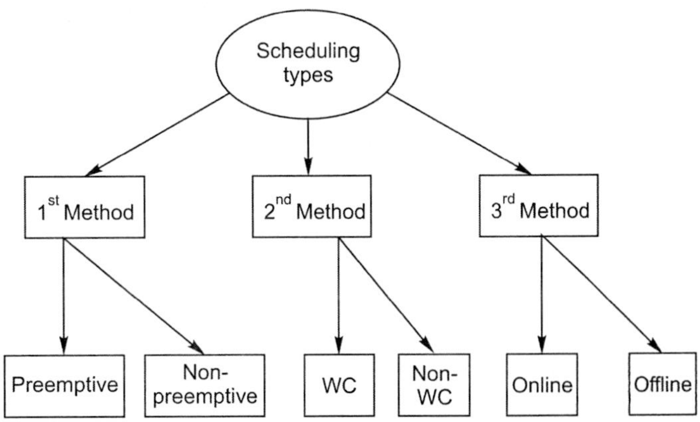

Fig. 3.3. Types of scheduling.

3.1.7 Feasibility and Optimality of Scheduling

A task set said to be feasible, if the timing constraints of an application task will meet during runtime. The schedule of a task set said to be feasible, if a scheduling algorithm can generate a schedule for a given set of tasks such that all tasks meet their deadlines. If scheduling is not feasible, then all the tasks will arrange again, so that it becomes schedulable. A scheduling algorithm said to be *optimal*, if it can feasibly schedule a task set whenever some other algorithm can schedule the same task set under the same scheduling policy.

Feasibility Condition (FC)

A task set said to be feasible, if the timing constraints of an application task will meet during runtime. The schedule of a task set said to be feasible, if a scheduling algorithm can generate a schedule for a given set of tasks such that all tasks meet their deadlines. A feasibility condition is a set of condition that determines whether a task set is feasible for a given Scheduling algorithm or not. The feasibility condition can be necessary and sufficient or it can be sufficient only.

Necessary and Sufficient FC

A task set said to be feasible if and only if, it passes the necessary and sufficient FC. If the necessary and sufficient FC is satisfied, then the task set is schedulable. Conversely, if the task set is schedulable, then the necessary and sufficient FC is satisfied. Therefore, if the necessary and sufficient FC of a task set is not satisfied, then it means that the scheduling algorithm cannot feasibly schedule the task set.

Sufficient FC

A task set will meet all its deadlines if it passes the sufficient test. A task said to be schedulable if the sufficient FC of a scheduling algorithm is satisfied. However, the converse is not necessarily true. If the sufficient FC of a task set is not satisfied, then the task set may or may not be schedulable using the scheduling algorithm.

3.1.8 Minimum Achievable Utilization

A processor is said to be fully utilized implies that a processor is fully busy. A processor said to fully utilized, when a processor cannot handle the increase in the computation time of any of the tasks in a task set, because the increase in computation time in task set makes the task set unschedulable. Utilization of one task is ratio between WCET and its period. Total utilization is the sum of all tasks utilization of a task set. This is the minimum achievable utilization or utilization bound of the scheduling algorithm and it must achieve to get a schedule feasible. A scheduling algorithm is said to be feasibly schedulable if the total utilization of the tasks is less than or equal to the minimum achievable utilization of the scheduling algorithm.

3.1.9 Scheduling Algorithms

Scheduling algorithms execute task set on a particular processor. These algorithms can be classified based on processors (uniprocessor or multiprocessors) used.

Uniprocessor Scheduling

Uniprocessor scheduling algorithm uses a single processor to execute set of tasks. Before executing the task, task feasibility condition is checked then scheduling algorithm feasibility checked to see that whether all the tasks in a given task set meet their required deadline or not.

Multiprocessor Scheduling

The multiprocessor scheduling algorithm uses multiple processors to execute set of tasks as shown in Fig. 3.4. For this, it uses two scheduling principles-global scheduling and partitioned scheduling:

Its examples are RM and EDF algorithm. RM algorithm is widely used in industry because of its simplicity, flexibility and its ease of implementation. RM algorithm supports execution of aperiodic tasks to meet the deadlines of the periodic tasks.

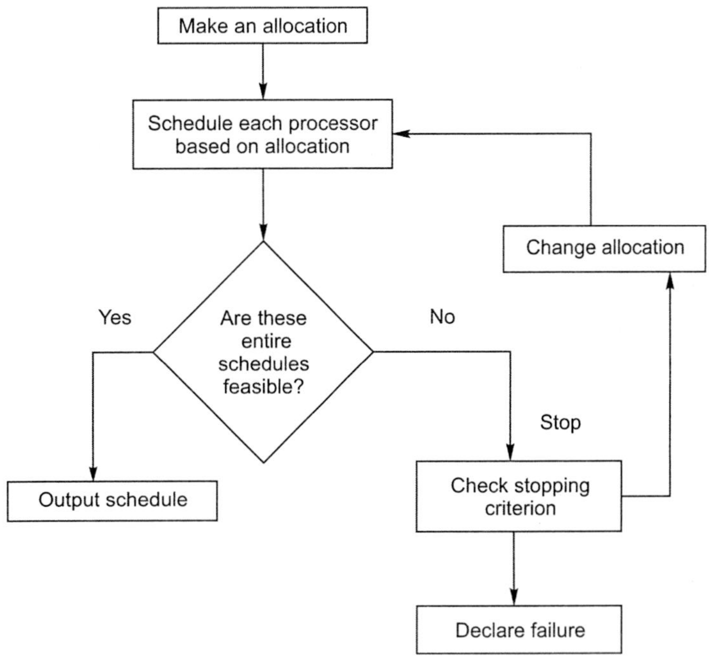

Fig. 3.4. A Multiprocessor schedule.

Global Scheduling: as the name implies, a task executed on any processor even it resumed after preemption. To perform this, all the preempted tasks placed in a global queue, and executed priority wise. In this scheduling, tasks can migrate as they placed in global queue.

Partitioned Scheduling: as the name implies, task set grouped in different task partitions and each partition has a fixed processor onto which all the tasks of that partition assigned. To perform this, tasks placed in the local queues of each processor. In this scheduling, tasks cannot migrate. A task can only execute in assigned processor, it cannot allow executing in another processor even if the other processor is idle.

3.1.10 Offline and Online Scheduling

Offline Scheduling also said to be static scheduling. In offline scheduling in advance (before executing the task set), we know that whether the given task set is schedulable or not. To check the feasibility condition, it requires the various static task parameters like period, execution time, and deadlines of different tasks in a given task set.

Online Scheduling also called as dynamic scheduling. Off line scheduling only used when before executing the task, we able to know whether the given task is schedulable or not. If all task parameters *not* known before the task execution, then the schedulability analysis is not possible to predict. When a new task arrives in the system with new period, deadline and timing constraints, then online scheduling used. For a newly arriving task can interfere with the execution of already existing tasks in the system, an admission controller is needed to determine whether to accept a new task that arrives online. Admission controller checks the feasibility condition of that task. This checking does not take a long time. This is because using processing capacity to check the feasibility condition could determinately affect the timing constraints of the existing tasks in the system. Portioned multiprocessor scheduling algorithm mainly used in online scheduling.

3.1.11 Scheduling Growth

Scheduling algorithms demand is increasing year by year, as they very effectively allocates CPU time to various processors to perform various tasks as shown in Fig. 3.5.

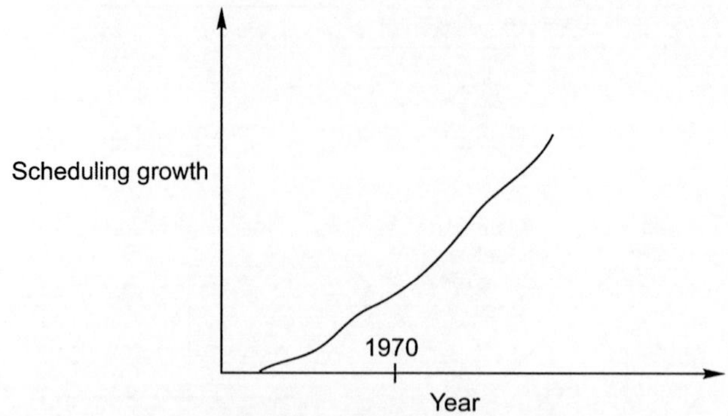

Fig. 3.5. Growth of scheduling.

3.2 SCHEDULING ALGORITHMS

A scheduling algorithm allocates CPU time to various processors to perform various tasks as shown in Fig. 3.6. Purpose of scheduling algorithm is:

- Each task must get CPU time.
- Only a high-priority task can preempt a low-priority task.
- The scheduler must scale well with a growing number of tasks.

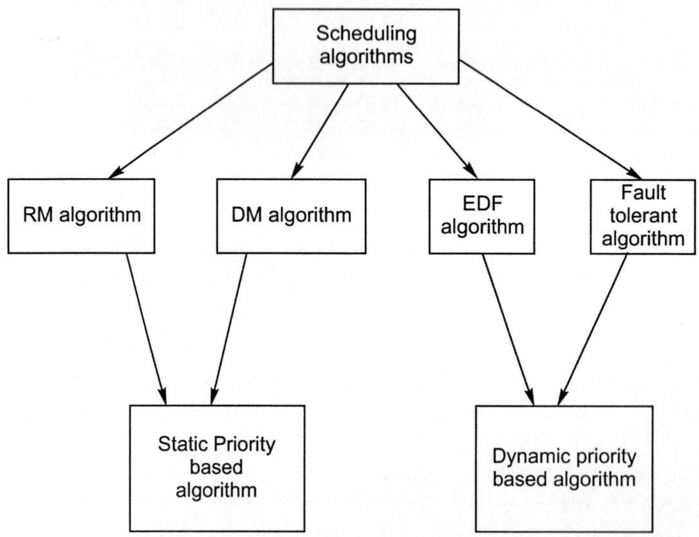

Fig. 3.6. Types of scheduling algorithms.

Real time Scheduling Algorithms schedules the various tasks in such an order that all tasks meet their deadlines. This algorithm checks the feasibility of all the existing tasks and new arriving task. Each task must get processor time to complete in a specific time. If each task is scheduled A_t times a second, or every bit millisecond, then $B_t = 1000 / A_t$. So each task executed at C_t milliseconds. This will create a load (is represented by L) of $L_t = C_t/B_t$. The total load on system (TL) the sum of loads of all the tasks. If the total load exceeds 0.7, then tasks unschedulable.

3.2.1 Rate Monotonic Scheduling Algorithm (RMA)

Rate Monotonic Algorithm is a static priority algorithm and mostly used in practical applications. It is a very simple algorithm and it is very easy to implement it. It is widely used in Industry. RMA assigns priorities to the various tasks based on their rates of occurrence. A task assigned lower priority according to its lower occurrence rate. A task assigned higher priority according to its higher occurrence rate. It is optimistic static priority real time scheduling algorithm. Optimistic means if all the tasks in a task set cannot scheduled then there is no any algorithm that can schedule them.

At RMA, task priority is directly proportional to the occurrence rate of the task and inversely proportional to task period. So task T_i priority p_i computed as:

$$\text{Priority} = \frac{n}{p_i}$$

where n is constant and p_i is the period of the task T_i

From the above stated formula, plots for different tasks having different priority values can be easily obtained as shown in Fig. 3.7(*a*) and Fig. 3.7(*b*). From this figure task priority linearly increases with the rate and inversely with its period.

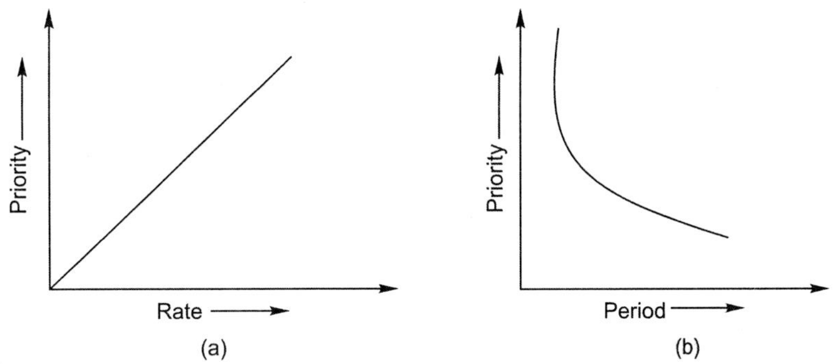

Fig. 3.7. (*a*) Priority vs. rate plot, (*b*) priority vs. period plot.

Necessary Condition:

Necessary condition for RMA schedulability is:

$$\sum_{i=1}^{n} e_i/p_i = \sum_{i=1}^{n} u_i \leq 1$$

where e_i is the execution time of a task can be worst-case execution time (WCET).

p_i is the period of a task T_i

n is the number of tasks that has to be scheduled

u_i is the CPU utilization achieved due to a task T_i in a task set.

The total CPU utilization must less than 1.

Sufficient Condition:

A set of n periodic tasks are schedulable under the RMA, if

$$\sum_{i=1}^{n} u_i \leq n(2^{1/n} - 1) \text{ ......Exp.3.1}$$

where u_i is the CPU utilization achieved due to a task T_i in a task set.

As task set satisfies the sufficient condition, then means that task set is RMA schedulable.

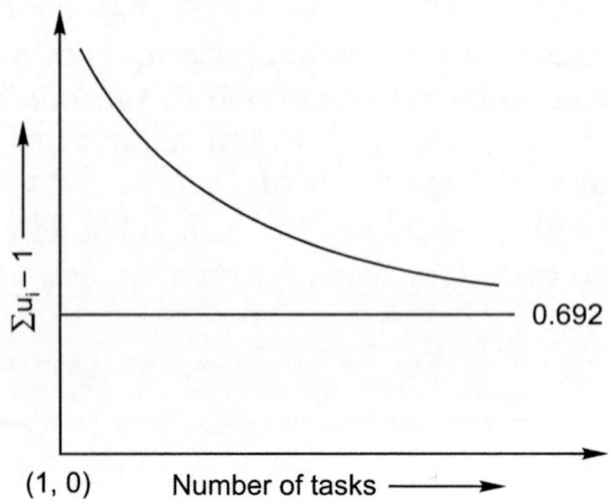

Fig. 3.8. Achievable utilization.

If there is only one task in the system, *i.e.*, $n = 1$.

Substituting $n = 1$ in Exp. 3.1,

$$\sum_{i=1}^{1} u_i \leq 1(2^{1/1} - 1) \quad \text{or} \quad \sum_{i=1}^{1} u_i \leq 1$$

Similarly for $n = 2$,

$$\sum_{i=1}^{2} u_i \leq 2(2^{1/2} - 1) \quad \text{or} \quad \sum_{i=1}^{2} u_i \leq 0.828$$

For $n = 3$

$$\sum_{i=1}^{3} u_i \leq 3(2^{1/3} - 1) \quad \text{or} \quad \sum_{i=1}^{3} u_i \leq 0.78$$

For $n \to \infty$,

$$\sum_{i=1}^{\infty} u_i \leq 3(2^{1/\infty} - 1) \quad \text{or} \quad \sum_{i=1}^{\infty} u_i \leq \infty.0$$

RMA gives the maximum CPU utilization equal to 1. This can achieve if there a single task in the system. If the number of tasks increases in the system then CPU utilization starts to decrease and when n goes to ∞, then it will get stabilized to $\log_e 2$, which is approximately 0.692. This plot is shown in Fig. 3.8.

Example 1: *Whether the following task set is RMA schedulable or not?*

$$T_1 = (e_1 = 10, p_1 = 100), T_2 = (e_2 = 90, p_2 = 450), T_3 = (e_3 = 30, p_3 = 150).$$

Sol. Firstly, compute for necessary condition (the total CPU utilization for given three tasks):

$$\sum_{i=1}^{3} u_i \frac{10}{100} + \frac{90}{450} + \frac{30}{150} = 0.5$$

Value is 0.5, which is less than 1. Therefore, it satisfies necessary condition. Now check for sufficient condition (the maximum achievable utilization):

$$3(2^{1/3} - 1) = 0.78$$

Substitute these values in exp. 3.1:

$$\sum_{i=1}^{3} u_i \leq 3(2^{1/3} - 1)$$

$$0.5 < 0.78$$

As sufficient condition satisfied, therefore, the task set is RMA schedulable.

Example 2: *Whether the following set of three periodic real time tasks are RMA schedulable or not?*

$$T_1 = (e_1 = 50, p_1 = 100), T_2 = (e_2 = 90, p_2 = 450), T_3 = (e_3 = 20, p_3 = 100).$$

Sol. Let us first compute the total CPU utilization due to the given task set:

$$\sum_{i=1}^{3} u_i = \frac{50}{100} + \frac{90}{450} + \frac{20}{100} = 0.9$$

Now check for exp. 3.1:

$$\sum_{i=1}^{3} u_i \leq 0.78$$

Since 0.9 is not ≤ 0.78, the task set is not RMA-schedulable.

Example 3: *Check whether the following task set is RMA schedulable or not?*

$$T_1 = (e_1 = 40, p_1 = 100), T_2 = (e_2 = 90, p_2 = 450), T_3 = (e_3 = 80, p_3 = 600).$$

Sol. Firstly, compute for necessary condition (the total CPU utilization for given three tasks):

$$\sum_{i=1}^{3} u_i = \frac{40}{100} + \frac{90}{450} + \frac{80}{600} = 0.7333$$

Value is 0.73, which is less than 1. Therefore, it satisfies necessary condition. Now check for sufficient condition (the maximum achievable utilization):

$$3(2^{1/3} - 1) = 0.78$$

Substitute these values in exp. 3.1:

$$\sum_{i=1}^{3} u_i \leq 3(2^{1/3} - 1)$$

$$0.73 < 0.78$$

As sufficient condition is satisfied, therefore, the task set is RMA schedulable.

3.2.1.1 Advantages and Disadvantages of RMA

Advantages of RMA

(*a*) It is optimistic static priority task scheduling algorithm.

(*b*) This algorithm is widely used in Industrial applications.

(*c*) Implementation of this algorithm is very easy.

(*d*) It used in all commercial applications.

(*e*) This algorithm is simple and efficient.

(*f*) RMA requires less data structure.

(*g*) RMA has good transient overload handling capability, which means that a higher priority task cannot miss its deadline. Whenever a higher priority task is ready, it can preempt any executing lower priority task, which makes RMA stable under transient overload.

Disadvantages of RMA

(*a*) RMA cannot support aperiodic and sporadic tasks.

(*b*) RMA is not optimal when task periods and deadlines differ.

Characteristics of Rate Monotonic Scheduling

- It is static priority based algorithm.
- Priorities assigned before the execution.
- Shorter period assigned a higher priority.
- A higher priority task can preempt lower priority tasks.

3.2.2 Deadline Monotonic Algorithm (DM)

Deadline Monotonic Algorithm (DMA) is a static based algorithm. When deadline and the period of a task differ, then DMA algorithm used. DMA assigns the priority to the tasks based on their shorter deadlines while in RMA priority assigned occurrence based. DMA is more capable than RMA. RMA and DMA give the same result, when deadline of a task is proportional to its period. When the deadline of a task is not proportional to its period, then DMA is more capable than RMA. When DMA does not succeed then always RMA cannot be succeed. Here is an example in which task set is DMA schedulable but not RMA schedulable.

Example 4: *Check whether the given task set is DMA and RMA schedulable or not?*

$T_1 = (e_1 = 10, p_1 = 50, d_1 = 35)$, $T_2 = (e_2 = 15, p_2 = 100, d_1 = 20)$, $T_3 = (e_3 = 20, p_3 = 200, d_1 = 200)$ *[time in msec].*

Sol. *e* refers to execution time a task.

p refers to period of the task.

d refers to deadline of the task.

RMA checks the schedulability of tasks based on their occurrence rate means their arrival rate:

Checking for T_1:

10 msec < 35 msec. Hence, T_1 would meet its first deadline.

Checking for T_2:

$$(10 + 15) > 20 \text{ (exceeds deadline)}$$

Thus, T_2 will miss its first deadline. Hence, the given task set cannot schedule under RMA.

Now check the schedulability for DMA:

In DMA, tasks assigned priority based on their shorter deadline. So for a given task set:

$$\text{priority } (T_2) > \text{priority } (T_1) > \text{priority } (T_3).$$

Checking for T_2:

15 msec < 20 msec. Hence, T_2 will meet its first deadline.

Checking for T_1:

$$(15 + 10) < 35$$

Hence, T_1 will meet its first deadline.

Checking for T_3:

$$(20 + 30 + 40) < 200$$

Therefore, T_3 will meet its deadline.

Therefore, the given task set is schedulable under DMA but not under RMA.

Characteristics of DMA

- It is fixed priority algorithm.
- Tasks assigned priority based on their shorter deadline.
- RM and DM produce identical result if the relative deadline is proportional to its period.
- RM always fails when DM fails.

Comparison between RM and DM Algorithm

Table 3.1. RMA vs. DMA.

S.No.	RMA	DMA
1.	Static priority algorithm	Fixed priority algorithm
2.	Assigns priorities based on tasks occurrence rate.	Assigns priorities based on task deadline.
3.	It is not used where deadline and period of a task differ	It can be used where deadline and period of a task differ
4.	Less reliable	More reliable
5.	RMA cannot succeed if DMA does not succeed	DMA succeed although RMA succeed or not

3.2.3 Earliest Deadline First (EDF) Algorithm

Earliest Deadline First (EDF) algorithm also called as least time to go algorithm. It is a dynamic scheduling algorithm and mostly used in real-time systems. It places tasks in a priority queue. Whenever a task finishes its execution, then the queue will search for the task closest to its deadline and the closest deadline task will execute first. Schedule the tasks in such a manner that all tasks complete on time and fulfill their respective deadlines. The ready task waits for the long time in the queue schedule first for the execution. When tasks deadlines and periods are same, then EDF gives a utilization bound of 100%. This algorithm is simple and very easy to understand.

In Earliest Deadline First (EDF) scheduling, the shortest deadline task first taken up for scheduling. For a task set to be EDF schedulable, the total utilization of the processor because of task set must less than or equal to 1.

For periodic tasks set $\{T_1, T_2, ..., T_n\}$, EDF schedulability can be:

$$\sum_{i=1}^{n} \frac{e_i}{p_i} = \sum_{i=1}^{n} u_i \leq 1$$

where u_i is the utilization of the processor because of the task T_i

n is the number of the tasks in the task set.

This expression used, when task period and deadline are similar. This expression is both necessary condition and sufficient condition for tasks set to be EDF schedulable.

EDF is an optimal uniprocessor scheduling algorithm means that if a given task set is not schedulable under EDF then no any other scheduling algorithm can make the given task set schedulable. When period of a task is not equal to its deadline, then above scheduling algorithm gets change. If task period is greater than task duration ($p_i > d_i$) then each task executes in e_i execution time, every min (p_i, d_i) duration of time. Therefore, above expression can be rewrite as:

$$\sum_{i=1}^{n} \frac{e_i}{\min(p_i, d_i)} \leq 1$$

This expression is only a sufficient condition and not a necessary condition. However, if $p_i < d_i$, then a task set is EDF schedulable. Although EDF is simple and optimal algorithm, it has few shortcomings because of which this algorithm cannot use for Industrial/practical applications. Therefore in case of EDF tasks scheduled based on the closeness of their deadline.

Example 5: *Find whether given task set is EDF schedulable on a uni processor or not?*

$$T_1 = (e_1 = 40, p_1 = 100), T_2 = (e_2 = 90, p_2 = 450), T_3 = (e_3 = 80, p_3 = 600).$$

Sol. The total processor utilization for three tasks is:

$$\sum_{i=1}^{3} u_i = \frac{40}{100} + \frac{90}{450} + \frac{80}{600} = 0.7333$$

As processor, utilization is less than 1. The given task set is EDF schedulable.

3.2.3.1 Implementation of EDF

EDF algorithm can implement in three ways:

1. **First method:** In the EDF algorithm, all the tasks must complete its execution before their deadline arrives. All tasks must complete in a specific time. Schedulability must doing in such a way that all the tasks meet their deadlines. A new arriving task will place or insert at the end position of the queue. When a task preempts the other task, the whole queue will read from the beginning of the queue to find that task which is having the shortest deadline and that task will execute first. EDF algorithm complexity is that task insertion achieved in $O(1)$ time, task execution and task deletion achieved in $O(n)$ time, where n is the number of ready tasks in the queue. This EDF implementation is not efficient.
2. **Second method:**

(*a*) Arrange the various tasks and then place them in a sorted priority queue, means the task is having a shorter deadline placed first in queue.

(*b*) A sorted priority queue can be implement using heap data structure.

(*c*) A new arriving task placed/inserted into the heap structure in $O(\log_2 n)$ time. Where n is the total number of tasks available in the queue. The task removed/deleted from the queue, before its execution. This deletion of the task from the pointy queue can be achieved in $O(1)$ time.

3. **Third method:**

(*a*) For each task, a FIFO queue maintained.

(*b*) Absolute deadline of a new arriving task calculated from task release time and task relative deadline.

(*c*) This new arriving task placed in the queue (at the end position of its corresponding relative deadline).

(*d*) Tasks inserted and arranged in queue according to their deadlines (specifically relative).

(*e*) The time to insert/place a new arriving task in the FIFO queue *O*(1) time. To find a task with the shortest absolute deadline in the FIFO queue will also be *O*(1) time.

3.2.3.2 Advantages of EDF

Although EDF has so many shortcomings, then also it is much better than RM algorithm. It is clearly shown in Fig. 3.9 (*a*, *b*). Here is an example, which illustrates it completely:

Example 6: *RM Scheduling vs. EDF Scheduling*

Sol. Schedule the following task set with RM Algorithm:

$$T_1 = (1, 4),\ T_2 = (2, 6),\ T_3 = (3, 8)$$

$$U = \frac{1}{4} + \frac{2}{6} + \frac{3}{8} = \frac{23}{24}$$

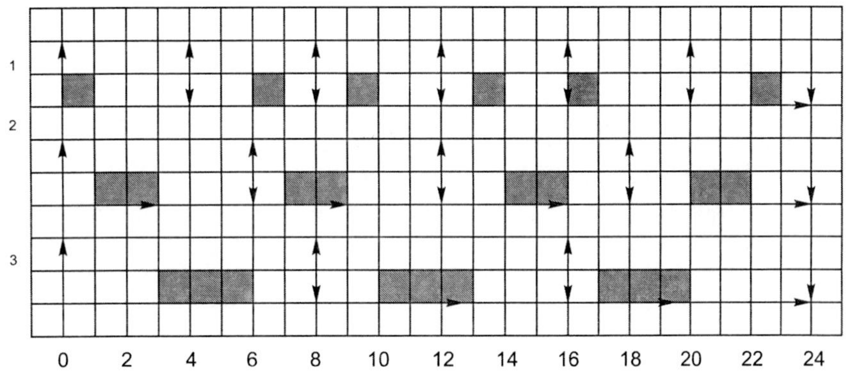

Fig. 3.9(a). RM algorithm.

The utilization is greater than the bound so a deadline can be missing in RM algorithm.

At time 6, although deadline of task T_3 is very close, RM scheduler decides to execute task T2 first. With this, T_3 misses its deadline.

Example: Schedule the same task set with EDF:

$$T_1 = (1, 4),\ T_2 = (2, 6),\ T_3 = (3, 8)$$

$$U = \frac{1}{4} + \frac{2}{6} + \frac{3}{8} = \frac{23}{24}$$

Again, the utilization is very high, but deadline cannot miss in the manic period.

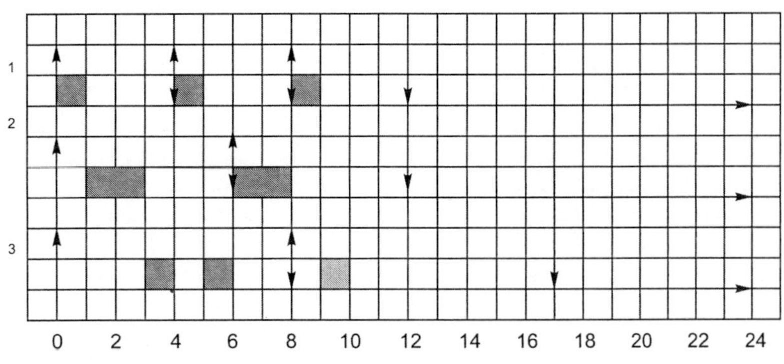

Fig. 3.9(b). EDF algorithm.

At time 6, EDF scheduler manages the all tasks and T_3 will finish its execution with in specific deadline.

3.2.3.3 Shortcomings/Disadvantages of EDF

EDF cannot use for practical applications because of its some shortcomings. These are:

1. **Resource sharing:** in case of high overhead, it cannot support resource sharing between different tasks.
2. **EDF implementation:** is not so easy. Tasks arranged based on their shorter deadline and placed in priority queue. When a new task arrives, placing the task in the priority queue based on its shorter deadline is bit complex and this insertion complexity is in the order of order $log_2 n$, where n is the total number of ready tasks that has to be scheduled. This creates high run time overhead.
3. **Transient overload:** this occurs in very short time. Some tasks of the system not able to complete their execution in specific time especially the time planned during their design time called transient overload. A task may take longer time to complete their execution because of many reasons. These reasons are:

(*a*) The task might enter an infinite loop.

(*b*) An unusual condition had arrived.

(*c*) The task had given some irregular input values.

When a task does not complete its execution on time, then it causes some other tasks to miss their deadlines. Sometimes a low priority task does not complete its execution on time and leads to transient overload. With this, it is possible that some high priority task miss its deadline. Therefore, it means that a high priority task has missed its deadline because of low priority task. This is the main drawback of EDF algorithm. With this serious drawback, this algorithm cannot use practically.

4. **Domino effect in EDF**

When $U > 1$, EDF can have the domino effect, with this effect all tasks will miss their deadlines.

An example of domino effect is shown in the following Fig. 3.10 (*a*, *b*):

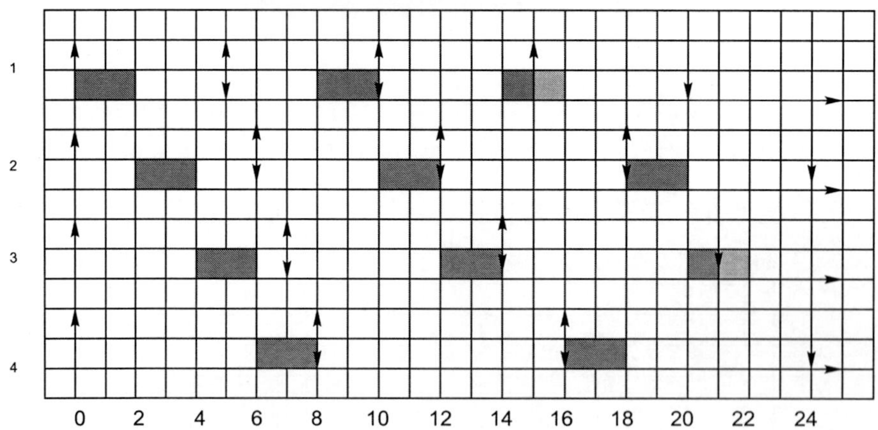

Fig. 3.10(a). EDF algorithm.

All tasks missed their deadline almost at the sametime.

Domino effect in RM

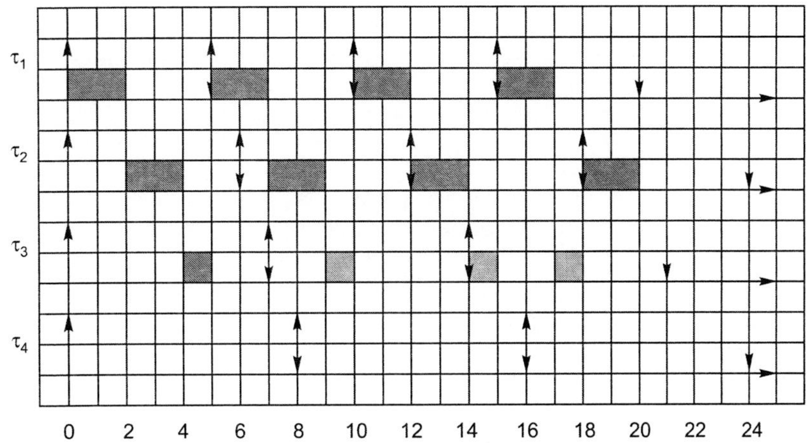

Fig. 3.10(b). RM algorithm.

RM has less domino effect. Only lower priority tasks miss their deadlines. In the previous example, if RM used:

As shown in Fig. T_1 and T_2 never miss their deadlines, T_3 misses lot of deadline, and T_4 does not execute.

Table 3.2. RM vs. EDF algorithm.

S.No.	Topic	RM Algorithm	EDF Algorithm
1	Priority	Static Priority Algorithm	Dynamic Priority Algorithm
2	Implementation	Multi-Level, Queue operation is $O(1)$	Priority Queue, $O(\log n)$, n is number of tasks
3	Processor Utilization	Guarantee only for 0:69, Practice 0:88	Full Utilization
4	Context Switches	Many	Few
5	Guarantee Test	Nontrivial	Simple
6	Predictability	Good	Bad
7	Processor Idle Times	More idle times	Less idle times (means full utilization of processor)
8	Industry Usage	More usage	Less usage in industry
9	Execution	More control over the execution.	Less control over the execution.
10	Response Time	Can be controlled	Cannot be controlled
11	Implementation overhead	Less implementation overhead	More implementation overhead

12	Platforms	RM is implemented on very small hardware platforms (for example, by using only interrupts)	RM is implemented on absolute deadline in a long data structure
13	Response Time Computation	The response time of a task depends only on its computation time and on the interference of higher priority tasks.	It depends on the parameters of all tasks.
14	Offset	If all offset are 0 in RM, then the maximum response time found in the first job of a task.	In EDF, the maximum response time not found in the first job, but in a later job.
15	Optimality	Optimal for fixed priority scheduling	Universal
16	Algorithm Time Complexity	$O(1)$ Job insertion is possible	Both job insertion and dispatch take $O(\log n)$ time.
17	Overload Survivability	High and predictable	Low and unmanageable
18	Responsiveness	High priority tasks always have shorter response time	Non-intuitive to reach Conclusions
19	Ease of Implementation	Easy to implement	Difficult to implement
20	Feasible schedule	May not give a feasible schedule even processor is idle at some points.	Give a feasible schedule

3.2.4 Fault Tolerant Scheduling Algorithm

Rate Monotonic (RM) scheduling algorithm is widely used in Industries because of its simplicity and ease of implementation. Initially uniprocessor RM scheduling algorithm provides efficient and good result even in the presence of faults. The multiprocessor scheduling algorithm provides efficient utilization of the processors while meeting the task deadlines. The purpose of the uniprocessor RM scheduling algorithm is to get good reliability of the system while the purpose of the multiprocessor RM scheduling algorithm is to get high performance of the system.

3.2.4.1 Fault Tolerant Systems

A system is an arrangement of different components, these components work together to achieve the goal of the system. A subsystem can be standalone or a system can be part of other systems (like a subsystem). The output of the system can directly give to the user or to another part of the system (like feedback of the system). For example, the human body in which different parts of the bodywork together to achieve the goal of the human body or the work which human body wants to perform. Another example is computer memory, provides various functionalities to the applications running on the computers.

A fault tolerant system must able to perform well even in the presence of hardware and software faults. A fault tolerant system must have normally or produce correct results, even in the presence of faults. The designer must care for this.

A real time fault tolerant system is able to perform well even in the presence of hardware or software faults, produce output in the specific time, and strictly follow the timing constraints.

3.2.4.2 Failure, Error and Faults

System failure: A system is said to be failed or in failure state, if a system or its components does not perform well and do not give require an output within a specific time. When a system comes across the fault, then failure occurs. For example, when a computer user is not able to read his stored data from a computer, a laser cannot find its designated target; aerial refueling system is not able to transfer its fuel at the proper flow rate.

System error: This error found by the operating system. When an error occurs in the system, then procedure rules of the system violated. System errors are inner instructions. This error produces incorrect result in the system. Its examples are certain portions of the computer memory that has been corrupted or broken, with which a user is not able to read the stored files

System fault: is an external instruction produces an error in the system. A fault in the system causes system failure. Some faults of the system are tolerable and some are not. When fault cause error in the system, then that fault must manage. There are mainly two types of faults. The fault affects the system functionality and produces incorrect result and cause errors in the system, these types of faults called active fault. When the occurrences of fault do not produce any error in the system, these types of faults are tolerable and negligible and called as passive fault. For example, impurities in the semiconductor devices may cause computer memory in the end to behave unpredictably. To tolerate faults, errors must detect in any fault tolerant system.

A fault tolerant system must have normally or produce correct results, even in the presence of faults. The designer must care for this. A fault can occur in hardware as well as software.

Hardware faults: This fault occurs in hardware. This type of fault can be permanent, temporary and for a short time. Permanent faults are permanent or hard faults and are stable and continuous. These faults occur because of failure in computing unit. Temporary faults are momentary or Transient faults occur because of error in computing unit. These types of fault occur for short time duration and disappear without causing a permanent damage.

Hardware transient faults sources: The main sources of transient faults in hardware are environmental disturbances like power fluctuations, electromagnetic interference etc. Transient faults are the most common, and their number is continuously increasing due to high complexity, smaller transistor sizes and low operating voltage for computer electronics.

Software faults: are also known as software bugs and these bugs are permanent. These faults are obvious. These faults can be permanent and temporary. Permanent faults always give incorrect results. Example: Initializing a global variable with incorrect value and use that value during execution of the program, as global variable value is incorrect so its execution always produce wrong results. Temporary fault may or may not give wrong results. For example, when different execution paths are used based on the different input values.

3.2.4.3 Fault Model (Recovery Block)

A real time system should be design in such a way that a system must able to work well even in the presence of hardware and software faults and even under the worst-case load condition and strictly follow the timing constraints. Scheduling of fault tolerant system must give this guarantee. To fulfill this guarantee, it works under the assumption of a faulty model.

This fault model mainly assumes that systems behave normally even in the presence of hardware or software fault. This system assumes that software transient fault can easily remove by resetting the system processor before re-execution. Therefore, that corrects input values given to the system produce correct result.

As the change in input parameters, the software execution path could be different from one execution to another. As a different execution path taken so it is expected the same error would not occur. These faults appear in short time, so these faults can be set easily. Fault model assumes that permanent software fault can also recover by using recovery blocks. When an error is detected and permanent fault found during task execution, then faulty task is re-executed or a recovery block corresponding to the faulty task executed.

The recovery block of a task has the same period as the original task but may have a different worst-case condition than that of the original task. When a task executed for the first time, it called the primary copy of the task. After an error detected the re-execution or execution of the recovery block called the *recovery copy* of the task.

3.2.4.4. FTRM (Fault Tolerance Rate Monotonic) Algorithm

A faulty task should treat to get efficient result. Fault tolerance rate monotonic algorithm mainly used to treat faulty tasks. This is a uniprocessor scheduling algorithm. This algorithm designed for scheduling n periodic tasks in task set T. Deadline and released time of the each task considered in a task set. Its feasibility condition is in terms of exact RM feasibility condition by considering the worst-case condition and when the system is much overloaded. This algorithm used for tasks having implicit deadline and RM priority, tasks with specific deadlines and fixed-priority. In this algorithm, higher priority task must execute first. This is the first fault tolerant algorithm that considers such a general fault model.

The scheduling analysis of FTRM considers occurrences of a maximum of f faults within any time interval of length $T_{max.}$ Where, T_{max} is the largest period of any task in the periodic task set T.

The run time complexity of FTRM is $O(n \cdot N \cdot f_2)$.

Where n is the number of tasks in a periodic task set.

N is the maximum number of jobs released within any interval of length T_{max}.

3.2.4.5. Task Model

The task model assumes a set of n implicit deadline periodic tasks $T = \{\tau_1, \tau_2, \ldots, \tau_n\}$. Each task $\tau_i \in T$ characterized by WCET, C_i and period T_i. The jth job of task τ_i is denoted by $\tau_{i,j}$. The job $\tau_{i,j}$ is released at time $r_{i,j}$ and has an absolute deadline by time $d_{i,j}$ as is defined in

$$r_{i,j} = (j - 1) \, . \, T_i$$

T_{max} to be the maximum period of any task in the task set $T = \{\tau_1, \tau_2, \ldots, \tau_n\}$, that is,

$$T_{max} = \max_{i=1}^{n} \{T_i\}$$

Without loss of generality tasks are sorted in set T in order of decreasing priority, that is, all tasks in set $\{\tau_1, \tau_2, \ldots \tau_{i-1}\}$ are of higher-priority than the priority of task τ_i. Moreover, denote the maximum number of jobs released within any time interval of length T_{max} by N.

3.2.4.6. Fault Model

Fault model considers all the types of faults. Its purpose is it to remove the fault or reduce the impact of the fault in the system so that system behaves in the normal way and produce effective and efficient output to the user. This model assumes that fault of always occurs at the end of execution either it occurs in primary task or recovery task. It also assumes that during execution of a primary or a recovery copy of a task, a fault can occur at once. These all assumptions are essential for the worst case schedulability analysis.

It considers occurrences of a maximum of f faults within any time interval of length $T_{max.}$ The faults can occur during the execution of any primary task and/or a recovery copy of a task. When a task executed for the first time, it called the primary copy of the task. After an error detected the re-execution or execution of the recovery block called the *recovery copy* of the task. The recovery copy could simply be the re-execution of the primary copy or it could be a different implementation of the same task, called a recovery block, in which case the WCET may not be same as the WCET of the primary copy.

To recover the task, each task must have f recovery copies, in case if all the f faults occur in the same job of a task. Therefore, a recovery copy recovers the faulty task. A fault f can occur in primary copy of the task τ_i or a recovery copy of the task τ_i. Priority of recovery task is same as that of the primary task (original task). If an error or fault detected in primary task, then the first recovery copy of the original task executed. If an error or fault may detect during execution of the recovery task then a trigger will generate and next recovery copy of the same task will execute and so on. If there are k faults occur on a job of task τ_i, then it means that the first fault occurs in the primary copy of the task τ_i and each of the subsequent $(k - 1)$ faults occurs in each subsequent recovery copy of the same τ_i.

Although for a faulty task, many recovery copies have to executed, the overhead for executing the recovery operation does not affect the system performance. All tasks either they are primary or recovery copy of the task, should be properly managed by a fault tolerant scheduling algorithm. This algorithm must give the guarantee of proper execution of all the tasks.

There are different possibilities of the occurrences of the f faults in the N jobs. One possibility is that all the f faults occur in one of the N jobs. Another possibility is that a different number of faults occur in different jobs. Each such possibility of fault occurrence called a *fault pattern.* Given a set of jobs in A, by k-fault-pattern, $k = 0, 1, 2 \ldots f$. For example, if $k = 0$, no fault occurs within the jobs in set A. To achieve fault tolerance, it has to ensure that all the jobs released within any interval of length T_{max} will meet the deadlines for any possible f-fault pattern.

According to combinatorial theory, there is a total of $\binom{N+f-1}{f}$ different ways the f faults can occur in N jobs.

A number of different fault patterns given by the binomial coefficient $\binom{N+f-1}{f}$ are equal to

$$\binom{N+f-1}{f} = \Omega\left(\left(\frac{N}{f}\right)^f\right) = O(N^f)$$

This fault model will not be useful for increasing values of N and f. Then, this model is difficult to implement and practically impossible.

3.3 TASK ASSIGNMENT

Tasks assigned to different processors. Task assigning done on task priorities basis. Before assigning the task to a processor, first check whether the schedule is feasible or not. All the tasks meet their specific deadlines or not. Arrangement or order of the tasks must in such a way that all the tasks meet their deadlines. Assigning tasks to different processors done by various algorithms.

These are:

3.3.1 Next Fit Algorithm Based on RM Scheduling

All tasks only need processor time. Tasks do not need any resources.

Utilization time of each task = $\frac{e_i}{p_i}$.

Each task class has some boundaries and task class can execute only in that boundary. Corresponding to each task class a processor assigned means a processor allocated to single class set.

Example:

There are four classes having boundaries as shown in table:

Class	Boundary
C1	(0.37 – 0.92)
C2	(0.22 – 0.37)
C3	(0.16 – 0.22)
C4	(0.00 – 0.16)

Each task has execution time and period. From this utilization of each task found. Using utilization from above table, class found.

Task	T_1	T_2	T_3	T_4	T_5
e_i	2	5	1	1	10
p_i	10	8	24	20	16
u_i	0.2	0.63	0.04	0.05	0.63
CLASS	C3	C1	C4	C4	C1

$T_1 - T_5$ represents tasks.

e_i is the task execution.

p_i is the period of each task.

Processor for each task then (same class assigned to a processor):

Processor	Tasks
P_1	T_1
P_2	T_2, T_5
P_3	T_3, T_4

3.3.2 Bin Packing Assignment Algorithm Based on EDF

In this algorithm, firstly u_i arranged in first fit decreasing algorithm, after that assigned to each processor.

Using the same above example:

u_i in decreasing order :

u_i	Tasks
0.63	T_2
0.63	T_5
0.2	T_1
0.04	T_3
0.05	T_4

Now assigned these tasks to processor:

Processor	Tasks
P_1	T_2, T_5
P_2	T_1
P_3	T_3, T_4

3.3.3 Focused Addressing and Bidding Algorithm

This algorithm used for both critical and non-critical tasks. It is a very simple algorithm. Critical tasks have a specific time for their execution and task must complete in this specific time even in the presence of heavy workload, while in case of non-critical tasks, task executed or not, it depends on the system's ability to do so. Priority of a task always gives to critical task.

When a critical task arrives then available processor time and resources checked so that critical task never misses its deadline. So a non-critical task can be executed later, but critical will always be executed on time. Critical task executed based on worst-case run time and non-critical task executed based on expected run time of the task.

Purpose of FAB algorithm is to shift the tasks to another processor, if it does not have sufficient time and resources.

FAB algorithm working

Each processor maintains a status table indicates that which critical and non-critical tasks system has to execute. First, of all critical tasks executed and if time left then only non-critical task executed. Processor time and resources provided for each critical task.

Purpose of FAB algorithm is to shift the tasks to another processor, if it does not have sufficient time and resources. If load of the system exceeds from its threshold value, then randomly a task shifted to another processor. This other processor called focused processor, means now this processor has to execute the shifted task. It may be the case that the selected processor (focused processor) did not have free time to execute the task.

Then focused processor will find lightly loaded processor. Lightly loaded processor sends request for bids (RFB) to focus processor, which means that lightly loaded processor have free time and resources to execute the task in a specific time (deadline). When focused processor receives the RFB, then it checks how much time a new task arrive and what its deadline:

T= current time + bid receiving time by focused processor + time taken by focused processor to make a decision + task transfer time + time taken by lightly loaded processor to either guarantee or reject the task.

3.3.4 Myopic Offline Scheduling Algorithm (MOS)

It is an assignment offline scheduling algorithm. All the tasks are non-preemptive. A task cannot preempt any other task although its deadline is near. This algorithm provides both processor time and resources to different tasks. As it is an offline scheduling algorithm, in advance user has the knowledge of task arrival time, execution time and deadlines. Its example is using and controlling the printer, access to memory blocks.

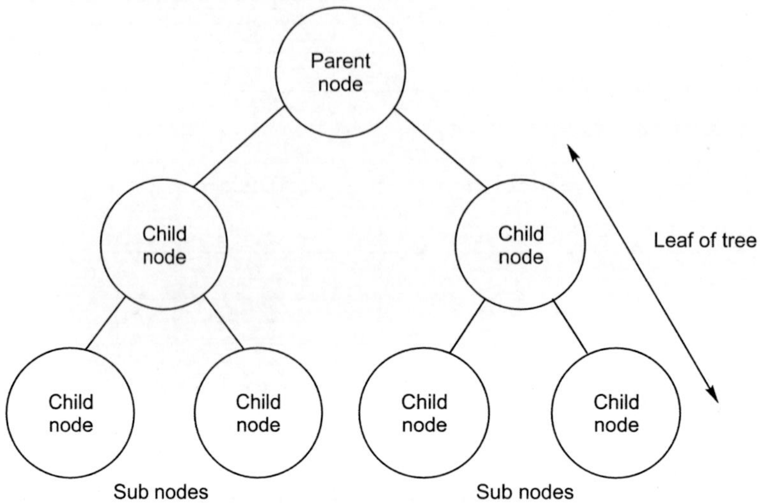

Fig. 3.11. MOS tree.

MOS creates a tree to schedule various tasks. Each node in the tree represents scheduled subset of tasks. The root node of the schedule in the tree is empty. Leaf of the tree contains a schedule of various tasks. This schedule can be feasible or not. Root node represented as level zero. Root node is empty node means contain no task. A tree is shown in Fig. 3.11.

Drawbacks

1. A tree practically cannot implement.
2. Schedule in the tree can be feasible or not. Schedule must feasible before executing the task. Therefore, practically a complete tree cannot generate.
3. Suppose if there are a number of tasks in the task set, then it is very difficult to decide which task placed first in the child node for execution. Sometimes this decision based on minimum task execution time, shorter deadline and earliest start time. However, this is not a practical approach. One condition (task execution time, shorter deadline and earliest start time) must mandatory for the completion of a tree.
4. If a node is not strongly feasible (means schedule is not feasible), then backtracking is done. This node is hopeless so back go to its parents. This task is very time consuming.
5. If numbers of tasks are very large, then it takes a long time to make a decision which node is feasible or which is not.

Example:

Construct a complete MOS tree for five tasks having two processors. Release time, execution time and deadline of each task given.

Time	T_1	T_2	T_3	T_4	T_5
r_i (release time)	0	12	0	16	0
e_i (execution time)	13	5	14	11	15
d_i (deadline)	13	23	17	28	40

Root node is an empty node. Now schedule the child nodes.

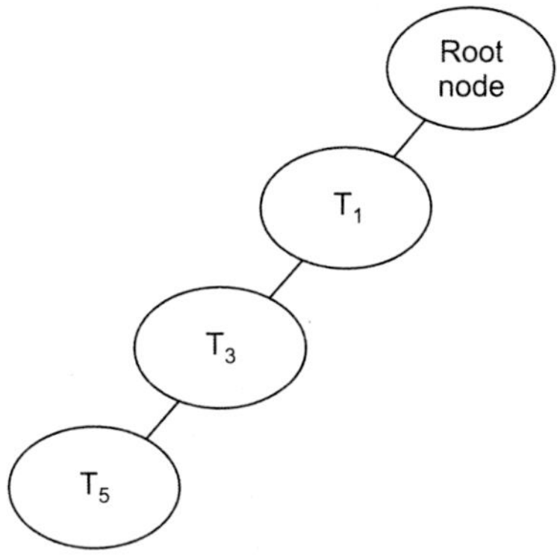

Fig. 3.12(a). Initial MOS tree (three levels with same release time).

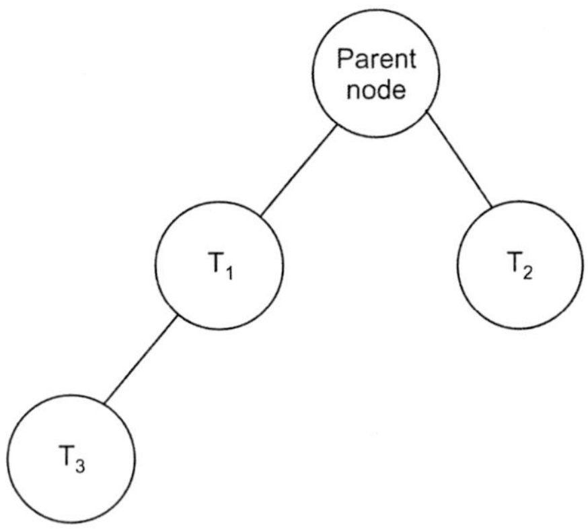

Fig. 3.12(b). MOS tree (T_5 cannot be executed).

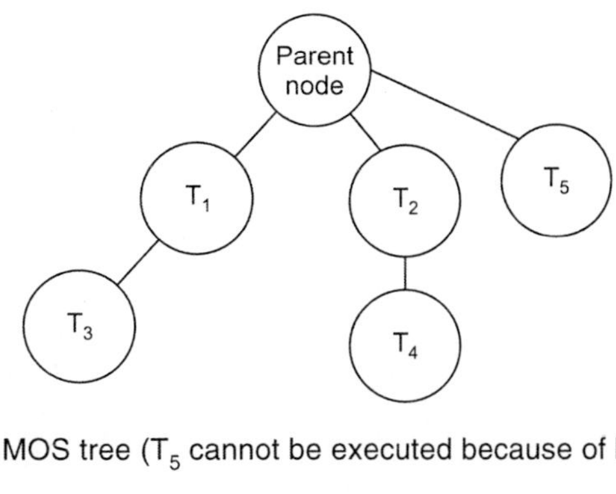

Fig. 3.12 (c). MOS tree (T_5 cannot be executed because of later deadline).

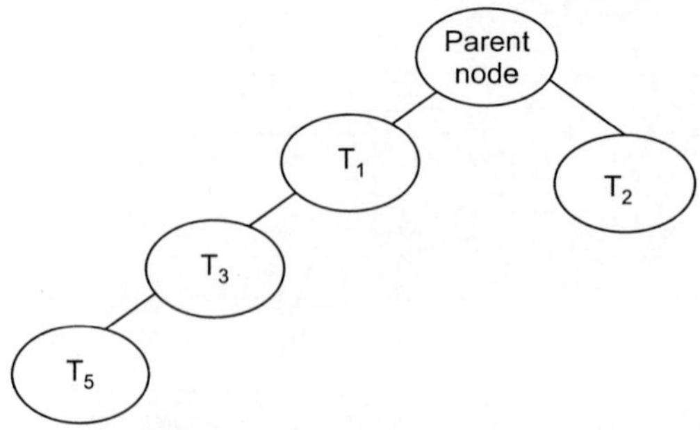

Fig. 3.12(d). A complete example based MOS tree.

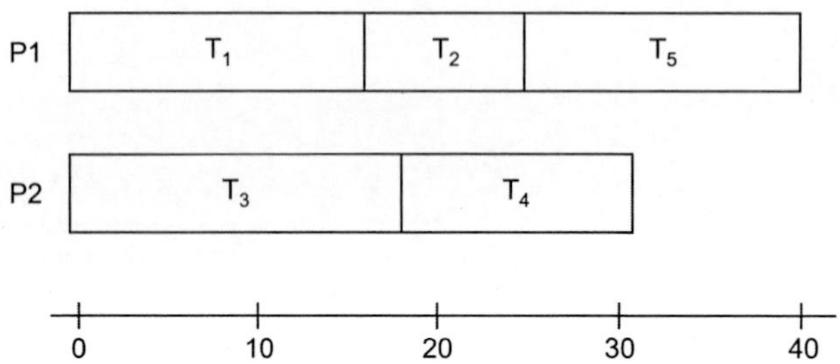

Fig. 3.12 (e). A complete MOS tree with timing constraints.

First, choose that task which is having release time equals to 0. These tasks are T_1, T_3 and $T_{5.}$ First, T_1 assigned to child node, executed first, and complete its task at 13 (as specified in deadline). Then T_3 start and complete its execution in 17. Then T_5 started according to its release time, but if T_5 started, then T_2 will not meet its deadline. T_5 is not a strongly feasible node, so backtracking done up to parent node. T_2 executed first according to its release time. T_2 will complete its task in 23. Then again, T_5 started according to its release time but with this T_4 will not meet its deadline. So T_4 will execute first and then T_5. It is clearly shown in Fig. 3.12 (*a, b, c, d, e*).

3.3.5 Buddy Strategy

Purpose of buddy strategy is same as that of FAB algorithm. It also shifts the tasks to another processor, if it does not have sufficient time and resources. The Buddy strategy way to find the lightest loaded processor is different from FAB algorithm. Each processor has three states. If Q is the processor queue length, then:

(*a*) Under load State (U): means the processor is lightly loaded. It can take the task from other processors. $Q \leq U$

(*b*) Fully Loaded State (F): means processor is fully busy. It has sufficient time and resources to execute its scheduled tasks. $F < Q \leq O$

(*c*) Overloaded State (O): means the processor is overloaded, which implies that there are many tasks in waiting queue of the processor. $Q > O$

When a processor wants to shift its task, then it can only shift to U state processors. Then it broadcast this information to only limited sets of processors (U state). These limited sets of processors called the buddy sets of the processors.

Example:

Each processor in a system connected to three other processors like in three-dimensional hypercube shown in Fig. 3.13.

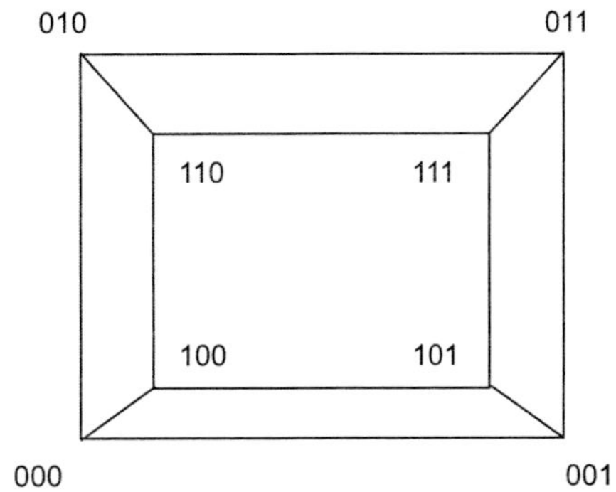

Fig. 3.13. 3-D hypercube network.

Buddy set given to its immediate neighbors. With 1 bit, each node is differing from its nearest neighbor. Give highest priority to processors differ in MSB, then middle bit and lowest priority to LSB. For example, if node 011 is heavy loaded then it search for lightly loaded processors by sending buddy sets to immediate neighbors according to their priorities. Therefore 011 firstly check 111 (MSB higher priority), then 001 (middle bit) and at last 010 (LSB-lower priority). Priority list given in table:

Table 3.3. Priority list.

Node	MSB	Middle Bit	LSB
000	100	010	001
001	101	011	000
010	110	000	011

SUMMARY

- When a fault occurs in the system, then hard real time system does not produce output on specific time. Output comes after the specific time, does not produce any significant effect, output should be on the time. For example, in stock market, if the stock trading halted for sometimes then it has no usage. Hard real time systems must satisfy all the timing constraints and should be fault tolerant in the presence of faults. The timing constraints of the real time applications achieved by using task scheduling and reliability achieved by means of fault tolerance.
- Task is the basic component of scheduling. Examples of task are reading sensor data, data processing and transmission of sensor data. The tasks occur at regular intervals of time. These tasks follow hard deadlines and their time occurs in worst-case execution. In each period, a task released. That task is ready to execute at the beginning of each period. This period called release time of the task. Each task must complete its execution before its completion time. In this, there are two types of deadline. A relative deadline is the time in which a task must finish its execution relative to its released time. The absolute deadline of a task is the time equal to released time plus the relative deadline.

- These tasks are ready to execute. These tasks have not completed their execution because of some reason and they placed in the queue (waiting queue) of ready tasks.
- When two or more ready tasks exist in waiting queue, then priorities assigned to these tasks before their execution. Priority of a task can be *static* or *dynamic*. Static priority when assigned to a task never changes during run time. For example, RM scheduling algorithm assigns static priorities to tasks such that shorter the period of the task higher is the priority. Dynamic priority when assigned to a task changes during run time. In dynamic priority, different jobs of a task may have different priorities relative to other tasks in the system. Its example is Earliest Deadline First (EDF) scheduling algorithm.
- Work conserving scheduling implies that a processor cannot be idle, if tasks are waiting for the processor in waiting queue. A processor is in busy state. If a ready task is waiting for a processor, then that task executed first and if there is no any task in waiting queue, then only a processor idle. RM and EDF algorithms are work-conserving algorithms. While in case of non-work-conserving algorithm, although there are number of tasks in ready queue but processor do not care for that, and get idle. A scheduling algorithm allocates CPU time to various processors to perform various tasks.
- A system is said to be failed or in failure state, if a system or its components does not perform well and do not give require output within specific time. When a system comes across the fault, then failure occurs. System error cannot found by operating system. When an error occurs in the system, then procedure rules of the system violated. System errors are inner instructions. This error produces incorrect result in the system. Its examples are certain portion of the computer memory that has been corrupted or broken, with which a user is not able to read the stored files. System fault is an external instruction produces an error in system.
- A fault in the system causes system failure. Some faults of the system are tolerable and some are not. When fault cause error in the system, then that fault must managed. There are mainly two types of fault. When occurrence of fault does not produce any error in the system, these types of faults are tolerable and negligible and called as passive fault. For example, impurities in the semiconductor devices may cause computer memory in the end to behave unpredictably. Hardware fault occurs in hardware. This type of fault can be permanent, temporary and for short time. Permanent faults are permanent or hard faults and are stable and continuous. These faults occur because of failure in computing unit. Temporary faults are momentary or Transient faults occur because of error in computing unit. These types of fault occur for short time duration and disappear without causing a permanent damage.

EXERCISES

1. Define online and offline scheduling algorithm.
2. Define static and dynamic priority.
3. Explain RM algorithm with an example.
4. Explain DM algorithm with an example.
5. Give an example in which RM and DM algorithm give identical results.
6. Give an example in which DM algorithm is better than RM.
7. Explain the implementation methods of EDF.
8. Define heap structure used in EDF.
9. Define fault.

10. Define period, deadline.
11. Define task, latency time.
12. List the various task assignment methods.
13. Which task assignment method is widely used in practices? Explain with an example.
14. Define MOS and FAB.
15. Explain MOS tree with an example.
16. Define periodic and aperiodic tasks.
17. Explain domino effect in RM and EDF with an example.
18. Give comparison between RM and EDF algorithm.
19. Give comparison between FAB and buddy strategy.
20. Explain why scheduling is done and which scheduling algorithm is mostly used.
21. Whether the following task set on uniprocessor is RMA schedulable or not?
    $T_1 = (e_1 = 20, p_1 = 90), T_2 = (e_2 = 50, p_2 = 150), T_3 = (e_3 = 60, p_3 = 750)$.
22. Whether the following task set is RMA schedulable or not?
    $T_1 = (e_1 = 10, p_1 = 190), T_2 = (e_2 = 20, p_2 = 250), T_3 = (e_3 = 30, p_3 = 350)$.
23. Whether the following task set is RMA schedulable or not?
    $T_1 = (e_1 = 34, p_1 = 450), T_2 = (e_2 = 25, p_2 = 180), T_3 = (e_3 = 45, p_3 = 650)$.
24. Check whether the given task set is DMA and RMA schedulable or not?
    $T_1 = (e_1 = 20, p_1 = 10, d_1 = 45), T_2 = (e_2 = 25, p_2 = 90, d_1 = 50), T_3 = (e_3 = 10, p_3 = 300, d_1 = 300)$ [time in msec].
25. Check whether the given task set is DMA and RMA schedulable or not?
    $T_1 = (e_1 = 20, p_1 = 60, d_1 = 15), T_2 = (e_2 = 35, p_2 = 200, d_1 = 45), T_3 = (e_3 = 10, p_3 = 50, d_1 = 35)$ [time in msec].
26. Check whether the given task set is DMA and RMA schedulable or not?
    $T_1 = (e_1 = 15, p_1 = 60, d_1 = 55), T_2 = (e_2 = 25, p_2 = 200, d_1 = 40), T_3 = (e_3 = 10, p_3 = 100, d_1 = 100)$ [time in msec].
27. There are four classes having boundaries as shown in table, check whether task assignment to each processor is feasible or not using next fit algorithm.

Class	Boundary
C1	(0.35 – 0.90)
C2	(0.19 – 0.35)
C3	(0.14 – 0.19)
C4	(0.00 – 0.14)

28. There are three classes having boundaries as shown in table, check whether task assignment to each processor is feasible or not using bin packing EDF algorithm.

Class	Boundary
C1	(0.31 – 0.80)
C2	(0.14 – 0.31)
C3	(0.10 – 0.14)

29. Construct a complete MOS tree for five tasks having two processors. Release time, execution time and deadline of each task are given.

Time	T_1	T_2	T_3	T_4	T_5
r_i (release time)	0	15	1	14	1
e_i (execution time)	16	10	15	12	18
d_i (deadline)	16	20	16	25	42

30. Construct a complete MOS tree for five tasks having two processors. Release time, execution time and deadline of each task are given.

Time	T_1	T_2	T_3	T_4	T_5
r_i (release time)	0	11	10	15	0
e_i (execution time)	22	15	22	20	25
d_i (deadline)	22	16	27	30	50

Fill in the Blanks

1. Period is the tasks occur at ______ intervals of time.
2. Each task must complete its execution before its ______ time.
3. ______ is the maximum time that a task can take to complete the execution of the task.
4. One task started before another task finishes called ________.
5. In ______ *graph,* all the tasks execute in an order.
6. A precedence graph is a ______ graph.
7. A priority when assigned to a task never changes during run time called ______ .
8. A priority when assigned to a task changes during run time called ______ .
9. In preemptive scheduling a task, can ______ the other task.
10. A processor cannot be idle, if tasks are waiting for the processor in waiting queue, called ______ .
11. A task set is ______ feasible, if the timing constraints of an application tasks meet during runtime.
12. A processor said to be ______ utilized implies that a processor is full busy.
13. ______ Algorithms execute task set on a particular processor.
14. A task can execute on any processor even when it resumed after preemption called ______.
15. A high-priority task can ______ a low-priority task.
16. The scheduler must scale well with ______ number of tasks.
17. Rate Monotonic Algorithm is ______ algorithm.
18. Total CPU utilization must less than ______ .
19. RMA cannot support ______ and ______ tasks.
20. Shorter period is assigned ______ priority.

True/False

1. A *precedence graph* cannot execute the tasks in an order. (T/F)
2. Precedence graph shows the dependency of different tasks. (T/F)
3. Uniprocessor scheduling algorithm uses a single processor to execute set of tasks. (T/F)
4. Multiprocessor scheduling algorithm uses multiple processors to execute set of tasks. (T/F)
5. In global scheduling, a task cannot execute on any processor even when it resumed after preemption. (T/F)
6. In RMA, task priority is directly proportional to task period and inversely proportional to occurrence rate of the task. (T/F)
7. In RMA, Total CPU utilization can be greater 1. (T/F)
8. RMA is widely used in Industrial applications. (T/F)
9. RMA requires large data structure. (T/F)
10. RMA has good transient overload handling capability. (T/F)
11. RMA can support aperiodic and sporadic tasks. (T/F)
12. RMA is optimal when task periods and deadlines differ. (T/F)
13. RM and DM produce identical result if the relative deadline is inversely proportional to its period. (T/F)
14. Earliest deadline first (EDF) algorithm also called as least time to go algorithm. (T/F)
15. EDF can support resource sharing between different tasks. (T/F)

MULTIPLE CHOICE QUESTIONS

1. WCET stands for
   (*a*) Well case execution time
   (*b*) Worst critical execution time
   (*c*) Worst-case execution time
   (*d*) None of the above
2. EDF stands for
   (*a*) Electronic data file
   (*b*) Earliest deadline first
   (*c*) Easy deadline first
   (*d*) Earliest demand first general metrics
3. RM stands for
   (*a*) Rate monotonic
   (*b*) Reverse monotonic
   (*c*) Both (*a*) and (*b*)
   (*d*) None of the above
4. DM stands for
   (*a*) Deadline monotonic
   (*b*) Degrade monotonic
   (*c*) Demand monotonic
   (*d*) All of the above
5. Heap data structure can be used for the implementation of
   (*a*) RM
   (*b*) DM
   (*c*) EDF
   (*d*) All of the above
6. FIFO queue used in
   (*a*) RM
   (*b*) DM
   (*c*) EDF
   (*d*) All of the above
7. Waiting queue contains which tasks
   (*a*) Ready tasks
   (*b*) Executing tasks
   (*c*) Error tasks
   (*d*) None of the above

8. With domino effect in RM, which tasks miss their deadlines
(*a*) Low priority task (*b*) High priority task
(*c*) Both (*a*) and (*b*) (*d*) None of the above
9. Which algorithm have many context switches:
(*a*) RM (*b*) DM
(*c*) EDF (*d*) All of the above
10. Which algorithm is more predictable:
(*a*) RM (*b*) DM
(*c*) EDF (*d*) All of the above
11. Fault model uses
(*a*) Paging scheme (*b*) Log methods
(*c*) Recovery blocks (*d*) All of the above
12. FTRM stands for
(*a*) Fault tolerance rate monotonic (*b*) Fixed tolerance rate monotonic
(*c*) Fault tolerance reverse monotonic (*d*) None of the above
13. Tasks are assigned to different
(*a*) Processors (*b*) Graphs
(*c*) Monitors (*d*) None
14. FAB algorithm stands for
(*a*) Focused addressing and bidding (*b*) Focused addressing and bidding
(*c*) Focused addressing and bidding (*d*) Focused addressing and bidding
15. Buddy strategy use
(*a*) Processor queue length (*b*) Processor length
(*c*) Waiting queue length (*d*) All of the above.

QUESTIONNAIRES

1. Define tasks.

Ans. Task is a function that a system has to perform. A task can be depends on other task or it can be standalone. Some algorithms give priority to various tasks based on their deadline, execution times and their arrival time. Tasks need various resources to complete their execution. All tasks require some execution time on a processor.

2. What is relative deadline?

Ans. Relative deadline of a task = Absolute Deadline – Release Time. Suppose a task T has relative deadline d_1 and released time a, then it must executed by time $t \pm d$. The absolute deadline is the time by which a task must completed.

3. Define schedule.

Ans. Schedule said to be feasible if all the tasks complete their execution in their specific time and before or on their deadlines. To manage this various scheduling algorithms used to get efficient output. Real time systems main purpose is to get feasible schedulability.

4. Explain static and dynamic priority algorithm.

Ans. Static means before execution, we know the deadline and arrival of all task. A task appear in between in static priority algorithm is difficult to manage. Task priority does not change with the new arrival of task. However, in case of dynamic priority algorithm, everything is in reverse. In this priority can change with time. Its examples are Rate Monotonic (RM) algorithm and the Earliest Deadline First (EDF) algorithm.

5. Explain utilization balancing algorithm.

Ans. This algorithm assigns tasks to processors one by one in such a way that at the end of each step, the utilizations of the various processors nearly balanced as possible. Tasks assumed to preemptable.

6. What is difference between preemptive and non-preemptive scheduling?

Ans. In case of preemptive scheduling, a higher priority task can preempt lower priority task. However, in non-preemptive scheduling a task cannot preempt by any other task. As shown in example, at time 4 when a task is released both processors are busy.

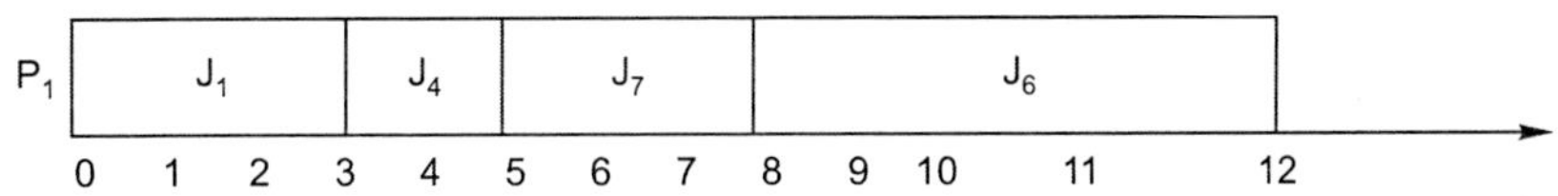

(a)

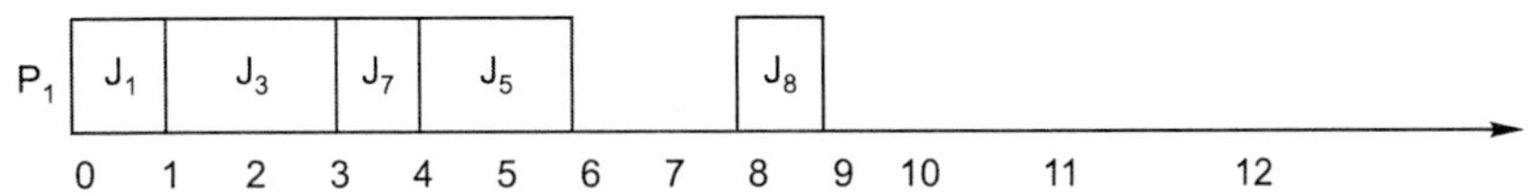

(Preemptive)

(b)

Non-preemptive scheduling is not much better than preemptive scheduling as with this number of higher priority tasks miss their deadlines. Preemptive scheduling is better when the cost of preemption ignored.

4 Real Time Databases

4.1 INTRODUCTION

Many real time applications have large amount of data, this data must be correctly processed, managed and stored for successful operation in real time system. Examples of real time database management systems are network management system, an industrial control system and an autopilot system. Real time database management system managed large quantity of data. These data should maintain and up to date regularly.

A real time database system is similar to a conventional database system in terms of queries, schemas, commit protocols, logs, transactions, and concurrency control and storage management. In a real-time database system, main is timing constraints related to transactions, and data available are valid for specific time intervals. Timing constraints means a transaction must complete before its deadlines. This timing constraint also related to start time and execution time of the transaction. Some transactions have time constraints and others may not have. Therefore, in real time database management system main is transaction timing constraints and validity of available data also called as time semantics of data. Time semantics mean that the data available is valid for only specific time interval. Examples of such available data are sensory data and stock market prices.

Absolute time consistency related to individual data items, some data values/data items used by those transactions are temporally valid. In contrast, Relative time consistency related with multiple data items, theses data items must update within a specified time interval of each other. For example, a chemical process needs two data items temperature and pressure, which closely related to the other and these data items, should be updated within a specific time to make the correct decision or perform the specific operation. To maintain the data and to meet system-timing constraints time-cognizant protocols used.

Figure 4.1 (*a*, *b*) shows working on a time-cognizant protocol, this protocol improves the processing of two transactions, *A* and *B*. In conventional database system, transactions scheduled based on their arrival time means FCFS (First Come First Served) basis. In this process, *A* arrives first, A locks the data, and then *B* arrives. Although B's deadline is earlier, *A* prevents *B* to do any transaction. *A* completes its transaction and meets the deadline; However, *B* misses its deadline. When a cognizant protocol used in the real time database system then *B* can preempt *A* transaction, as B's deadline is earlier. Therefore, with this first of all *B* will complete its transaction, meet the required deadline and then *A* complete its transaction, and meet the specific deadline. Therefore, both the transactions complete in time and meet the specific deadlines.

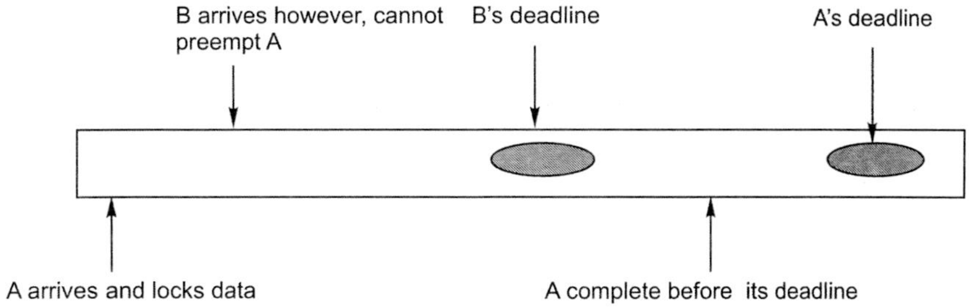

Fig. 4.1 (a). A conventional database system.

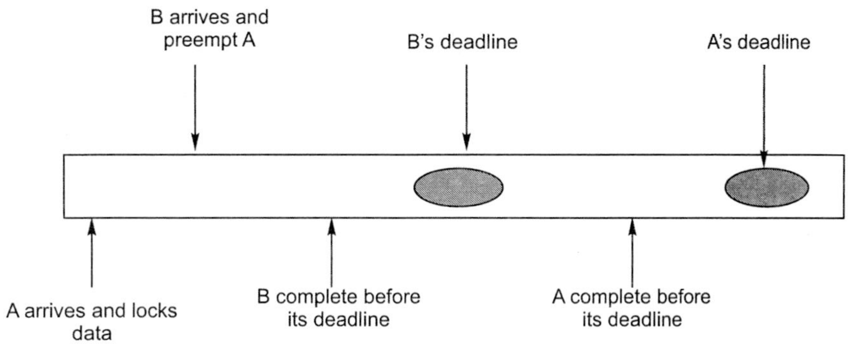

Fig. 4.1 (b). A time cognizant protocol used in RTDB.

Conventional database systems by simply adding some functional methods cannot use for real time applications, because real time applications need timing constraints, and timing constraints deals with the lowest level database schema. Therefore, it affects the overall structure of database systems. Some real time applications also need real time operating systems instead of conventional operating systems.

4.1.1 Real Time Database Model

A real time database transaction goes through various components or steps before its completion. As shown in Fig. 4.2, various components are discuses with its issues.

- Task functionality: Whether the task is Hard, Soft and Firm real time system?
- If a transaction has locked the data, then other transactions have to wait and those transactions will place in waiting queue. When the first transaction will be committed then transactions in the waiting queue will reactivate, based on the priority and after that, transactions performed its operation.
- Suppose a transaction request for a data value and that value is currently not available in main-memory. Then, I/O request generated and demanding transaction will place into a waiting queue. When requested data become available, then demanding transaction will reactivate, while seeing there is no any other higher-priority transaction in waiting.
- When a transaction completes, then it stores the result using commit command. After committing transaction will releases all of the data items used by that transaction.
- A transaction may abort many times, before its commit operation. Aborts mainly are of two types. These are:

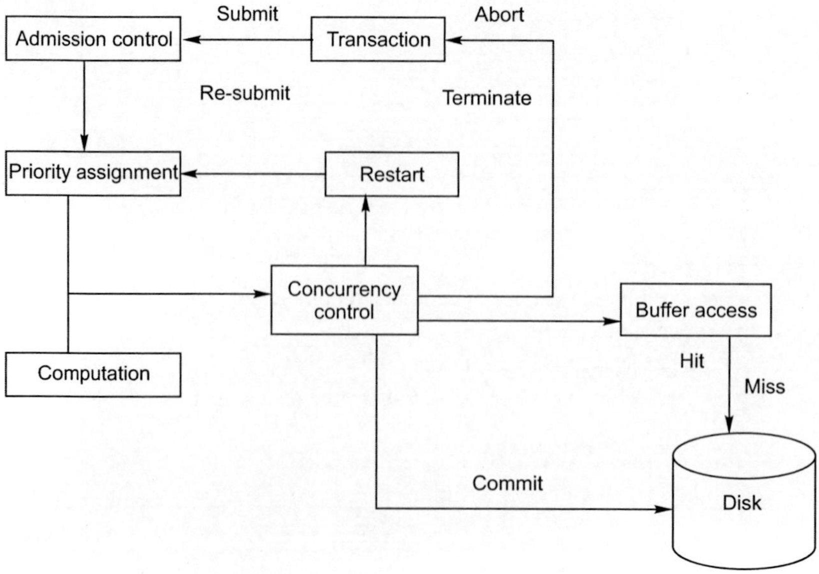

Fig. 4.2. Real time database model.

1. **Terminating abort:** There are two other aborts:

(*a*) This abort occurs due to missing the deadline.

(*b*) Self-abort—a transaction has aborted itself because of some outstanding (exceptional) conditions.

2. **Non-terminating abort:** This abort occurs due to deadlock and data conflict. In this case, the transaction can restart if its deadline remains feasible.

4.1.2 Real Time Databases Vs. Conventional Databases

1. In conventional database systems, transactions will access an arbitrary subset of data objects. In real time database systems, transactions will access a fixed subset of data objects.
2. In a real time database system, transaction invocation is much more predictable than conventional database systems. In a real time database, transactions can be periodic and sporadic transactions.
3. Conventional databases have discrete data, changed in a stepwise manner and this data cannot use for any other application. Real time database has control data, which is not changing in nature and mostly used in other applications.
4. Conventional databases contain static data while real time databases contain dynamic, valid and up to date data.
5. Conventional databases have *functional* consistency (are defined over the values stored in data objects) while real time databases have temporal consistency (concerning time).
6. Transaction scheduling in a conventional database allows any ordering which preserves functional consistency. In a hard real time database, the scheduling must also preserve temporal consistency.
7. Real time databases are more secure than conventional database system.

8. Real time databases have time semantics means the available data valid for a certain time, called as temporal validity. A conventional database system did not have this concept.
9. Real time databases deals with the timing constraints, however, conventional databases does not deal with it.
10. Real time databases deals with the deadlines, however, conventional databases does not deal with it.
11. A real time database has time semantics However; a conventional database does not have this concept.
12. Real time databases have time cognizant protocols to handle database operations while conventional databases have conventional database protocols.
13. Real time databases give good estimates of worst-case execution time (WCET), although it is very complex to obtain WCET for each transaction because transactions have multiple resources, such as CPU, I/O, buffers and data.
14. Real time databases use the time cognizant protocol to maintain and control the concurrent transactions. Conventional database uses normal protocol for maintaining and controlling the concurrent transactions. Therefore, real time databases can better handle concurrency control and the scheduling of various transactions.
15. In conventional databases, *serializability* is the main concern, which means that produced results will be correct and in serial order. However, in case of real time database, cost of maintaining serializability is very high. In this case, producing a useful result on time with a non-serializable schedule is better than producing a result too late with a serializable schedule.
16. In conventional database systems, buffer management used to reduce transaction response times. The real time database system does not use this concept because this approach degrades system performance. With the approach there may be the case that transactions can miss their deadlines or can be too late in the execution.

4.1.3 Examples of Real Time Databases

1. **Industrial Control Systems:** These systems managed by sensors and actuators. Sensors since the data; they generate input which used by controlled process-to-process specific task. The sensor takes the input and the controlled process manipulates the valves. Control decisions based on the input data and controller configuration parameters. For successful operation of a typical process control application, the controlled process has to run fast and complete its operation within a specific time. A database transaction has to be complete their deadlines, regardless of the workload.
2. **Internet Service Provider:** Today ever person is using the internet. So today's world is internet world. Internet Service Providers (ISPs) provide various services to different users. In today's worlds, service providers are increasingly implementing Service Management Systems (SMS). With an SMS, IP provides various services such as e-mail, VPN (Virtual Private Network) etc. It allocates various resources to subscribers, does resource management and provides single centralized control for the network. The real time database system widely used SMS for performing authorization, authentication and accounting for the different users.
3. **Network Management System:** These handle large amount of data for the purpose of network topology, configuration and equipment settings, etc. This system provides various applications for controlling and storing the data.

4.2 SCHEDULING OF REAL TIME DATABASE TRANSACTIONS

Real time database provides encapsulation and central control to the data. Data managed structurally, instead of managing data in an application-dependent manner, real time database have following features:

- Redundancy elimination: it removes the redundant/duplicated data. Data shared among different users and each user maintains its own version.
- Maintenance and integrity control: data containing errors rejected first before recording in the permanent database, thereby eliminating corruption of information.

RTDBMS has several policies and mechanism to handle the data. Data encapsulated and abstracted to meet the required deadline. RTDBMS should be managed regularly and follow Serializability to control the concurrent processing. Scheduling policies uses Rate Monotonic and Earliest Deadline First algorithm. When tasks with different priority access shared resources in an exclusive mode, then a problem known as the priority-inversion can occur, and it must correct by using various corrective measures. These corrective measures are not only required to manage priority inversions, however, also to handle emergence conditions.

Types of Transactions

There are three types of transactions:

(*a*) *Hard Real Time Transaction:* This transaction cannot miss the deadline. Timing constraints must follow.

(*b*) *Soft Real Time Transaction:* Response can produce over specific time; however, with this system performance degrades.

(*c*) *Firm Real Time Transaction:* This transaction has no value, if deadline expires.

4.3 SOFT AND HARD TRANSACTIONS

Real time database consists of schemas, tuples, records, record statements and various transactions on these records. Record statements applied to the value of the records called as consistency constraints. Maintaining the consistency of the database by applying various read and write operations on the database called ***a transaction.*** Each transaction must be getting a consistent view of the database. There can be a single transaction and multiple transactions in the database.

Concurrency means multiple transactions executed in parallel. With concurrency, maximum throughput and resource utilization achieved. To maintain the consistency in the database, a schedule must follow. A schedule is the particular order or sequence in which number of the transactions will execute. Each transaction must get a consistent view of the database and it is only possible with a schedule. A schedule provides a consistent view of the database to the transaction called consistent schedule.

A conventional Database Management System (DBMS) provides consistencies by satisfying *ACID* properties.

A **Atomicity:** Operation on each transaction is atomic (means single or indivisible). Sometimes all or none of the operations performed on the transactions.

C **Consistency:** Each transaction must be able to view a consistent database regardless of the failure. Data must be consistent.

I **Isolation:** Multiple transactions can execute concurrently without the interference of any other transaction.

D **Durability:** When a transaction committed, all of its changes must be stored permanently in the database regardless of failure.

4.3.1 Concurrency Control

Concurrency control techniques for real time databases are in the extension or combinations of traditional concurrency control techniques, *i.e.* Two phase locking (2PL), optimistic concurrency control (OCC), pessimistic concurrency control, or timestamp ordering (TO), which provides serialization among conflict transactions.

4.3.1.1 Soft Transactions

In the real time database, a transaction must meet its deadline. In soft transactions, a transaction can produce its output over specific time However; it leads to degrade system performance.

Soft transactions have the following phases during their executions as shown in Fig 4.3.

1. **Transaction Start Phase (TSP):** means the transaction is in ready state or active state.
2. **Lock Phase (LP):** A transaction gets the required read/write lock.
3. **Commit Phase (CP):** When a transaction commits, then all the changes made by that transaction will be stored permanently in the database. To maintain the consistency of the database it is a mandatory step.
4. **End Phase (EP):** After the commit phase, a transaction will complete by releasing all the locks that it has acquired. With the end phase, all changes made by the transactions will also be now visible to other transactions.

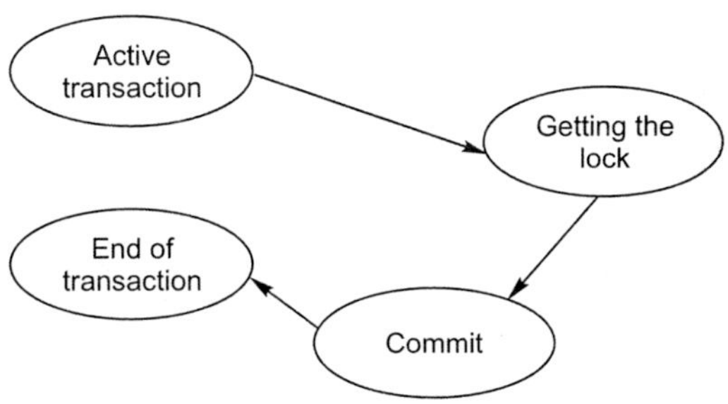

Fig. 4.3. Soft transaction execution phases.

There are some locking rules for soft transactions. These are:

Rule 1: Active soft transactions read data from the database after obtaining read or write lock.

Rule 2: After obtaining the write lock, soft transactions can change the data values.

Rule 3: Active soft transaction will get the required read/write lock.

Rule 4: Multiple soft transactions can have read locks, and all these transactions can read particular data elements at the same time.

Rule 5: Multiple soft transactions cannot have write locks at the same time. A write lock once assigned to a transaction for a particular data element, cannot access by any other soft transactions.

Rule 6: When a transaction has write lock on the particular data element, then any other soft transaction cannot make changes in it.

Rule 7: When a transaction reaches to end phase, then only its data element will be visible to any other transaction.

Rule 8: Two soft transactions will conflict with each other, if they violate rules 4, 5 and 6.

4.3.1.2 Hard Transactions

Database pointers used by hard transactions as shown in Fig. 4.4.

Soft transactions cannot preempt hard transactions. There are some locking rules for hard transactions. These are:

Rule 1: A hard transactions can preempt soft transaction. A hard transaction can have read/write lock for the data element; either that data element locked by a soft transaction.

Rule 2: Conflicts do not come in hard transactions.

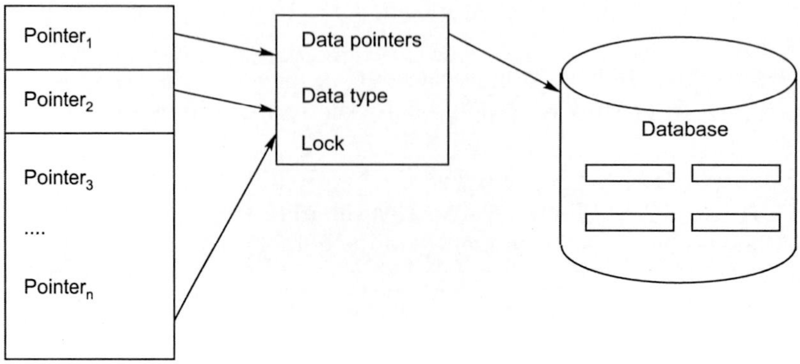

Fig. 4.4. Hard real time transactions using data pointers.

4.3.1.3 Transaction conflicts

In hard transactions, no data conflicts occur. However, in case of soft transactions, chances of occurring data conflicts are more (specified in rule 8). So here, some rules depicted to resolve these conflicts. These are:

Rule 1: If conflicts arise in soft transaction, then that transaction will abort unless that transaction has not committed yet.

Rule 2: If a higher priority soft transaction appears, then the lower priority transaction will abort unless that transaction has not committed yet.

4.3.1.4 Optimistic Concurrency Control

(*a*) For Conventional Databases

In optimistic concurrency control, a transaction goes through three phases during its execution. These phases read validation and write phase. After accessing the data object, optimistic concurrency control (OCC) detects a conflict.

If conflict detected at documentation time, then the conflict is resolved at this time, so that transactions will complete its execution. After completion, a transaction reaches to commit phase so that all the changes will be stored in the database and all other transactions will be able to see the updated and consistent data. If a transaction abort before the commit phase, then it lost whole data.

There are two types of OCC, to understand this concept takes two transactions T_i and T_j.

1. **Backward-oriented OCC (BOCC):** It checks during the validation phase. It checks whether read set RS (T_j) intersects with write sets WS (T_i) of all transactions. T_i read phase has been finished before T_j.
2. **Forward-oriented OCC (FOCC):** It also checks during the validation phase. It checks whether to write set WS (T_j) intersects with read set RS (T_i) of all transactions. In this Ti has not finished its read phase.

(*b*) Extended Optimistic Concurrency Control for RTDBs

Optimistic Concurrency Control (OCC) are non-blocking and deadlock free, that is why it is widely used in real time transaction processing. OCC performs priority based CPU scheduling. Main concern of OCC is to handle priorities, time constraints and deadlines into conflict resolution. Optimistic concurrency control decides whether the transaction is valid or not in validation phase. Transaction validation can do in one of two ways: Forward validation and backward validation. Backward validation not used for real time applications. Because if a transaction has conflict, then that transaction may be aborted or committed, as there is no any surety of it. Therefore, it is less used.

4.3.1.5 Pessimistic Concurrency Control or 2PL

The basic *2PL* protocol is a pessimistic locking technique, which guarantees the Serializability of an execution by controlling the lock and unlocks operations that performed on the transactions. It divides a transaction execution into two phases. During the first phase, also known as the *growing-phase*, a transaction can acquire all its locks dynamically as the need arises, however, cannot release any of the holding locks. During the second phase, also known as the *shrinking-phase*, the transaction dynamically starts releasing the locks it holds, and cannot acquire any more locks. It means that in the first phase, a transaction acquires the lock and in second phase transaction releases the lock. If a transaction releases a lock, it cannot get any more locks. A transaction can change from a read lock to a write lock only during the first phase.

Under *2PL*, when a transaction requests a lock and that lock is being held by any other transaction, the requestor waits (blocks) until the release of the lock. Blocked transactions are queued in the *DBMS* lock manager. The technique used in organizing this queue is of great concern in time-critical systems in which deadline maters. If every transaction in a schedule follows the *2PL* protocol, the schedule guaranteed to be serializable and does not need to verify.

A close look at 2*PL* reveals that transactions cannot release locks as soon as they are using the corresponding data objects, rather, they must wait until they enter their second phase. The period between transactions finishes using a data object and releasing the lock bounded by the lifetime of the transaction, during which other transactions might block on that particular unused data object. Thus, 2*PL* can limit the degree of concurrency in the system, which lowers the system's utilization level. Such delay gets even worse under *conservative* and *strict* 2*PL* protocols.

The Priority Ceiling Protocol

Priority-Ceiling Protocol (*PCP*) used to solve the priority inversion problem in locking-based protocols. The *PCP* protocol is as follows:

1. When a lower-priority transaction, TL, blocks the execution of a higher-priority transaction, TH, TL inherits the priority of TH and executes at such elevated priority until completion. If there is more than one higher priority transaction blocked on the same data object, then the lowest-priority transaction inherits and executes at the highest-priority among all blocked transactions.
2. A total priority ordering must establish among all active transactions, which can achieve by defining three parameters for each data object in the database: *write priority ceiling*, *absolute priority ceiling*, and *read-write priority ceiling*.
    - *Write ceiling* of a data object is the highest priority that may write the object.
    - *Absolute ceiling* of a data object is the highest priority that may read or write the object.

- *Read-Write ceiling* of a data object is set dynamically at run time. When a transaction writes a data object, the read-write ceiling is set equal to the absolute ceiling. However, the read-write ceiling is set equal to the write ceiling for read operations.

A transaction cannot obtain a read or write lock on a data object unless the *ceiling-rule* is satisfied, which states that the priority of the requesting transaction must be higher than the read-write ceiling of all data objects.

4.3.1.6 Optimistic Vs. Pessimistic Concurrency Control

- Pessimistic concurrency control or pessimistic locking considers data conflicts, it assumes that in each transaction there may be the chances of occurring the conflicts However, Optimistic concurrency control or optimistic locking assume that although data conflicts are possible, However, they occur very rarely. Pessimistic concurrency control locked the record by assuming that two or more users will update the same record at the same time. This prevents the user to update the data at the same time. Record can read However, cannot update. In optimistic concurrency control records not locked, system do not care for this. Suppose if two users want to update the same record at the same time than one user data will be updated and other user's updating are rejected and the user is informed. For example, if User1 wants to update a record and User2 only wants to read the same record, then User2 simply reads the data, User1 updates the records However, do not commit it, then User2 will read out of date information, as this record has not locked by User1.
- Pessimistic locking mainly used in resolving the problem of data conflicts, when there are a number of updates has to perform then this technique used. If number of users want to update the same record at the same time then preferably this technique used. For example, a bank adds interest rate earnings to every account at the end of each month. These applications are *hot spots* and widely used pessimistic technique while optimistic technique cannot use in these applications.
- Optimistic concurrency control wastes effort in rolling back conflicting transactions, however, pessimistic control does not.
- Optimistic concurrency controls mostly used in read and write operations, very few updates, while pessimistic control mostly used in a lot of updates.
- Optimistic concurrency control aborts the transactions. In optimistic control, if no transactions follow the serializability and recoverability, then it rolls back the whole transactions, while pessimistic control avoids aborting the transaction.
- Pessimistic control blocks an operation of a transaction, which leads to performance reduction.

4.4 SERIALIZABILITY

Serializability implies that all the transactions must execute in a particular order so that all transactions will meet specific deadlines. Purpose of serialization is also to resolve data conflicts occurs between concurrent transactions. Serializability maintains the serialization of different transactions. In conventional database system, transactions must be committed in serial order to avoid data conflicts and maintain a consistent view of the database, however, in real time database system freshness of the data is important rather than its serial Oder. Here are some rules for serializability in real time databases. These are:

Rule 1: If all the transactions completed (End phase) in the serial order, then they follow the rule of serializability.

Rule 2: A hard transactions change the data element currently locked by soft transaction serialized after that transaction.

Rule 3: A hard transaction on particular data element serialized before all hard transactions have read/write lock on that particular data element.

Serializability Example:

Three transactions T_1, T_2 and T_3 are executed in a serial order by locking data element X and Y in different ways:

Table 4.1. Serializability example.

Transactions	Action
First Transaction Start	T_1 starts and get write lock on data element (X)
Write_ Lock (X)	T_2 preempts T_1 and made changes in X as X writes locked by T_1, so T_2 is serialized after T_1.
Write_ Lock (Y)	T_3 starts and get write lock on data element Y and update it. As Y is not write locked by T_1. Therefore, T_3 is serialized before T_1. T_3 now committed and reaches to end phase.
Write_ Lock (Y')	T_1 obtain write lock on y'.
T_1 Executes(X, Y')	T_1 executes Y and X'. T_1 does not update X' as T_2 has preempted it and not saved the changes made.
T_1 Updated (Y')	T_1 updated Y' and make it Y''
End Phase of T_1	After committing phase and end transaction phase, all other transaction can view the changes made in Y.

Performance Measure

The load increased from zero to low and from low to high.

As shown in Fig. 4.5. At zero conflict, both optimistic and pessimistic have identical results. As load, become higher pessimistic give good result than optimistic.

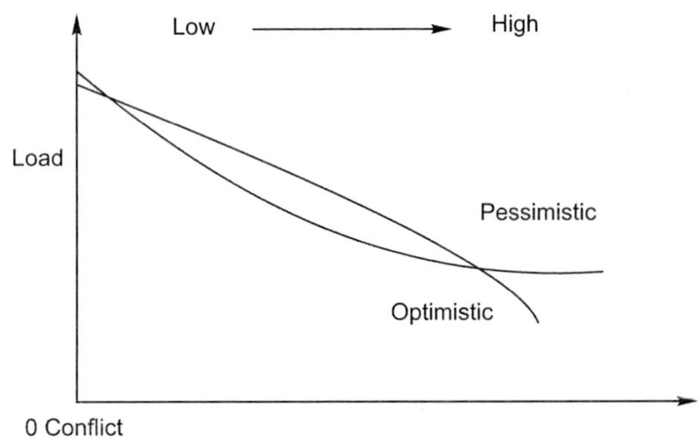

Fig. 4.5. Performance graph.

4.5 MAIN MEMORY DATABASES (MMDB)

Main memory databases represented as MMDB and conventional databases or disk residential databases represented as DRDB. In MMDB, data exist permanently in physical main memory while in DRDB data exist on disk. In DRDB, disk data can place into main memory for faster access while in MMDB the memory data can place for a backup purpose on disk. Therefore, MMDB and DRDB both can have the same data (*i.e.*, Copies of data) on both disk and main memory.

MMDB contains permanently primary copy of the data, which this main memory densities increase, which implies that larger and larger database, can be stored in memory makes main memory a reality. As data can directly access from memory, MMDB can provide much better response times and transaction throughput as compared to DRDB data. This is essential requirement for real time applications, as they have to complete their transactions on time.

4.5.1 MMDB Vs. DRDB

1. The access time for main memory is orders of magnitude and this order is less than for disk storage.
2. Main memory is volatile and disk storage is non- volatile.
3. Disk storage devices are block oriented while main memory is not block oriented.
4. The disks have a high, fixed cost for data accessing, the volume of data accessed does not matter.
5. Data layout on a disk is much more critical than the data layout in main memory. Main memory can access randomly. A disk has sequential access much faster than random access.
6. Main memory data can be directly accessed which increase throughput, while disk data cannot directly access.
7. Main memory data are more susceptible than disk data, as disk data also leads to software errors.
8. Main memory needs periodic back up, because content of main memory can be lost if the system crashes.
9. Main memory reliability can increase by adding special hardware.
10. Main memory database has very large cache. These cached data can access through indexes designed for disk access.

Real time applications mainly need faster access to complete the transaction in time. Therefore, in case of real time applications main memory database is preferred. Example of real time applications is telecom, radar tracking and securities trading.

4.5.2 MMDB Usage in Real Time Database

Main memory data have more impact on the transactions and database components. So its usage and impact discussed here:

Concurrency Control

Main memory data can access much faster than disk data. Therefore, main memory has faster response than disk data. Main memory used very large lock granules (records or fields). Some system wants to reduce contention, for that they choose small locking granules. When memory data used, then contention is already, low makes system response time and throughput better than disk data.

Access Methods

In access main memory database, index structures like B-Trees, hashing of trees used. Although hashing provides fast lookup and update, however, it is space inefficient and it cannot support larges queries like a tree. Access methods of B-trees and hashing are different.

Data Representation

Main memory databases use the pointer for data representation. Pointer usage has many features. With the help of pointers variable length field can be easily handled. Pointers are space-efficient when large values appear multiple times in the database, as actual value is stored only once in the memory.

Recovery

Data in memory can be lost, if the system crashes. Therefore, memory data must place in a disk or any other storage device for the purpose of recovery. Data must periodically update in the recovery blocks.

Commit Processing

Before a transaction commits, its updated records must write to the log for the purpose of recovery from failure. This log provides a back copy of the data, if failure occurs. As main memory data can be lost if the system crashes. Therefore, the log is the main requirement in transactions. Memory data must place in a disk or any other storage device for the purpose of recovery. Data must periodically update in the recovery blocks. However, placing the data in disk degrades system performance, because the transaction has to wait once for writing its data in log before committing. Sometimes this wait can be longer and cause bottlenecks in the system. There are many solutions to solve bottlenecks. The method makes a small portion of the main memory as a log. Storing the data in the log, before committing is now faster operation than another does. The transaction has not to wait for a long time and so bottleneck never occurs.

4.5.3 MMDB Applications

Main memory databases mainly used in IP network routing and telecom switches. These databases mainly require a real time operating system for effective real time applications. It used in set-top boxes, MP3 players, social networking sites, e-commerce, securities trading etc.

4.5.4 Market Available MMDB Software

1. **Oracle's Ten Times:** It is memory residential database software. Times Ten designed for low latency, high-volume data and transaction management.
2. **Birdstep Technology formerly Raima Corporation's RDM Embedded:** This handles Raima Database Manager, RDM Server and RDM Mobile.
3. **Enea's Polyhedra:** It is memory residential software. It used to handle fault tolerance in the system. It is available in 32-bit and 64-bit versions of different platforms.
4. **McObject LLC:** It is extreme database, specially designed for Embedded Database.
5. **HSQLDB:** It is memory residential database software. It is open source software used for database transactions.

4.6 DATABASES FOR HARD REAL TIME SYSTEM

4.6.1 MDARTS: Multiprocessor Database For Hard Real Time Systems

MDARTS is the example of a hard real time database. Conventional/traditional database does not support high speed and hard real time applications. Conventional/traditional database uses client server overhead for all the transactions. For this, object-oriented database system needed. This database provides concurrent data access and well-defined interfaces between software modules. Object oriented database also support for high speed and hard real time applications. This object-oriented database called as MDARTS—Multiprocessor Database Architecture for Real Time Systems. MDARTS avoids client server overhead. Transactions executed into application tasks. It eliminates extra overhead and focuses on basic data management services such as concurrent access, serializability, and multiprocessor transaction support. MDARTS uses several prototypes; these prototypes provide hard real time transaction and theses transactions are three times faster than conventional and existing real time database systems.

MDARTS disable preemption, when a transaction wants to acquire a lock and waiting for it. MDARTS provides real time features and all the semantic constraints needed inside the application code. MDARTS contains a library and this library checks all the declarations at application initialization time and constructs that objects which are suitable for the real time requirements. MDARTS is also helpful in remote transactions, these transactions uses remote procedure calls for data access within specific time and provide information in prescribed deadline. MDARTS implemented in C++ and executed on VME based multiprocessors and Sun workstations.

In today's world, real time applications are becoming more and more complex and process large volumes of data. Database systems used to manage data and shared data between different software components like tasks, processes and modules.

MDARTS framework used for developing object oriented data management services. It is suitable for high speed, hard real time applications on uniprocessor and multiprocessor platforms. MDARTS provides flexible data management services that are compatible with the extremely demanding performance requirements of high-speed real time systems. MDARTS transaction is composed of two components. The first component signifies local task execution time required to perform a transaction. The second component signifies blocking delays caused by a transaction for either concurrency control or communication with other processes. These two components perform real time scheduling of various tasks performed by MDARTS.

Some unique features of MDARTS (Compared to other RTDBSs) include:

- MDARTS used for both Hard real time applications and for high speed applications.
- Guaranty to know transaction execution times before performing a transaction.
- MDARTS is a convenient application programming interface (API).
- MDARTS support for both remote procedure call transactions and local shared memory transactions.
- MDARTS did not support the client server architectures.
- MDARTS support multiprocessor without performance bottleneck overhead.

Since traditional ACID properties are expensive and so they are not used by real time system. There are some transaction which is no need of serializabilty, some transaction need so. Some transaction no need of persistence However, some need so. MDARTS does not follow a single transaction while it works for multiple transactions. It supports all the transactions.

MDARTS uses following methods to provide high performance real time data management:

- Use memory rather than disks.
- Use multiprocessor than uniprocessor.
- Avoid the overhead associated with the client server architecture.

4.6.1.1 MDARTS Access to Shared Memory Data

Some real time applications timing constrains are very hard and these transactions should execute much faster than conventional system. Its example is NGC manufacturing machine has one controller, two or more tasks monitoring sensors and computing control signals. An NGC control tasks are periodic in nature and follow hard deadlines. When the task of the system executed, then sensor extracted the value from the database and calculates new control signals for the actuators.

To calculate the control signals at each cycle, number of real time database transactions used. Therefore, the worst-case transaction times must be less than one millisecond. Conventional database and database used in virtual memory cannot provide so much high speed. Therefore, if we want to access data at high speed, then that data should place in shared physical memory.

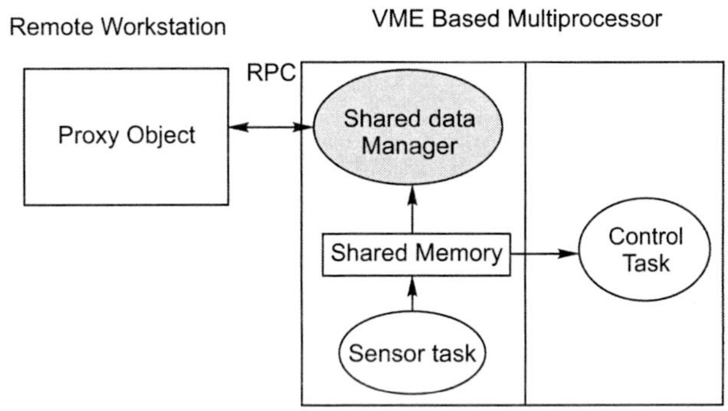

Fig. 4.6. Shared memory data acess.

Real time control systems provide data locally to the control tasks, by placing the data in memory as ordinary variables and making the data unavailable to other software modules. To permit flexible data sharing, pointers used or declaring global data structures at predefined absolute memory addresses. This is clearly shown in Fig. 4.6. Shared data manager manages the whole data. Remote procedure calls used for remote processing. When the data shared among multiple users, using pointers then there may be the case that some data can misuse or interpret or corrupted. Such error leads to catastrophic failure.

Therefore, a better approach is to encapsulate access to the common memory using object-oriented techniques. Since all manipulations of the data performed by the object methods, application code never uses the raw memory addresses. The object methods can thus ensure that the shared data accessed consistently by all tasks. Instead of shared memory, shared object technique is more valuable and mostly used in case of object-oriented databases. However, it is very difficult to implement in practices. This problem is highly solved by MDARTS. MDARTS provides applications with the shared objects without exposing the complexity of their implementation.

4.7 THRASHING EFFECT

When load increase in the system, then system performance degrades, which called as thrashing and it is shown in Fig. 4.7.

(*a*) **Under Load:** means more transactions can execute in the system. Processor is free and waiting for more tasks.

(*b*) **Saturation:** When the system is full busy then saturation point occurs.

(*c*) **Overload:** When a system cannot handle more transactions, then overloading situation occurs which called thrashing.

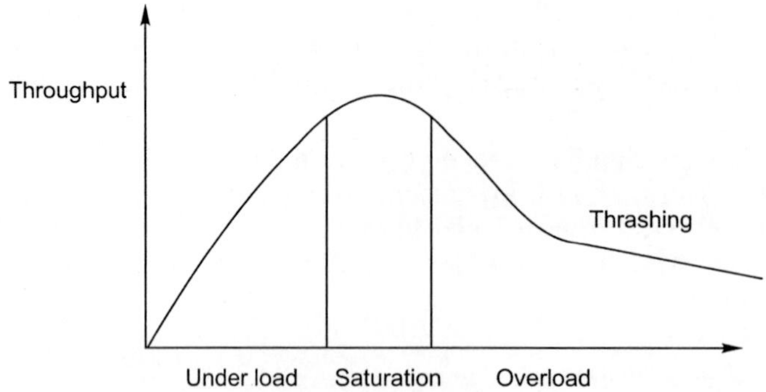

Fig. 4.7. Thrashing effect.

SUMMARY

- This chapter deals with real time database, in which real time transactions are scheduled. Concurrency control algorithms used to manage consequent data. In Real time database, main important consideration is time, missing deadline is very effective, and a deadline cannot miss. Consistency can ignore at some moments However, time cannot be. Real time database is temporal consistent while conventional database is functional consistent. Only a high priority task can preempt low priority task.
- In a real time database system, transactions invocation is much more predictable than conventional database systems. In a real time database, transactions can be periodic and sporadic transactions. Real time databases give good estimates of Worst Case Execution Time (WCET) although; it is very complex to obtain WCET for each transaction because transactions have multiple resources, such as CPU, I/O, buffers and data. Real time databases use time cognizant protocol to maintain and control the concurrent transactions. Conventional database uses normal protocol for maintaining and controlling the concurrent transactions. Therefore, real time databases can better handle concurrency control and the scheduling of various transactions.
- In conventional databases, *serializability* is the main concern, which means that produced result will be correct and in serial order. However, in case of real time database, cost of maintaining serializability is very high. In this case, producing a useful result on time with a non-serializable schedule is better than producing a result too late with a serializable schedule.
- In conventional database systems, buffer management used to reduce transaction response times. Real time databases system does not use this concept because this approach degrades system performance. There may be the case that transactions can miss their deadlines or can be too late in execution.
- Real time database consists of schemas, tuples, records, record statements and various transactions on these records. Record statements applied on the value of the records called as consistency constraints. Maintaining the consistency of the database by applying various read and write operations on the database called ***transaction.*** Each transaction must be get consistent view of the database.
- Concurrency control techniques for real time databases are in extension or combinations of traditional concurrency control techniques, *i.e.* two phase locking (2PL), optimistic concurrency control (OCC), pessimistic concurrency control, or timestamp ordering (TO), which provides serialization among conflict transactions. In optimistic concurrency control,

a transaction goes through three phases during its execution. These phases read validation and write phase. After accessing the data object, Optimistic Concurrency Control (OCC) detects a conflict.

- If conflict detected at documentation time, then conflict is resolved at this time, so that transaction will complete its execution. After completion, a transaction reaches to commit phase so that all the changes will be stored in the database and all other transaction will be able to see the updated and consistent data. If a transaction aborts before the commit phase, then it lost whole data. Optimistic Concurrency Controls (OCC) are non-blocking and deadlock free, that is why it is widely used in real time transaction processing. OCC performs priority based CPU scheduling. Main concern of OCC is to handle priorities, time constraints and deadlines into conflict resolution. Optimistic concurrency control decides whether the transaction is valid or not in validation phase.
- Under *2PL*, when a transaction requests a lock and that lock is being held by any other transaction, the requestor waits (blocks) until the release of the lock. Blocked transactions are queued in the *DBMS* lock manager. The technique used in organizing this queue is of great concern in time-critical systems in which deadline maters. If every transaction in a schedule follows the *2PL* protocol, the schedule guaranteed to be serializable and does not need to verify.
- Pessimistic locking mainly used in resolving the problem of data conflicts, when there are number of updates has to perform then this technique used. If number of users wants to update the same record at the same time then preferably this technique used. For example, a bank adds interest rate earnings to every account at the end of each month. These applications are *hotspots* and widely used pessimistic technique while optimistic technique cannot use in these applications.

EXERCISES

1. Define time cognizant protocol.
2. Define WCET.
3. Explain Real time databases.
4. Explain 2PL with an example.
5. Give an example in which OCC and PCC used.
6. Give an example in which OCC is better than PCC.
7. Explain real time database model with diagram.
8. Give comparison between conventional and real time database.
9. Define functional consistency.
10. Define temporal consistency.
11. Define deadline.
12. List the various examples of real time database.
13. Which concurrency control method is widely used in practices? Explain with an example.
14. Define ISP and SMS.
15. Explain scheduling of real time transactions.
16. Define soft and hard transactions.
17. Explain four phases of soft transactions.
18. Give comparison between soft and hard transactions.
19. Give comparison between OCC and PCC.
20. Explain why scheduling done and which scheduling algorithm is mostly used.

Fill in the Blanks

1. Real time database use ______ protocol.
2. Conventional database processed transactions based on ______ basis.
3. Using time cognizant protocol, transaction cannot miss its ______ .
4. Buffer access used in ______ model.
5. Waiting queue placed the ______ tasks.
6. A transaction can abort itself because of some ______ conditions.
7. *Non-terminating abort occurs* due to ______ and ______ .
8. In real time database systems, transactions will access ______ subset of data objects.
9. Conventional databases contain ______ data.
10. Real time databases have ______ consistency.
11. Transaction start phase used in ______ transaction.
12. A commit transaction cannot be ______ .
13. Active soft transactions read data from the database after obtaining ______ lock.
14. Database printers used by ______ transaction.
15. During growing-phase, a transaction ______ all its locks dynamically.

True/False

1. Conflicts do not come in hard transactions. (T/F)
2. A hard transaction cannot preempt soft transactions. (T/F)
3. Active soft transaction will get the required read/write lock. (T/F)
4. ACID property used by real time system. (T/F)
5. In Firm Real Time Transaction, missing deadline is tolerable. (T/F)
6. Pessimistic concurrency control wastes effort in rolling back. (T/F)
7. Pessimistic control cannot block an operation of a transaction. (T/F)
8. When system loads increases then higher, pessimistic cannot give good result than optimistic. (T/F)
9. MMDB contains permanently primary copy of the data. (T/F)
10. The access time for main memory is orders of magnitude and this order is less than for disk storage. (T/F)
11. Main memory is not required periodic back up. (T/F)
12. Oracle's Ten Times is disk residential database software. (T/F)
13. MDARTS is the example of hard real time database. (T/F)
14. MDARTS cannot be used for both Hard real time applications and for high speed applications. (T/F)
15. MDARTS support the client server architectures. (T/F)

MULTIPLE CHOICE QUESTIONS

1. MDARTS is the example of which database.
   (*a*) Hard (*b*) Soft
   (*c*) Firm (*d*) None of the above
2. ACID property used in
   (*a*) Conventional database (*b*) real time database
   (*c*) Both (*a*) and (*b*) (*d*) None of the above

3. Recovery done to
   (*a*) Find the errors
   (*b*) easy transaction
   (*c*) Recover data
   (*d*) None of the above
4. Commit command
   (*a*) Save
   (*b*) Roll back
   (*c*) Robot
   (*d*) All of the above
5. OCC stands for
   (*a*) Optimistic Concurrency control
   (*b*) Optimal Concurrency control
   (*c*) Optional Concurrency control
   (*d*) All of the above
6. Log files used
   (*a*) Store the data
   (*b*) Recover the data
   (*c*) Robot the data
   (*d*) All of the above
7. Soft transactions has phases
   (*a*) 3
   (*b*) 4
   (*c*) 5
   (*d*) 6
8. Real time database use which locking method
   (*a*) 2PL
   (*b*) 3PL
   (*c*) 4PL
   (*d*) None
9. TSP stands for
   (*a*) Transaction switched phase
   (*b*) Transaction stop phase
   (*c*) Transaction start phase
   (*d*) All of the above
10. TO stands for
    (*a*) Time stamp ordering
    (*b*) Time queue ordering
    (*c*) Time phase ordering
    (*d*) All of the above
11. Real time database use which protocol
    (*a*) Time cognizant protocol
    (*b*) Time inversion protocol
    (*c*) Time phases protocol
    (*d*) All of the above
12. VPN stands for
    (*a*) Variable private network
    (*b*) Virtual public network
    (*c*) Virtual private network
    (*d*) None of the above
13. ISP stands for
    (*a*) Internet service provider
    (*b*) International service provider
    (*c*) Intra service provider
    (*d*) None
14. Database pointers used by
    (*a*) Soft transaction
    (*b*) Firm transaction
    (*c*) Hard transaction
    (*d*) All of the above.

QUESTIONNAIRES

1. **Define real time database.**

Ans. A real time database system is similar to conventional database system in terms of queries, schemas, commit protocols, logs, transactions, and concurrency control and storage management. In a real time database system, main is timing constraints related with transactions, and data available are valid for specific time intervals.

2. Give the applications of real time database.

Ans. Applications of Real Time database are:

(1) Airline reservations

(2) Banking

(3) Stock market systems

3. Define transaction.

Ans. Maintaining the consistency of the database by applying various read and write operations on the database called ***transaction.*** Each transaction must be get consistent view of the database. There can be a single transaction and multiple transactions in the database.

4. Define atomicity.

Ans. Operation on each transaction is atomic (means single or indivisible). It may be that all or none of the operations performed on the transactions.

5. Define consistency.

Ans. Each transaction must be able to view consistent database regardless of the failure. Data must be consistent.

6. Define isolation.

Ans. Multiple transactions can execute concurrently without the interference of any other transaction.

7. Define durability.

Ans. When a transaction committed, all of its changes must be stored permanently in the database regardless of failure.

8. Define absolute consistency.

Ans. Absolute time consistency related with individual data items, these data values/data items used by those transactions are temporally valid.

9. Define relative consistency.

Ans. Relative time consistency related with multiple data items, theses data items must update within a specified time interval of each other.

10. Explain database for hard real time system.

Ans. MDARTS is the example of hard real time database. Conventional/traditional database does not support high speed and hard real time applications. Conventional/traditional database uses client server overhead for all the transactions. For this, object-oriented database system needed. This database provides concurrent data access and well-defined interfaces between software modules. Object oriented database also support for high speed and hard real time applications. This object oriented database called as MDARTS—Multiprocessor Database Architecture for Real Time Systems.

5 Real Time Communication

5.1 INTRODUCTION

Real Time Communications (RTC) deal with reality. It means that data used in real time applications will be real or live data. Real time communication purpose is to exchange the information between different users with minimum delay. Delay means latency and it must be less as possible for proper flow of data. Data should not deliver late. In real time communications, time constraints and deadlines are very important. Given task must perform on time to minimize catastrophic failure. Each message must be given a priority (priority is based on deadline, nearest is deadline high will be the priority) RTC deliver the message in time. In real time communication, reliability has less effect; important data must reach in time.

RTC is a peer-to-peer communication (person to person), *i.e.*, RTC is Unicast. RTC always has a direct path between the source and the destination. In this direct path, a path can contain several intermediate nodes. Data delivered reached to the destination directly, without saving at intermediate nodes as shown in Fig. 5.1.

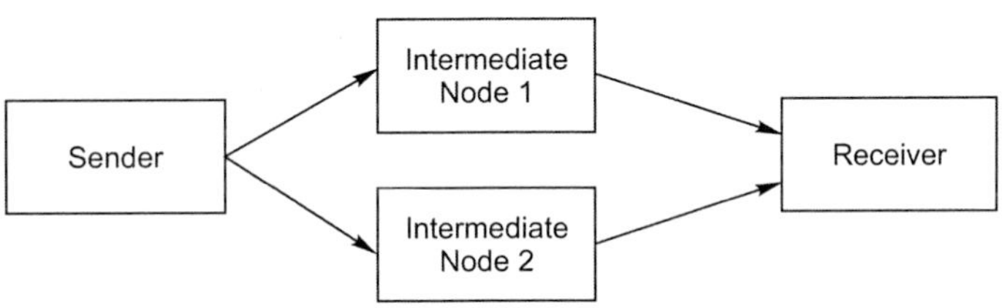

Fig. 5.1. Unicast communication.

RTC can take place in both half-duplex and full-duplex modes. In half-duplex RTC, real time data or live data can transmit in both directions on a single carrier. However, not at the same time as shown in Fig. 5.2 (*a*, *b*).

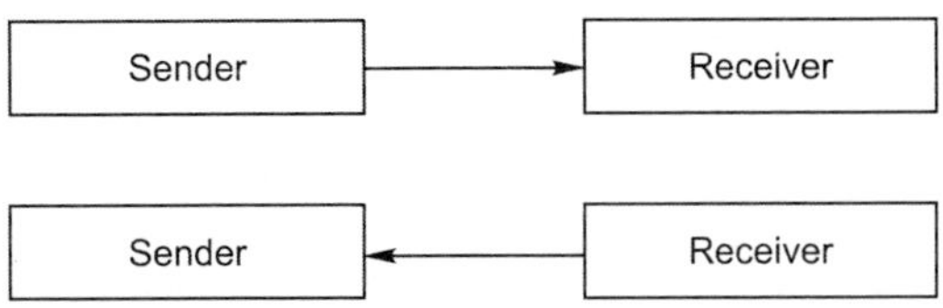

Fig. 5.2 (a, b). Half-duplex mode.

In full-duplex RTC, live data can transmit in both directions simultaneously on a single carrier as shown in Fig. 5.3.

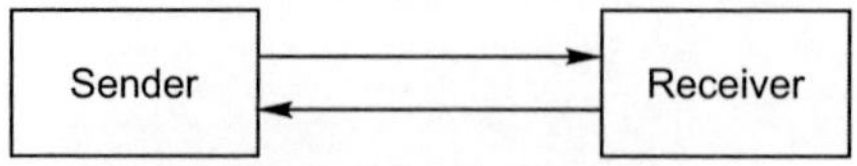

Fig. 5.3. Full-duplex mode.

Real time communications include:

- Traditional Telephones
- Internet Telephone called VoIP (Voice over IP)
- IRC (Internet Relay Chat)
- Live audio and video conference
- Mobile and cellular telephone
- Amateur radio
- Robotic tele presence
- Instant Messaging.

Factors that affect RTC

1. **Throughput:** is a measure of the number of packets that the network can deliver per unit time.
2. **Delay:** Also known as, latency is the time taken to deliver a packet.
3. **Jitter:** is variance of the latency. This can be of two types. First, fixed minimum propagation delay due to the speed of light and the second is variation due to waiting on the path.

Delay matters for some applications, however not for others, such as:

- Interactive applications need low delay
  - o Audio and video conferences
  - o Games
  - o Control applications need a low delay in the sensor, controller and in actuator.
- Non-interactive applications are less delay sensitive
  - o Video on demand
  - o TV and radio.

Throughput, delay and jitter vary according to router scheduling algorithms. Throughput and delay depend on the capacity of each path and waiting hop at each hop. Waiting or queuing depends on the traffic in the network. Throughput variation may lead to bottleneck at the links. Throughput, latency, and jitter should be within appropriate bounds for the real time communications. Examples of such networks are CAN (Control Area Network) and Ethernet.

5.2 CONVENTIONAL COMMUNICATION Vs. REAL TIME COMMUNICATION

1. In Conventional Communication Systems, bandwidth and throughput are important. However, in case of real time communication systems delivery of content by specific deadline is important.

2. Real time communication systems are economical, while conventional communication systems are not.
3. Conventional Communication Systems use Circuit switching, Message Switching and Packet Switching techniques while real time communication systems use Circuit switching, Message Switching and Wormhole Routing.
4. The real time communication service provided through connection oriented communication while non-real time communication service can be connectionless or connection oriented.
5. Real time traffic like audio and video usually arrives regularly or periodically and a real-time session/connection usually lasts for a long time, as compared to randomly arriving non-real time traffic.
6. In real time communication request is per connection based while in non-real time communication it is message based.
7. In real time communication, scheduling is Deadline Driven while in non-real time communication scheduling is Round Robin Variant.
8. It is desired to guarantee the requested delivery-delay bound for *each* real time packet, and hence, there is a need to set up a real time connection. However, in non-real time traffic it is not necessary.
9. Real time communication examples are voice and video transmission that requires bounded delays, while non-real time communication examples are remote login and e-mail in which there is no need to bounded delay. The only purpose is to transmit the data, deadlines does not matter.
10. In real time communication, there can be loss of data, however in non-real time communication there is no loss of data (zero loss).

5.3 COMMUNICATIONS MEDIA

- Electrical Medium
- Optical Fibres
- Wireless

Characteristics of Electrical Medium are:

- In this, there are twisted pair and coaxial cables.
- They are cheap to implement.
- Easy to wire
- In this, many topologies exist.

Characteristics of Optical Medium are:

- LED/laser diodes, light pulses
- High data rates even over long distances
- Immune to electromagnetic interference
- Only direct wiring or passive star topologies known to work.

5.3.1 Network Topologies

In the network, many topologies exist as in conventional communication system. These are:

- **Star topology:** All the nodes are connected in the form of a star. They are connected to a central point called hub.

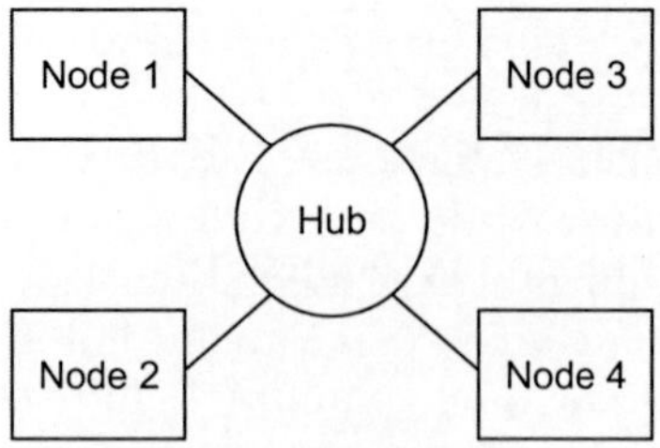

Fig. 5.4. Star topology.

As all the nodes are connected to a single point, so communication is done through this single channel which leads to collision in the network as shown in Fig. 5.4.

- **Ring topology**: All the nodes are connected in the form of a ring. In this, a token is used to transfer the data, as a connection if from one computer to another as shown in Fig. 5.5.

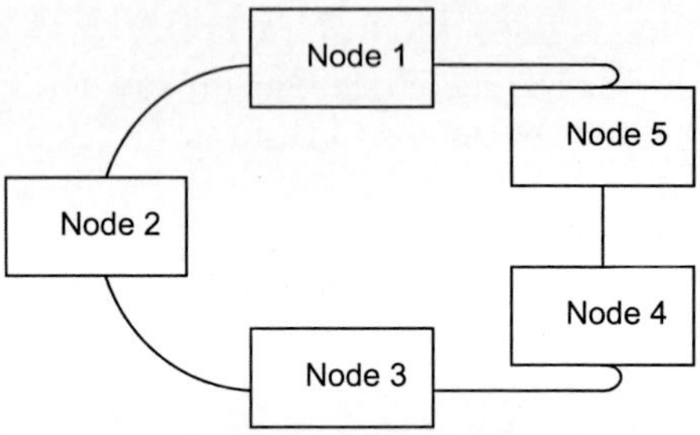

Fig. 5.5. Ring topology.

- **Bus topology**: In this, all the nodes are connected through single cable as shown in Fig. 5.6.

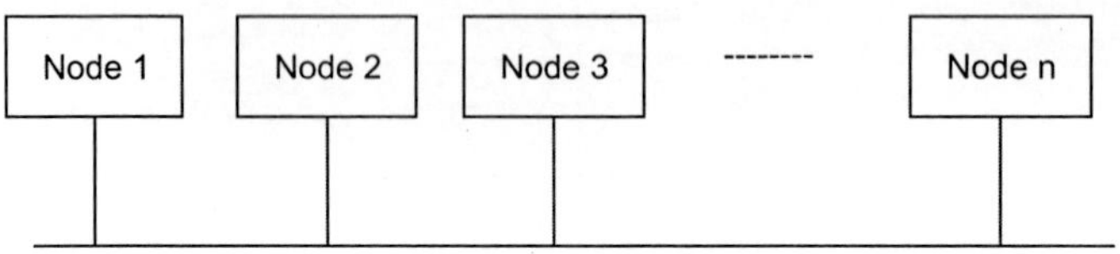

Fig. 5.6. Bus topology.

- **Tree topology**: A parent node has child nodes and these child nodes can have sub child nodes as in the tree as shown in Fig. 5.7.

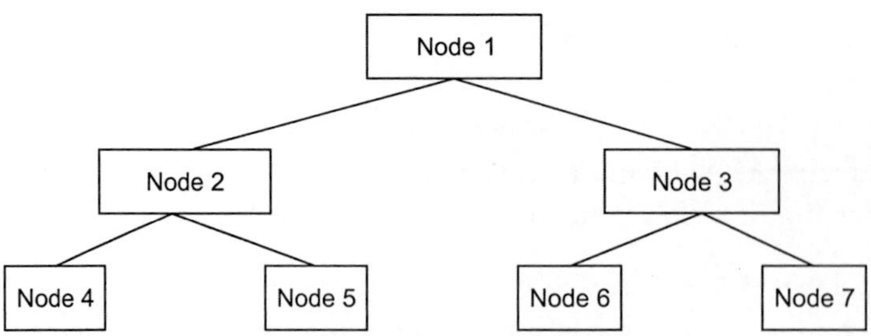

Fig. 5.7. Tree topology.

- **Meshed net:** In this, all the nodes are connected with each other. Meshed net is shown in Fig. 5.8.

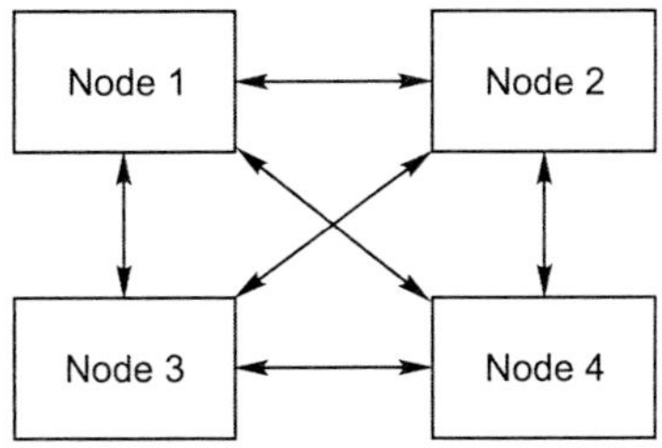

Fig. 5.8. Mesh net topology.

- Mixed forms of topologies

Network Topology effects the system response time & Reliability. The following features are important:

- **Diameter:** The maximum distance (number of hops) between any two nodes as a function of the number of nodes. It must increase slowly.
- **Node degree:** The number of edges adjacent to each node and determines the number of I/O ports per node and the number of links in the system.
- **Fault tolerance:** The network can withstand the failure of individual links and nodes remain functional.

1. Point-to-Point (Unicast) shown in Fig. 5.9.

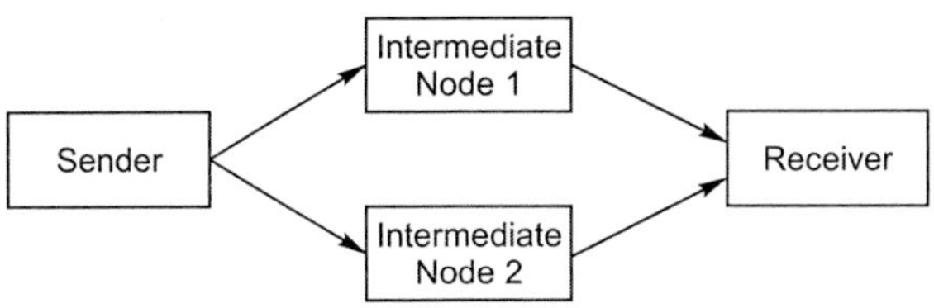

Fig. 5.9. Unicast communication.

  - Dedicated links
  - If no connection, utilize the intermediate nodes

2. Shared (Broadcast) shown in Fig. 5.10.

All the nodes share a common channel called broadcast channel.

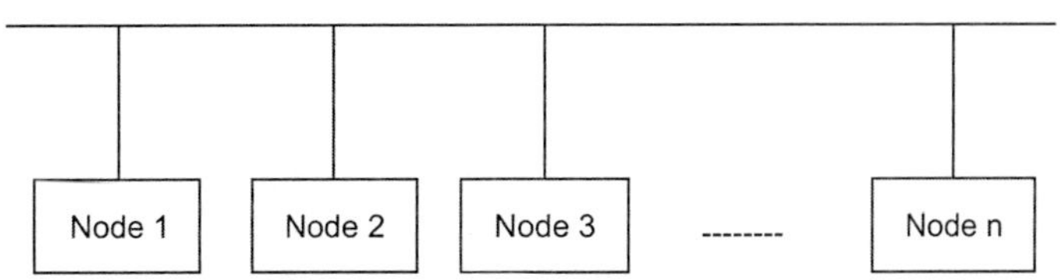

Fig. 5.10. Broadcast communication.

- Nodes have access to all communication channels
- Only one node can transmit at any time over a channel.

5.3.2 Purpose of Real Time Communication

Purpose of real time communication is to deliver the message with either zero or negligible latency shown in Fig. 5.11. The following are some properties of real time communication:

1. Less Variation
2. Less Delay
3. Ability to integrate non-real time and real time services
4. Best buffer requirement within the network.
5. High effective bandwidth utilization
6. Less overhead in header bits per packet or cell.
7. Less processing overhead per packet within the network and at the end system
8. Adaptable to dynamically changing network and traffic conditions
9. Good performance for large networks
10. Good performance for large number of connections.

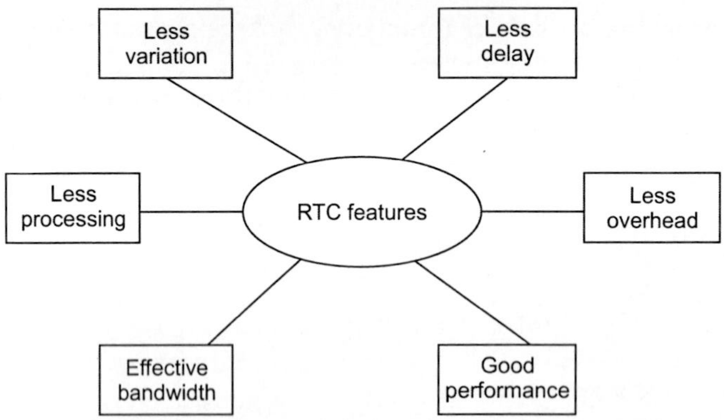

Fig. 5.11. RTC features.

5.4 TYPES OF NETWORK

In real time communication, mainly there are three types of network: Controller Area Network (CAN), LAN and Internet. This classification is based on the size of the network and the communication technology used.

1. **Controller Area Network (CAN):** These networks are smaller than a LAN and mainly used to connect the different components of embedded controllers. In general, a CAN behaves like a local bus in a computer. In an automotive system the different components such as engine, brakes; etc.; are connected and controlled through a CAN. The end-to-end length of a CAN is usually less than 50 meters. CAN is mainly used to handle the noise. CAN specifies only the physical and data link layers of the ISO/OSI model and higher layers perform the required specific implementations. In controller, control modules control the whole process by sensing the data through sensors and giving feedback to actuator as shown in Fig. 5.12. CAN bus is different from other computer buses as it carries the message related address.

   Now, CAN is widely used in various applications, such as industrial automation systems, trains, ships, agricultural machinery, household appliances, office automation systems, etc. CAN now is international standard under ISO 11898 and ISO 115192.

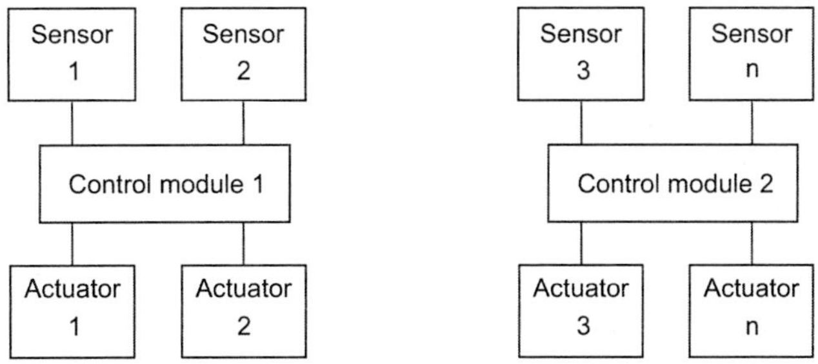

Fig. 5.12. Controller area network.

2. **Local Area Network (LAN):** It is within a building or a campus and usually privately owned. A LAN used to connect a number of computers within an organization to hardware and software resources as shown in Fig.5.13. In hardware resources scanner, printer and fax machines can share and in software files, folders and other data can share. LAN typically operates at data rates exceeding 10 Mbps and present day LAN (like Gigabit Ethernet) operates at 1 Gbps. LANs are usually implemented using broadcast networks.

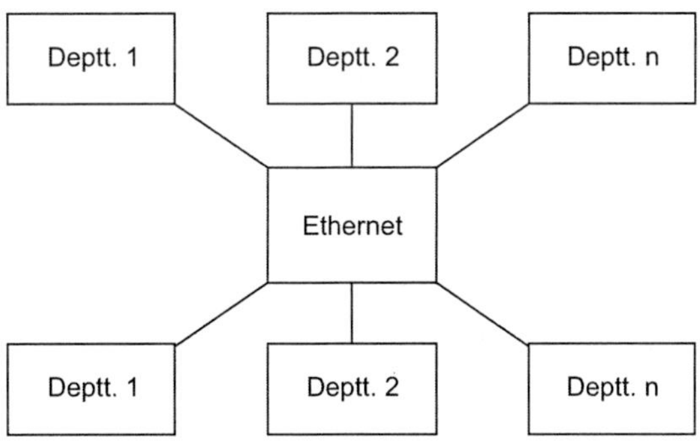

Fig. 5.13. Local area network.

3. **Internet:** Internet is also known as net. It is a worldwide system of computer network. A user of one computer can directly send or receive data from other computer. Sometimes permissions may need in some applications. A user of one computer can also direct talks with the user of other computer, known as Internet Telephony. The internet, originally named as ARPANET, uses internet protocol to link the various physical networks into a single logical network.

5.4.1 Quality of Service (QoS)

Service quality is often in terms of QoS. Real time communications must deliver packets within specific time and must guarantee the service quality of the underlying network as shown in Fig. 5.14.

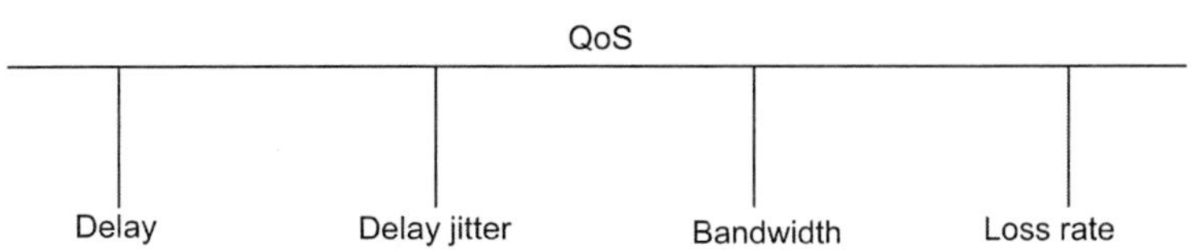

Fig. 5.14. QoS parameters.

These are the following parameters of QoS:

(*a*) **Delay:** It means latency, a packet must deliver within a specific time. In delay packet, receiving time is also noticeable. If a packet is received after the specific time limit, then it can result in time out and data receiving failure in case of hard real time applications and service will degrade in case of soft real time applications.

(*b*) **Delay Jitter:** When source sends the packet to the receiver and packet reaches for the receiver with different delays. This variation is due to queuing or waiting on path or traffic on the network. This variation can be randomly. This variation can affect the quality audio and video flow. This variation in delay is called jitter.

(*c*) **Bandwidth:** The amount of data that can carry from one station to another station in a given time (usually a second). Bandwidth is usually expressed in bits (of data) per second (bps). This parameter indicates the rate at which a connection would service by the network. Sufficient bandwidth is required to sustain the required throughput for an application.

(*d*) **Loss Rate:** Loss rate denotes the percentage of all transmitted packets that may be lost during transmission. Packets can be lost because of several reasons such as fixed delay, delay jitter, traffic in the network, buffer overflow and data corruption. In controlled applications zero loss rates is required while in the case of multimedia data loss is tolerable. Data corruption can be ignored in fibre optics, while in case of wireless media it is significant, and cannot be ignored.

5.4.2 Traffic Classification

Traffic is classified based on its traffic generation characteristics. Traffic classification is based on the data generated by the source of transmission on the network. CBR and VBR are shown in Fig. 5.15 (*a*, *b*). The following are the important classifications of traffic:

(*a*) **CBR Traffic:** implies Constant Bit Rate generation Traffic.

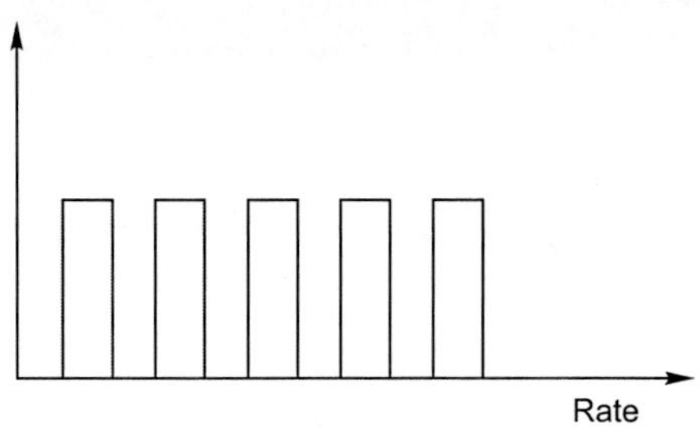

Fig. 5.15 (a). CBR traffic.

Its example is periodic data generated by sensors. This type of traffic appears in hard real time applications. In this, constant data rate is generated.

(*b*) **VBR Traffic:** It implies Variable Bit Rate generation. Its example is compressed audio and video signals. In this, traffic, data source alternates between periods. In this, data is transmitted in varying rates in which silence can occur.

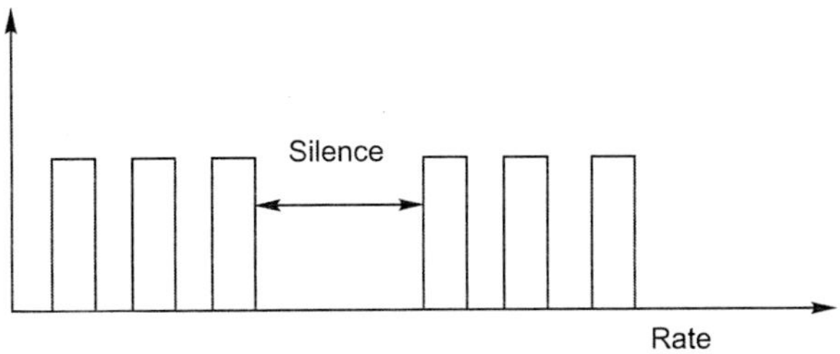

Fig. 5.15 (b). VBR traffic.

(*c*) **Sporadic Traffic:** Variable sized packets generated in bursts. Its example is traffic generated by alarm message.

5.4.3 LAN in Soft Real Time Applications

In soft real time applications, the message must deliver within specific time with or without minimum delay. If the message delivered over a specific time, then it can degrade message or service quality. These applications transfer real time CBR and VBR traffic. These applications do not ensure service quality (QoS), however they only refer that the data should be delivered within a specific time with or without minimum delay.

5.4.4 LAN in Hard Real Time Applications

In hard real time applications, messages must be receive by to the receiver in time, a little delay in delivery or receiving can cause catastrophic failure. Therefore, data must reach in time. These applications transfer real time CBR traffic such as periodic sensor signals. Hard real time applications mainly use three classes of protocols: global priority based, calendar based and bound access protocols.

5.5 ARCHITECTURE OF REAL TIME COMMUNICATION SYSTEM

In real time communication, all the nodes transfer their packets by using one common channel called broadcast channel. When single channel is used, the chances of occurring collision will be more. It is an example of Industrial Robots.

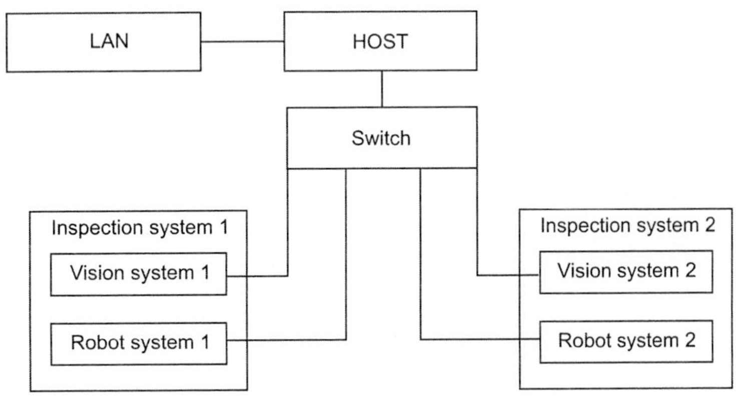

Fig. 5.16. Architecture of real time industrial robot.

When one node is transferring the packet it does not know that other is also transmitting the data, as data flows through a single channel, it leads to collision in the network. This collision can be detected by the Ethernet network and could be solved. To solve this collision, messages are delivered with little delay. However, with this message will not be received by the receiver in time. To do this, a protocol called Carrier Sense Multiple Access with Collision Detection (CSMA/CD) is used. If no collisions occur on the network, then message-receiving time will be known. TCP acknowledges data, so the time for sending acknowledgment data should be known. UDP does not acknowledge the data.

There are two methods to avoid collisions on the network:

1. By dividing one collision domain into several smaller ones
2. By managing medium access on application level.

In Fig. 5.16, the network topology of the real time industrial robot is shown. The host is the computer/PC which in on LAN network. A switch is used to control collision on the network. The switch directly transfers the packets from the robot system 1 to the vision system 1 independently from concurrent network traffic between host and robot system 2 or vision system 2. Therefore, use of switches provides collision free point-to-point communication between different components in the network.

5.6 TOKEN BASED PROTOCOL OR TIMED TOKEN PROTOCOL (TTP)

Token-based protocol is also known as timed token protocol. It is a MAC protocol. This protocol is widely used in various network standards such as the IEEE 802.4 token bus and the Fiber Distributed Data Interface (FDDI). This is the main protocol used in a real time communication system. It is a token passing protocol, in which each node must guarantee a share of the network bandwidth, because of this property, timed token-based protocol transfer synchronous based message. Synchronous messages used in real time communication have deadline constraints. However, sometimes this protocol can also be used to transfer asynchronous messages.

The IEEE 802.4 standard is Manufacturing Automation Protocol (MAP), which has been widely used in computer-integrated manufacturing and industrial applications. The medium access layer should properly control to deliver packets in specific time. In the timed-token protocol, the token manages and control the whole communication process of MAC layer. This token is also passed among the various nodes in a network in a circular fashion.

This protocol is used to manage real time traffic, by guaranteeing a reasonable share of the unused bandwidth for the best-effort traffic. It is a token passing protocol, in which each node must guarantee a share of the network bandwidth to get best effort traffic. In the timed-token protocol, token passes among the various nodes in a network in a circular fashion and it is given to each node until it reaches its destination.

An important parameter in this is, a protocol is the Target Token Rotation Time (*TTRT*). It is the expected time taken by a token to rotate around an entire network. Node is represented by *i*. Each node *i* has an associated time NT_i; whenever a node receives the token, it can transmit its messages for a time not greater than NT_i.

Figure. 5.17 shows a timed token-based network, in which there are four nodes. These nodes are arranged in a logical ring and they share a common channel.

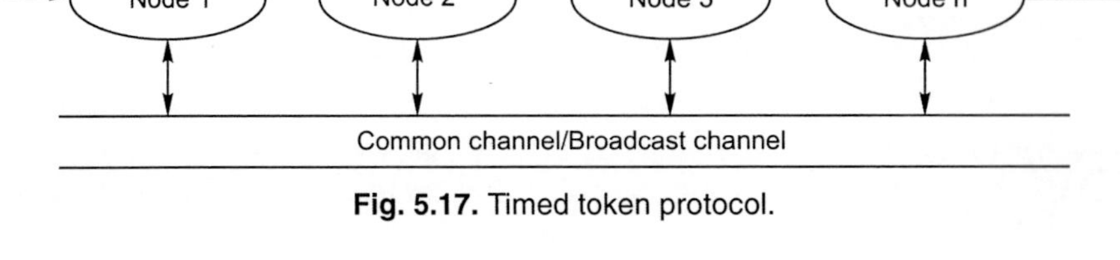

Fig. 5.17. Timed token protocol.

This protocol has n nodes and these nodes share a common channel like buses, in which each node can transmit synchronous real time traffic. In this network, node is represented by *i*, synchronous message is denoted by S_i, which is further described by three parameters (C_i, D_i, T_i), where:

- C_i is the maximum amount of time taken by node to transmit synchronous message S_i. This includes the time to transmit both the message payload and the message headers/ footers.
- *DI* is the maximum amount of time that a message S_i can wait in the transmission queue before its transmission is complete. It is also known as the relative deadline of the message. Hence, the transmission of the *j-th* message, which is queued at time $t_{i,j}$, must be completed no later than its absolute deadline $d_i = t_{i,j} + D_i$.
- T_i is the generation period of messages in stream S_i. If the *j-th* message in the Stream S_i is put in the transmission queue at time $t_{i,j}$, then the $(j + 1)$*-th* will arrive in the transmission queue at time $t_{i,j} + 1 = t_{i,j} + T_i$.

The channel utilization of each message in S_i is:

Definition 1: *Target Token Rotation Time (TTRT). The expected time taken by a token to rotate around an entire network.*

Definition 2: *The total bandwidth allocated to the nodes must be less than the available network bandwidth for efficient bandwidth utilization, i.e.*

$$\frac{\sum_{i=1}^{n} H_i}{TTRT} \le 1 - \frac{\tau}{TTRT}$$

This definition is protocol constrainted.

Definition 3: *τ is the time needed to transmit the token between various nodes, including the overhead introduced by the protocol.*

Definition 4: *If $S_{i,j}$ denotes the time at which the transmission of the j-th message in stream S_i is completed, the deadline constraint requires that for i = 1, ..., n, and j = 1, 2, ..., where $t_{i,j}$ is the message arrival time and D_i is its relative deadline.* It is a deadline constraint which ensures that every periodic message is transmitted before its absolute deadline.

Definition 5: *A stream set $\Gamma = \{S_1, S_2, ..., S_n\}$ is said to be feasible or schedulable when both Deadline Constraint and Protocol Constraint are met.* Deadline Constraint means all the messages have transmitted before its absolute deadline. In the Protocol Constraints sum of each node time should not be greater than the *TTRT* minus the overhead τ.

Definition 6: The average token rotation time does not exceed *TTRT* and the maximum rotation time does not exceed 2*TTRT*. If *D* is the minimum deadline among stream deadlines, then $D = min\ (D_i)$, it means that $TTRT = D/2$. From the Protocol Constraint it follows that:

$$\sum_{i=1}^{n} H_i \le TTRT - \tau = \frac{D}{2} - \tau$$

The bandwidth available for the real time traffic can be obtained dividing the above equation by *D*:

$$\frac{\sum_{i=1}^{n} H_i}{D} \le \frac{1}{2} - \frac{\tau}{D}$$

Since the total available bandwidth is $1 - \tau/TTRT$, the *TTP* can guarantee at most half of the total available bandwidth for the real time traffic.

5.6.1 Timed Token Protocol Rules

Here are some rules for proper functioning of the protocol. These are:

1. When a connection established in the network (so that the sender and receiver can transmit messages with each other), each node i declares a *TTRT*. This *TTRT* value should be equal to one-half of the deadline D_i related to its message S_i. Each node *i* has an associated time NT_i. The minimum declared value is chosen as *TTRT* and this value depends on NT_i.
2. Each node has two timers:
   (*a*) **Token Holding Timer (THT):** It is the time a node can hold a packet. THT counter will increase each time, when the node is delivering real time traffic or best-effort traffic, otherwise its value will not increase.
   (*b*) **Token Rotation Timer (TRT):** It is the time a token rotates in the given network by reaching each node. *TRT* counter increases always. When *TRT* = *TTRT*, it is reset to 0 and the token is signed as "late" by incrementing the node's late counter *Lc* by one. To initialize the timers and *Lc*, no messages are sent during the first token rotation after the ring initialization.
   (*c*) When node *i* gets the token, it performs the following operations:
   0 If $Lc > 0$, it sets $Lc = Lc - 1$ and $THT = TTRT$.
   Otherwise, $THT = TRT$ and $TRT = 0$.
3. Only the node holding the token can transmit messages. Timers control whole transmission process. In progress, transmission cannot interrupt until its completion.

As shown in Fig. 5.18, each node waits for the token. If there is synchronous data transfer, then the token will transfer to the node. Late token means token has to wait for sometime; otherwise, the token will pass immediately.

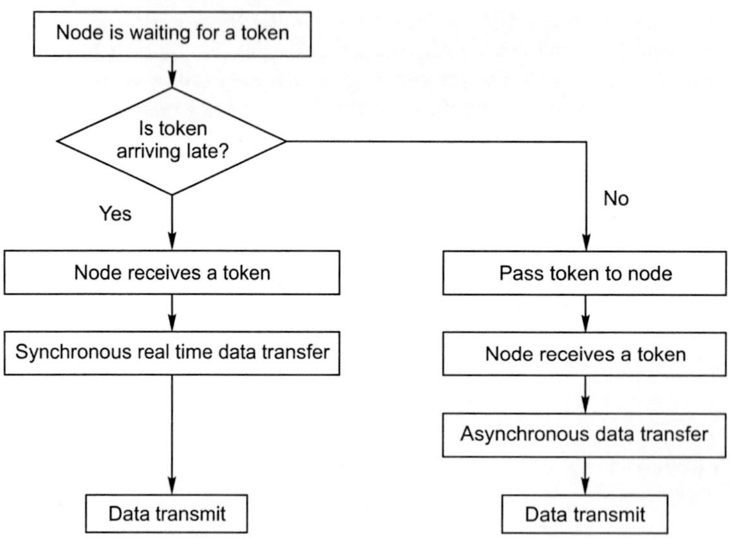

Fig. 5.18. Flowchart of timed token protocol.

The main drawback of *TTP* is the inability of guaranteeing the total available bandwidth for the real time traffic.

5.7 DEADLINE BASED PROTOCOLS

Real time systems respond to the input immediately. They have some specific time called timing constraints in which they have to give their outputs. Producing the output, after specific time degrade system performance, leads to catastrophic failure and sometimes output is useless for both system and user. They have to respond in order of milliseconds or in microseconds. Deadlines are necessary and must be fulfilled for the proper functioning (output) of the system. A failing system is not able to achieve its tasks in specific deadlines. Therefore, the output must be achieved in a specific time. Deadlines of all the tasks must meet, regardless of system load. Examples are a printer, phone and fax machines, driving vehicle such as cars and others. Non-real time system does not follow these conditions; it does not have any timing constraints and can respond to output at any time.

A deadline base protocol can be preemptive and non-preemptive. This protocol guarantees that all tasks must be complete before its deadline. To do this feasibility of all tasks must be checked before executing the tasks. Arrival time, start time, execution time, release time of all tasks must be known before the execution of tasks. Deadline based protocol knows the release time of an operation, however, not its start time. For set of tasks, S is the scalability of task T and A is the operation of a task T, S_A is the start time (the time instant when the operation starts its execution) of the task T. An operation can schedule if its start time is known. A system of operations is schedulable if there is at least one schedule satisfying the constraints of the system.

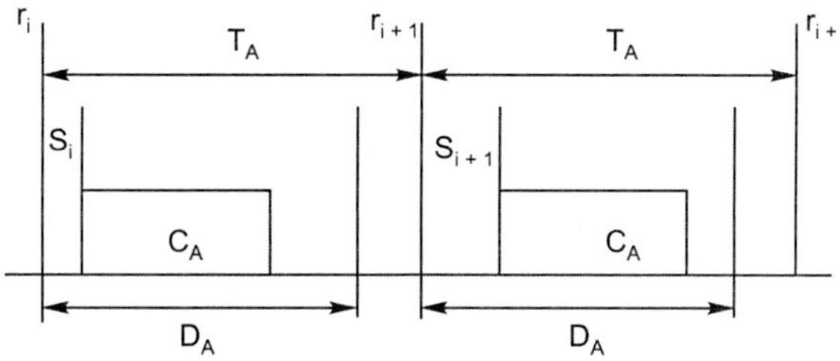

Fig. 5.19. Deadline based model.

An operation A starts its execution at its release time r_A. The release time is periodically repeated with a period T_A. Therefore, if the first release of an operation A is $r_0 = r_A$ then the ith release time of the operation is $r_i = r_A + iT_A$, for all i greater than or equal to 1 as shown in Fig. 5.19. Each instance of an operation A which requests its execution at $t = r_i$ must finish its execution by $r_i + D_A$, where D_A is the deadline of A. C_A is its computation time and is worst-case execution time.

For the latency-based model, the operations are always executed as soon as they are available and they are repeated periodically with a period T_A (as shown in Fig. 5.20). So if the first start time $s_0 = s_A$ of an operation A is known, then the ith start time of the operation is $s_i = s_A + iT_A$, for all i greater than equal to 1.

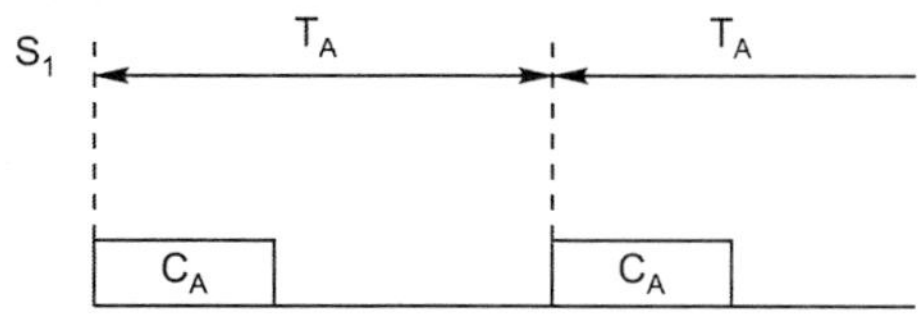

Fig.5.20. Latency based model.

In Latency based protocol only the start time of the first instance of an operation is unknown. Once the start time of the first instance is known, the start times of all the instances are also known and their release times are useless for this model. The difference between the two models is depicted for an operation A in Fig. 5.21.

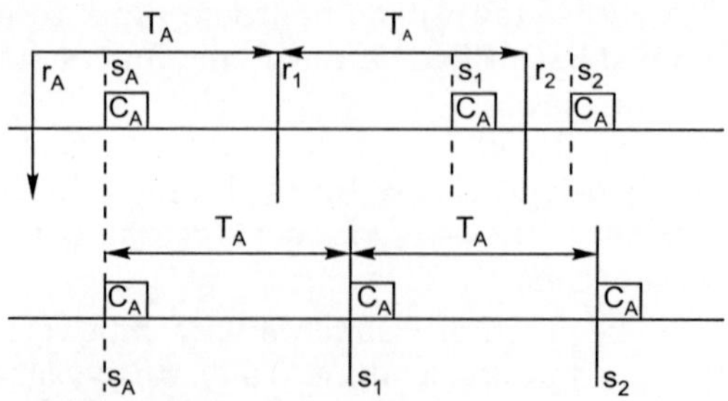

Fig. 5.21. Difference between deadline and latency based protocol.

5.8 POLLED BUS PROTOCOL

Polled bus protocol is a priority based protocol and is non-preemptive. Polling is performed on a set of tasks so that all tasks will meet its deadline. To do this, a poll number is assigned to each task, based on its deadline and task priority. The task having nearest deadline and higher priority will assign a high polled number so that it will execute first in the ready queue. Polling performed to minimize the probability of real time messages is missing its deadlines. When a token bus is used instead of a polling bus, then chances of getting missing deadline is more. Therefore, that is why it is preferred to use the polling bus in the network. Each node of the system consists of multiple processors interconnected by a broadcast bus and individual nodes are interconnected through an arbitrary network. All the nodes in the network share a common channel called common bus or polled bus. Using the common bus in the network and giving a different polling number of different tasks provides a high degree of flexibility in scheduling messages.

When the bus is free, the various tasks at a node write the poll number onto the bus and read it back, one bit at a time, starting from the most significant bit. If at any time the bit read back is different from the bit written, then that particular task will drop. This polling bus method provides decentralized control of the intra-node bus.

When the bus is busy, it gives a signal of *busy-line*, which means that, this line is used for transmitting the messages based on task priorities and polling numbers and imposing mutual exclusion on the broadcast medium. The busy-line has two states, dominant and recessive. If one node assigned dominant, then the entire node remarked as dominant. Time is equally divided among all the nodes. As shown in Fig.5.22, *R* is for recessive, *D* is for dominant. Once a node is given value *D*, then all other nodes are also noticed as *D*. *A, B, C, D* are the different nodes in an arbitrary network.

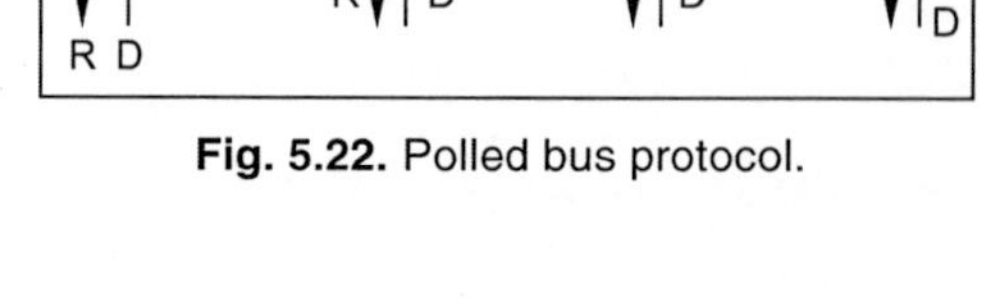

Fig. 5.22. Polled bus protocol.

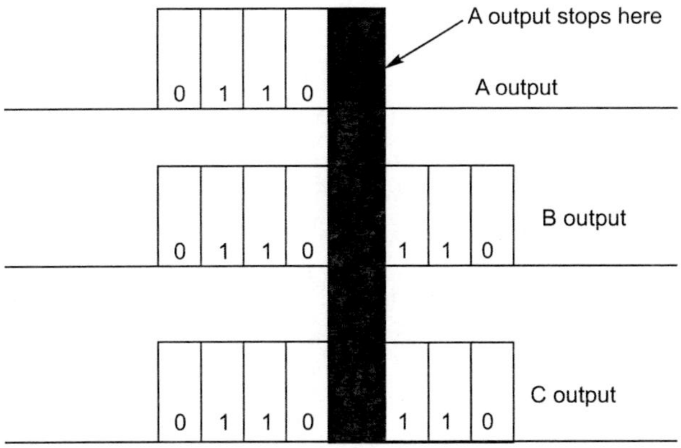

Fig. 5.23. One output stops in polled bus protocol.

Mutual exclusion implies:

- During a message transmission, the sending node keeps the busy signal dominant.
- When a node gets the busy signal *dominant,* it cannot start a new transmission.

Bus-arbitration implies:

- A node can start sending messages, if it detects no *dominant* signal on the busy-line for one bit-time.
- For one per bit-time, node starts sending a unique bit 1 for dominant and 0 for recessive. The node also sends poll number of the message based on the message deadline, time constraints and message priority on busy-lines.
- Then at the same time, node listens to received values. If listen value is different from the sending value, then the node will drop that value.
- If all bits-values have transmitted successfully, it keeps the busy-line *dominant* and sends its message.

When there are chances of occurring collision in the network, then collision must detect as we are using a common or polled bus. In this case, two nodes, suppose A and B want to send messages at the same time, then these two nodes must be provided unique polling number or priority so as to deliver the message effectively. In contrast, if A and B send data at the same time, however these two nodes have not assigned a unique polling number, then output will be stopped at some time as shown in Fig.5.23. Message priorities or polling numbers assigned by priority server. A message in the polling bus protocol can get delayed by a message already on the polled bus and by any pending message having higher priority.

Suppose that for each message m in node, the maximal transmission time is C_m and the minimal period is T_m, then the worst-case response time for message m will be R_m:

$$R_m = C_m + w_m$$

where, $$w_m = B_m + \sum_{\forall j \in hp(m)} \left\lceil \frac{w_m}{T_j} + 1 \right\rceil C_j \text{ with } B_m = \max_{\forall k \in lp(m)} (C_k)$$

$hp(m)$ is the set of messages having higher priority than m.

$lp(m)$ is the set of messages having lower priority than m.

w_m is the waiting time for messages having higher priority than m, messages will remain in queue before transmission.

B_{um} the time that message m blocked by a lower priority message on the medium that started before *m* became queued. With this, for each message a worst-case delay can compute.

5.8.1 Polled Bus Protocol Implementation on CAN Bus

CAN is Control Area Network, in which a number of processors are connected through a common bus called CAN bus. All these processors have a common controller interface. CAN architecture is shown in Fig. 5.24. Purpose of CAN bus is to deliver the messages from all the nodes within specific time so that all messages meet deadlines and timing constraints. CAN bus is designed in such a way that network should be able to work in worst-case condition too.

CAN Architecture

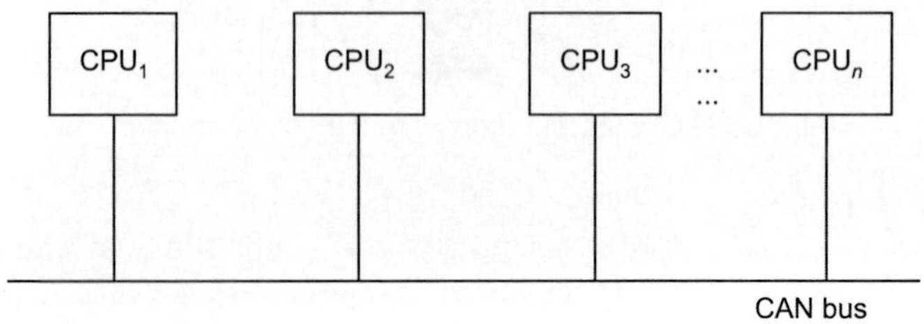

Fig. 5.24. CAN architecture.

5.9 CONTENTION BASED PROTOCOL

A contention based protocol and Media Access Control (MAC) protocol used in Ad hoc wireless networks shown in Fig. 5.25.

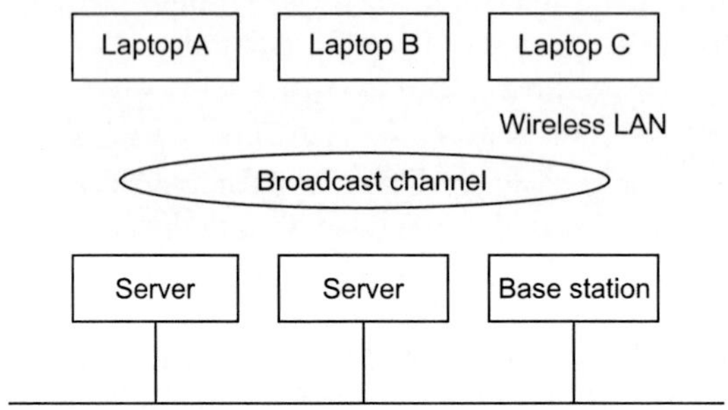

Fig. 5.25. Contention based protocol in MAC.

5.9.1 MAC Protocol Designing

Quality of service: Ad hoc networks provide limited quality of service, due to the high movements of mobile nodes. Once a node moves with respect to another node, it losts its reservation.

Synchronization: MAC protocol must provide synchronization among the various nodes. Synchronization is important for efficient bandwidth.

Bandwidth efficiency: Purpose of this network is to provide efficient bandwidth and guarantee the equally transmission of bandwidth to all nodes. This network provides limited bandwidth, and all the nodes adjusted within this bandwidth.

Nodes movements: In Ad hoc networks, nodes are moveable. Therefore, to manage, QoS and efficient bandwidth utilization, information between different nodes must manage properly. It should not be over burden on a single node.

No central coordination: In Ad hoc networks, as nodes are moveable, there is no central point of coordination. It means that the record of the node is lost when a node moves from one position to another. Information must be exchanged between different nodes.

Common channel: As both wired LAN and wireless LAN share a common channel (if one node is transmitting the data, then another node cannot send data at the same time. If it does, it leads to interference called a collision.), so chances of occurring collision is more. Therefore, MAC protocol must be designed in such a way that it minimizes the collision.

Hidden station problem: Station/Terminal *B* is sending data to Station *C*. A wants to send data to *B*, however is not able to hear that *B* is busy. Therefore, *A* sends data to *B* and cause collision in the network (as data passes through a common channel). It hides station problem as *B* is not bearable to *A*. It is shown in Fig. 5.26 (*a*).

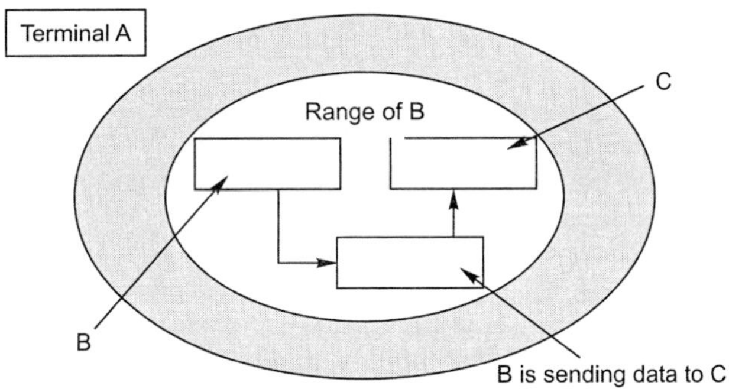

Fig. 5.26 (a). Hidden station problem.

Signal propagation delay: Signal propagation delay is the amount of time needed for the transmission to reach the receiver. Sender node is sending the data, however receiver node due to mobility has not reached yet. The Ad hoc networks that utilize the synchronization will have to expand the time slot to accommodate the propagation delay.

Exposed station problem: Station *B* is sending data to Station *C*. Station *B* also wants to send data to *A*, however, *B* think transmission would fail. It is exposed station problem and shown in Fig. 5.26 (*b*).

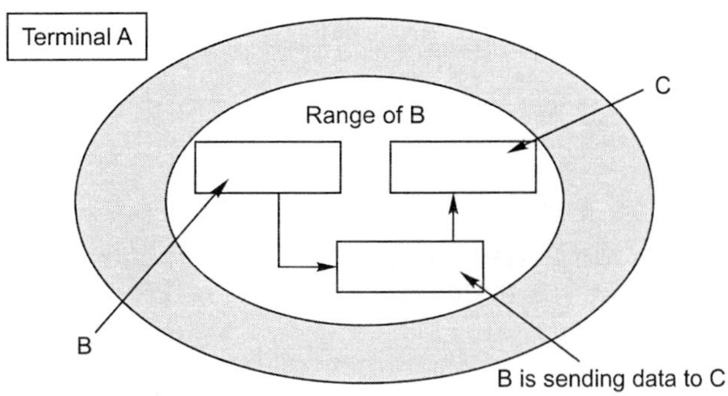

Fig.5.26 (b). Exposed station problem.

Classifications of Ad hoc network protocols:

These protocols can be classifies into three basic types:

- Contention based protocols
- Contention based protocols with reservation mechanisms
- Contention based protocols with scheduling mechanisms.

5.9.2 Contention Based Protocols

Ad hoc networks provide limited quality of service, due to the high movements of mobile nodes. Once a node moves with respect to another node, it losts its reservation. Common channel is available to all nodes. Therefore, to manage, QoS and efficient bandwidth utilization bit difficult in this, network, since access to the network cannot guaranty beforehand.

Sender-initiated protocols: A sender initiates packet transmission.

- *Single-channel sender-initiated protocols:* A node that wins the channel can make use of the entire bandwidth.
- *Multichannel sender-initiated protocols:* The available bandwidth divided into multiple channels.

Receiver-initiated protocols: A receiver initiates packet transmission.

Contention based protocols with reservation mechanisms:

These protocols reserve the bandwidth ahead; therefore, they can provide better QoS. These networks further subdivided into:

- **Synchronous protocols:** All the nodes in the network synchronized at the same time. All the nodes informed about reservations. With this, all the nodes synchronized. It is difficult to achieve global time synchronization.
- **Asynchronous protocols:** Instead of synchronized the node at the same time, relative time is used for the reservations.

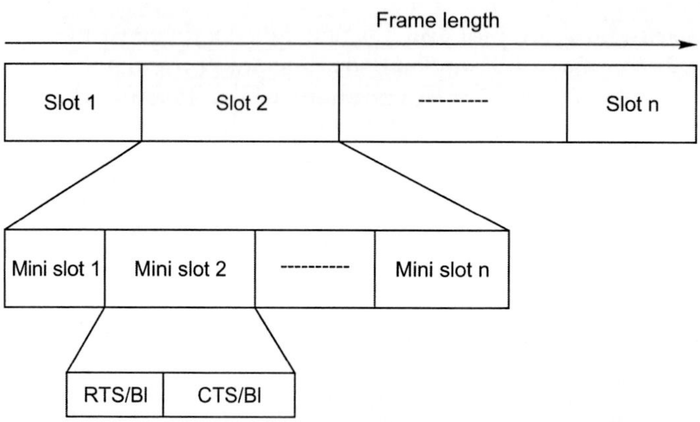

Fig. 5.27. D-PRMA protocol.

Reservation scheme use D-PRMA (Distributed Packet Reservation Multiple Access) protocol. This protocol is based on TDMA, therefore transmission of packet between sender and receiver is done through Time Division Duplexing (TDD), or by Frequency Division Duplexing (FDD). The time division channel is divided into frames, then further into slots, then further into mini slots. Each mini slot contains two control fields, RTS/BI—Request To Send/Busy Indication and CTS/BI—clear To Send/Busy Indication as shown in Fig 5.27. Voice traffic is first prioritized while giving reservation.

A mini slot wants to send data to other mini slot, sends RTS/BI to receive. After receiving it, the receiver sends CTS/BI to the sender. Once the path is clear and senders start sending the data to the receiver, then it will be continued to send data, until the entire mini slot and slot of that frames are not sent.

Contention based protocols with scheduling mechanisms:

- This network provides limited bandwidth, scheduling done to adjust all the nodes in fixed bandwidth.
- Priorities can use to schedule the packets.
- If one node is transmitting the data, then another node cannot send data at the same time. If it does, it leads to interference called collision. MACA (Multiple Access Collision Avoidance) Protocol avoids collision in the network.

5.9.2.1 MACA

Sender node if wants to transmit a packet, then it first transmits **RTS (Request To Send)** frame. Suppose, *B* wants to send data to *C*, so *B* first sends RTS to *C* as shown in Fig. 5.28 (*a*).

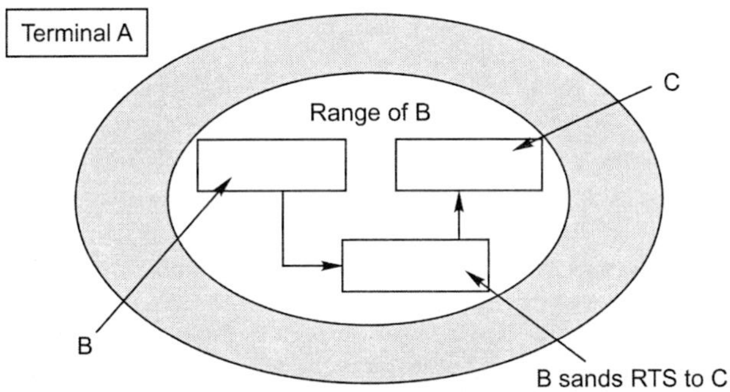

Fig. 5.28 (a). B is sending RTS to C.

The receiver node, on receiving the RTS, if ready to receive the packet, transmits **CTS (Clear to Send)** to sender as shown in Fig 5.28 (*b*).

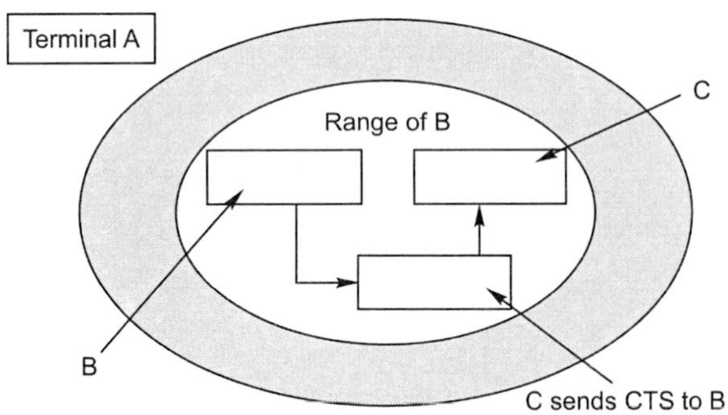

Fig. 5.28 (b). C is sending CTS to B.

- Once the sender receives the CTS packet without any error, it starts transmitting the packet.
- If a packet transmitted by a node is lost, the node uses the binary exponential back-off (BEB) algorithm to back off a random interval of time before retrying.

5.10 STOP AND GO MULTIHOP PROTOCOL (SGMP)

This protocol is a static priority based method. This protocol can be work conserving or non-work conserving. Work conserving means, a link cannot be idle if it has packets to send and numbers of the packets are waiting for that link. Work conservation gives lower average end-to-end delay for packets. In contrast, in non-work conserving, a link can be idle if it has no packet to send and no packet is waiting for that link. Non-work conserving gives minimum jitter.

In this is protocol, a new connection assigned a target link deadline. For each link, the connection assigned a priority according to its link deadline, where small link deadline is given low priority number and high link deadline is given high priority number. First, scheduling of all the connection checked, if it is possible to get deadline of a new connection without missing a deadline of other connections, then only a connection will be admitted/entered into the network. A higher priority connection cannot miss the deadline. This protocol provides the easiest means of admission control. Let T_F represent the frame period and i represent for each connection then simple bandwidth check will be:

$$\sum_{k \in \Omega j} \tau_k / TF_k \le 1$$

The packet is sent on the decided priority connection. At a switching node, the packet is multiplexed onto the next link along its path, along with the packets of other connections using the same link. Information about a new connection is stored at each node, called descriptor. The descriptor must contain packet periods/interval times, maximum lengths, maximum bursts size and resource allocated on that connection. Each incoming packet must contain a connection ID as part of its header.

5.10.1 SGMP Message Handling Method

SGMP handles the message at the output link of each node. Input arriving parameters take shapes and features as input. Then demultiplexer does demultiplexing. This demultiplexing inserts a packet into one of a set of queues. Packets inserted based on FCFS or deadline based priority. Then Multiplexer is used to depart the messages. Multiplexer selects queue from which packets will transmit and queue in which packets have to wait as shown in Fig. 5.29. SGMP does this scheduling. It will be discussed later on.

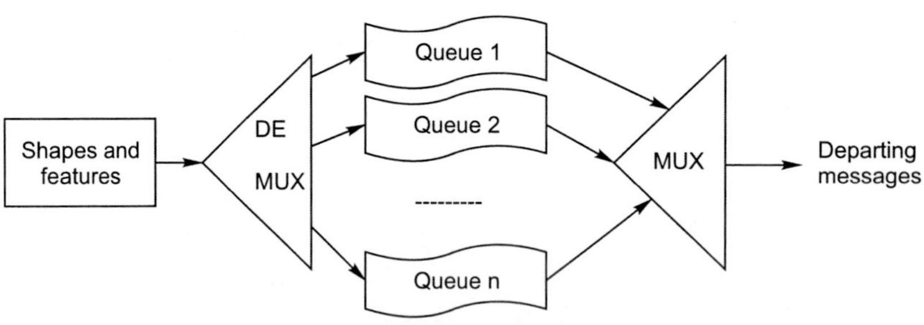

Fig. 5.29. Node processing per output link.

5.10.2 SGMP Scheduling

SGMP scheduling decides which packet has to stop and which packet has to go. So this protocol is named as Stop and Go protocol. The SGMP scheduling assigned priorities to the various packets placed in different queues. The packets are arranged in FCFS order or they can be arranged according to the nearest deadline. The packets having nearest deadline will assign higher priority and the packets having a late deadline will assign lower priority. A lower priority task cannot preempt the higher priority task. Only high priority task can preempt lower priority tasks. The output queues multiplex in priority order and messages will be departing from the queue. SGMP schedules packets as a group by clustering them into frames.

For each connection *i*, a frame *F* having frame size T_F is stored in its connection descriptor, in *H* hop network. There is a clock for each frame size, which produces a signal after every T_F second. When a packet arrives, it has buffered in queue until the clock for its frame produces its signal. As soon as the signal is produced; frame is transferred to the output queue. Based on priority frames are departed from the queues. In this, case, jitter is limited to only the last link and cannot be greater than $2T_F$. End to end delay with this method is approximately H_iT_F. This scheduling is mainly preferred in hard real time traffics and gives deterministic delay bounds. Scheduling decides which packet to stop and which packet to go, so H_i network falls between lower and upper delay bounds of stop and go queuing.

In networks, there can be fixed length packets to send or can be variable packets to send. The former comes in ATM networks and later comes in *H* hop networks. ATM network processor sharing is equivalent to weighted round robin scheduling. For *H* hop networks, scheduling is the most important part, because scheduling decides which packet has to go and which packet has to stop.

Queuing delay for each connection *i*, a frame *F* having frame size T_F, a share of bandwidth pi_s in *H* hop network will be:

$$D \leq \frac{\sigma_i + H_i \tau_i}{\rho_i}$$

5.10.3 SGMP Framing (An Example)

SGMP schedules packets as a group by clustering them into frames.

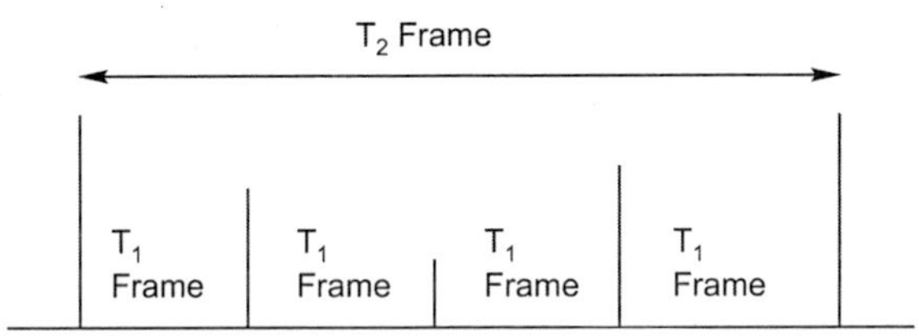

Fig. 5.30. Two level framing with $T_2 = 4{*}T_1$.

SGMP is based on multilevel framing strategy. In this, time axis is divided into frames, which are period of some constant length *T*. For *n* level framing, frame sizes are $T_1 \ldots, \ldots, T_n$ and packets are represented by *p* in network. According to SGMP, *p* packets arrive at an output link during a T_p frame will not transmit until the start of next T_p frame. It means that the link becomes idle, although packets are waiting for that link. This is the main problem of this protocol however; it can be resolved by a larger frame time as shown in Fig.5.30.

The packets having nearest deadline will assign higher priority and the packets having a late deadline will assign lower priority. A lower priority task cannot preempt the higher priority task. The only high priority task can preempt lower priority tasks. At each switch, the arriving frame of each incoming link is mapped to the departing frame of the output link by introducing a constant delay θ, where $0 \leq \theta < T$.

Another problem of this protocol is that delay bound and bandwidth allocation cannot achieve simultaneously. Suppose, delay of any packet is bounded by two frame times. To reduce the delay, smaller T is desired. T is also tied to bandwidth allocation. For fixed packet size (P), bandwidth allocation is P/T. For smaller bandwidth allocation, larger T is preferred. Both statements contradict each other.

5.11 HIERARCHICAL ROUND ROBIN PROTOCOL (HRR)

Hierarchical Round Robin Protocol scheduled the tasks based on their rates. It is mainly used in hard real time communication and is very similar to Stop and Go Protocol (SGMP). While sending data, two types of scheduling mechanisms are used. These are:

1. **Work Conserving Discipline:** In this discipline, the server can never be idle, if data is present to send. Work conserving discipline needs fewer buffers, as data is processed simultaneously. This scheme can cause shorter delay, however, not bound delay jitter tightly.
2. **Non-Work Conserving Discipline:** In this discipline, server can be idle, if data is not available for transmitting purposes. Each packet is assigned some duration for sending the packet. When all the packets are sent, the server becomes idle for sometime and waits for the new arriving data. This discipline can cause large delay as it needs larger buffers. This discipline can bound delay jitter tightly.

In HRR scheduling, packets are grouped into frames. HRR is a non-working conserving scheduling. Each task is assigned a level. Level I is used for highest priority. Each task is also assigned a fixed rate level called g. Each level k of a task corresponds to a frame of size n_k slots. kth level frame starts transmission after every FT_k seconds, where $FT_1 < FT_2 < \ldots < FT_g$. For each frame size n_k, b_k slots reserved for frames having lower or higher priorities. Lower priority packets transmitted after the higher priority packets. A connection i assigned to a level k allocated s_i slots, out of which each n_k slots allotted to that frame. As packets for connection i arrive, the input regulator will only release s_i of them for transmission during each interval of FT_k seconds. FCFS output queue can use in each level. The rate allocated to connection i assigned to level k is s_i/FT_k slots per second. Packets at lower priority levels than k are transmitted after the first $n_k - b_k$ slots of the frame for level k. Delay end and jitter are both less than or equal to $2HFT_k$ for a connection assigned to level k. Its alternative implementation is to have one FCFS queue per size frame, with one reference clock for each queue.

5.11.1 Characteristics of Hierarchical Round Robin Protocol

- This algorithm is also known as the processor-sharing algorithm
- This protocol is mainly used for scheduling time-shared applications.
- When there are n tasks for execution, each task gets $1/n$th share of the processor.
- A FIFO method is used to execute different tasks present in ready queue.
- Every task presents in ready queue gives a chance to execute. When there are n ready jobs in the queue, each job gets one time slice in n.
- As length of the time slice is relatively short (typically tens of milliseconds) the execution of each task begins almost immediately after it becomes ready.
- The task at the head of the queue executes for at most one time slice.
- If the task is not complete by the end of the time slice, it is preempted and placed at the end of the queue to wait for its next turn.

5.11.2 Weighed Round Robin Protocol

Weighed round robin protocol gives weight or priorities to different ready tasks. Giving different weights to different tasks decreases processor speed, which is the main drawback of this algorithm. So with this effect, this algorithm can also not use to schedule precedence-constrained tasks, as precedence constraint tasks are depending on each other. In that case, this protocol nearly becomes useless. This protocol is mainly used for scheduling real time traffic data in high-speed switched networks. Weight provides portions of the processor time to the task. A task with weight wt gets wt time portions at every time. Before execution, each task is assigned weight. From this, total time of execution can easily be calculated. It will be the sum of the weights of all the ready tasks.

5.11.3 An Example

For example, consider two sets of tasks.

$$T_1 = [T_{1.1}, T_{1.2}\} \text{ and } T_2 = [T_{2.1}, T_{2.2}]$$

All tasks execution times are 1 and release times are 0.

$T_{1.1}$ and $T_{2.1}$ execute on processor P_1.

$T_{1.2}$ and $T_{2.2}$ execute on processor P_2.

Suppose $T_{1.1}$ is predecessor of $T_{1.2}$ and $T_{2.1}$ is the predecessor of $T_{2.2}$.

Therefore, for these sets of tasks, precedence graph will be:

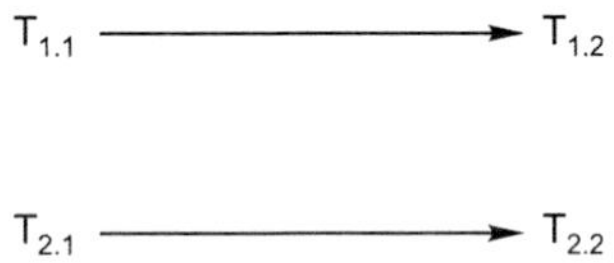

When round robin scheduling is applied on these set of tasks, then all the tasks will complete few time slices after time 2, as shown in Fig. 5.31 (*a*).

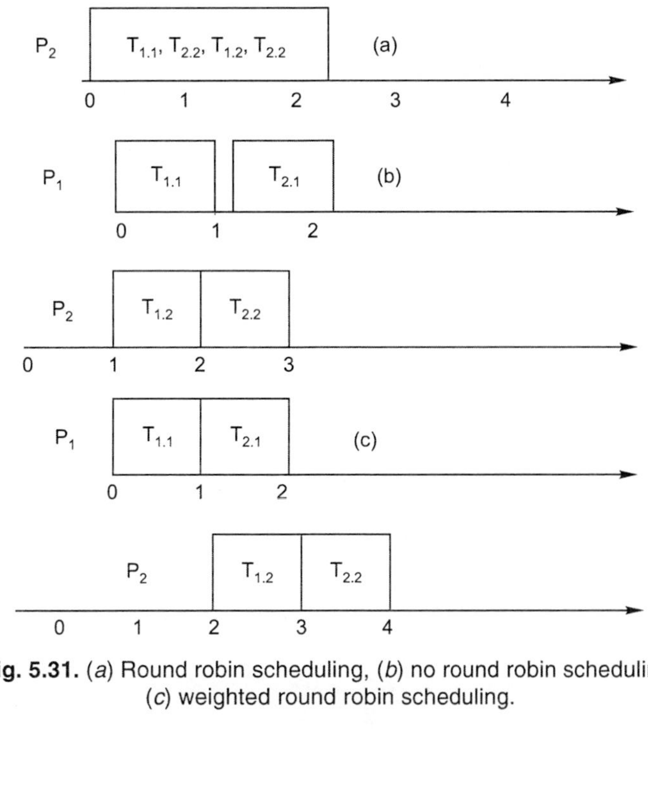

Fig. 5.31. (*a*) Round robin scheduling, (*b*) no round robin scheduling, (*c*) weighted round robin scheduling.

When round robin scheduling is not applied, then the task executed according their precedence order (one after the other). Then one set of task will complete at time 2 and other task set will complete at time 3, as shown in Fig. 5.16 (*b*).

When weighted round robin scheduling applied on these set of tasks, then one set of task will complete at time 2 and other task set will complete at time 4, as shown in Fig. 5.31(*c*).

Therefore, it is better to use round robin scheduling algorithm.

5.11.4 Advantages of Round Robin Scheduling

This protocol is widely used in switched network and in ultra high-speed networks.

This protocol is less expensive.

This protocol does not use sorted priority queue.

This protocol only requires round robin queue.

This protocol transmits an earlier portion of the message as soon as it receives the portion. It does not wait for the arrival of the rest of the message.

5.12 VIRTUAL TIME CARRIER SENSED MULTIPLE ACCESS (VTCSMA)

It is a broadcast network in which all the nodes share single or common channel. This network uses bus and ring topology. In this, algorithm priority is used and this priority can calculate as a function of current time. This protocol is used for hard real time communication. This algorithm implementation has done with FCFS. Data must transmit without any delay.

VTCSMA Algorithm

This algorithm uses two clocks for communication. One clock is a real time clock and second clock is a virtual clock. Real time clock synchronized with the clocks at other nodes. When the channel is busy, then virtual clock congeal and when the channel is free, virtual clock starts to send the data. Speed of transmission of virtual clock is faster than real time clock. Data is mainly transferred through virtual clock.

5.13 WINDOW BASED PROTOCOL

Window based protocol is used in CSMA/CD and token ring networks. Each node is given a common time interval called window. If there is one message in the window, then that message will transmit and window duration will be kept as it is. If there are two or more messages in the window then collision can occur, in that case window time shortened for all the nodes. If there is no message in the window, then bus becomes idle and in that case, window duration increased for all the nodes as shown in Fig. 5.32.

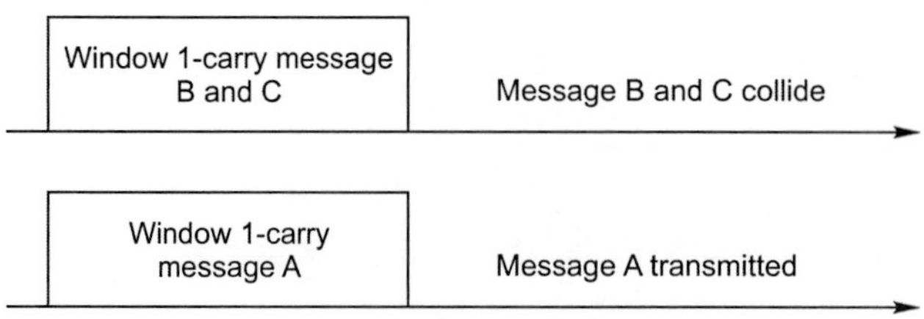

Fig. 5.32. Window based protocol.

Table 5.1. Comparison table.

S.No.	Protocol Name	Topology Used	Deadline Guarantee
1.	Time token	Ring	Yes
2.	Stop and go	Point to point based	Yes
3.	Polled bus	Bus	No
4.	Deadline based	Point to point based	No
5.	Latency based	Point to point based	No
6.	Hierarchical round robin	Point to point based	Yes

SUMMARY

In real time communication, all the nodes transfer their packets by using one common channel called broadcast channel. When single channel is used, the chances of occurring collision becomes more. When one node is transferring the packet it does not know that other is also transmitting the data, as data flows through a single channel, it leads to collision in the network. This collision can be detected by the Ethernet network and can be solvd. To solve this collision, messages are delivered with little delay. However, with this message will not be received by the receiver in time. To do this, a protocol called Carrier Sense Multiple Access with Collision Detection (CSMA/CD) used.

A token-based protocol is also known as timed token protocol. It is a MAC protocol. This protocol is widely used in various network standards such as the IEEE 802.4 token bus and the Fiber Distributed Data Interface (FDDI). This is the main protocol used in a real time communication system. It is a token passing protocol, each node must guarantee share of the network bandwidth, because of this property, timed token-based protocol transfers the synchronous based message.

Real time systems respond to the input immediately. They have some specific time called timing constraints in which they have to give their outputs. Producing the output, after specific time degrade system performance, leads to catastrophic failure and sometimes output is useless for both system and user. They have to respond in order of milliseconds or in microseconds. Deadlines are necessary and must be fulfilled for the proper functioning (output) of the system. A failing system is not able to achieve its tasks in specific deadlines. Therefore, the output must be achieved in specific time. Deadlines of all the tasks must meet, regardless of system load. Examples are a printer, phone and fax machines, driving vehicle such as cars and others. Non-real time system does not follow these conditions; they do not have any timing constraints and can respond to output at any time.

Polled bus protocol is a priority based protocol and is non-preemptive. Polling performed on a set of tasks so that all tasks will meet its deadline. To do this poll number assigned to each task, based on their deadline and task priority. The task having nearest deadline and higher priority will assign a high polled number so that it will execute first in the ready queue. Polling minimizes the probability of real time messages missing their deadlines.

This protocol is a static priority based method. It can be work conserving or non-work conserving. Work conserving means, a link cannot be idle if it has packets to send and numbers of the packets are waiting for that link. Work conservation gives lower average end-to-end delay for packets. In contrast, in non-work conserving, a link can be idle if it has no packet to send and no packet is waiting for that link. Non-work conserving gives minimum jitter. In this, protocol, a new connection assigned a target link deadline. For each link, the connection assigned a priority according to its link deadline, where small link deadline is given low priority number and high link deadline is given high priority number.

EXERCISES

1. What is a real time system?
2. List the important considerations while selecting a processor.
3. List out the uses of RTC.
4. What are the two essential units of a processor on an embedded system?
5. Give examples for general-purpose processor.
6. Differentiate synchronous communication and iso-synchronous communication.
7. What are the two characteristics of synchronous communication?
8. What are the three ways of communication for a device?
9. What is a CAN bus? Where is it used?
10. Draw the data frame format of CAN.
11. Define Real Time Clock (RTC).
12. Name the important terms of RTOS.
13. Define task and task state.
14. Define Task Control Block (TCB).
15. Draw the process state transitions.
16. What are the goals of RTOS?
17. What is the difference between real time sharing and time-sharing?
18. Consider a real time system comprising 7 independent periodic tasks; assume that all task deadlines are equal to their periodicity, and context switch times are negligible.
    (*a*) If the system utilization is 0.60, what can you conclude about the schedulability of this system?
    (*b*) What if the system utilization were increased to 0.70?
19. Explain the difference between a system that is fault-tolerant and one that is reliable. Illustrate with an example.
20. Consider the following real time system composed of 5 concurrent tasks and 3 shared resources. The system is scheduled according to DMPO, and uses simple priority inheritance prevent priority inversion.

Table 5.2. Real time system tasks.

Task	Computation Time (worst-case, msec)	Period (msec)	Deadline (msec)	Resources Used
A	4	11	10	K_1, K_3
B	5	16	20	K_1, K_2, K_3
C	6	56	30	K_2
D	9	50	45	K_1
E	10	70	50	K_2

Table 5.3. System resources.

Resource	Computation Time (worst-case)
K_1	2
K_2	5
K_3	2.5

For the system described above:

(*a*) List the priority order of the tasks.

(*b*) Compute the blocking time of each task.

(*c*) Compute the worst-case response time for the highest priority task.

(*d*) Compute the worst-case response time for the lowest priority task.

21. Draw and explain basic system of an Automatic chocolate vending system:
    - Diagram
    - Case definition, multiple tasks and their function
    - Creating a list of tasks, functions and IPCs.
22. Explain the case study of an embedded system for a smart card.
23. What does the term "real" in a real time system signify?
24. What is the Quality of Service (QoS) parameters underlying network for satisfactory operation in real time application?
25. Explain how a real time operating system differs from a traditional operating system.
26. Name a few real time operating systems that are commercially available.
27. What is a real time CORBA Concept? Explain any two specifications of CORBA that are required for implementing any real-time system.
28. What is Remote Procedure Calls (RPC)? Explain with example, how it is useful in protocol design.

    (*a*) Real time systems have to interact with real world entities. These interactions can get complex. State different issues in real time system design and explain those in detail.

    (*b*) What is real time scheduling? Explain taxonomy of real time scheduling algorithms with examples.

    (*c*) What is the significance of multiprocessor in real time system? In addition, list kind of potential difficulties observed with multiprocessor system.

    (*d*) What is the importance of "kernel" in a real time operating system?
29. Explain different types of threads commonly available for performance measurement in real time systems.
30. List and explain capabilities of commercial real time systems.
31. How can we say the First Come First Served scheduling algorithm is non-preemptive?

Fill in the Blanks

1. Real time communication purpose is to exchange the information between different users with minimum ______ .
2. RTC is ______ to ______ communication.

3. ______ is a measure of the number of packets that the network can deliver per unit time.
4. ______ is a the time taken to deliver a packet.
5. ______ is a variance of the latency.
6. In real time communication, scheduling is ______ .
7. Token-based protocol also known as ______ protocol.
8. ______ is a the expected time taken by a token to rotate around an entire network.
9. A deadline base protocol can be ______ and ______ .
10. In Latency based protocol only the ______ instance of an operation is unknown.
11. When numbers of processors connected through a common bus called ______ bus.
12. Contention based protocol and Media Access Control (MAC) protocol used in ______ .
13. Ad hoc networks provide limited ______ , due to the high movements of mobile nodes.
14. SGMP schedules packets as group by ______ them into frames.
15. ______ method used to execute different tasks present in ready queue.

True/False

1. RTC stands for real time communication. (T/F)
2. CBR deals with conversion bit rate. (T/F)
3. Larger delay in delivery or receiving can cause catastrophic failure. (T/F)
4. Token-based protocol is also known as timed token protocol. (T/F)
5. Target Token Rotation Time (TTRT) is not the expected time taken by a token to rotate around an entire network. (T/F)
6. A deadline based protocol can be preemptive and non-preemptive. (T/F)
7. Polling is performed on set of tasks so that all tasks will meet their deadline. (T/F)
8. When a node gets the busy signal dominant, it cannot start a new transmission. (T/F)
9. CAN bus does not deliver the messages from all the nodes with in specific time. (T/F)
10. Weighted round robin protocol cannot give weight to different ready tasks. (T/F)

MULTIPLE CHOICE QUESTIONS

1. RTC stands for
   (*a*) Real time communication (*b*) Real time conversation
   (*c*) Real time conversion (*d*) None of the above
2. Ad hoc network is used in
   (*a*) MAC (*b*) CBR
   (*c*) VBR (*d*) None of the above
3. Other name of latency is
   (*a*) Delay (*b*) Throughput
   (*c*) Jitter (*d*) None of the above
4. Wormhole routing used in
   (*a*) Real time communication (*b*) Conventional communication
   (*c*) Traditional methods (*d*) All of the above
5. CAN is used in
   (*a*) Local network (*b*) Wide network
   (*c*) Embedded network (*d*) All of the above

6. Variation in delay is known as
   (*a*) Delay (*b*) Throughput
   (*c*) Jitter (*d*) None of the above
7. Token-based protocol manage
   (*a*) Conventional traffic (*b*) Real time traffic
   (*c*) Nominal traffic (*d*) All of the above
8. SGMP is used for
   (*a*) Start and Go (*b*) Stamp and Go
   (*c*) Stop and Go (*d*) None of the above
9. Server can never be idle
   (*a*) Work conserving discipline (*b*) Non-work conserving discipline
   (*c*) In work conserving discipline (*d*) All of the above
10. Processor sharing algorithm is also known as
   (*a*) TO (*b*) HRR
   (*c*) Deadline based protocol (*d*) All of the above.

QUESTIONNAIRES

1. Define communication in real time system.

Ans. Real time communications (RTC) deal with reality. It means that data used in real time applications will be real or live data. Real time communication purpose is to exchange the information between different users with minimum delay. Delay means latency and it must be less as possible for proper flow of data. Data should not be delivered late. In real time communications, time constraints and deadlines are very important. Given task must perform on time to minimize catastrophic failure. Each message must be given a priority. (priority is based on deadline, nearest is deadline high will be the priority.) to deliver the message in time. In real time communication, reliability has less effect; important is data which must reach in time. RTC is a peer-to-peer communication (person to person) *i.e.* RTC is Unicast. RTC always has a direct path between the source and the destination.

2. Explain the reasons for message delay.

Ans. (1) Formatting and packetizing the message.

(2) The message is in queue and waits for access to the broadcast channel.

(3) Due to presence of number of switching nodes.

(4) DE formatting the message.

3. Define constant rate.

Ans. In constant rate, fixed size packets generate at periodic intervals. Its example is traffic generated through constant bit rate. CBR example is periodic data generated by sensors. This type of traffic appears in hard real time applications.

4. Define variable rate.

Ans. In variable rate, variable size packets are generated at regular intervals. VBR Traffic: It implies Variable Bit Rate generation. Its example is compressed audio and video signals. In this traffic, data source alternates between periods.

5. Define fault tolerance.

Ans. Real time systems must be fault tolerant, means they should be able to handle worst-case condition or should be able to work properly regardless of workload.

6. Define token.

Ans. A token is a grant of permission to a node to transmit its packets on the network when the token holding node completes its transmission; it passes this token to another node. Only a node present in the network can hold the token.

Packet transferred between sender and receiver. Packets can be of fixed size or variable length.

7. Explain packet switching.

Ans. Packet transferred between sender and receiver. Packets can be of fixed size or variable length. Packets have headers, source and destination address and message. Packets are sent by using routers and flow control algorithms.

8. Define circuit switching.

Ans. A circuit is established between source and destination. The sender sends the data and receiver after getting the data, acknowledges the sender. Message not saved in intermediate nodes. Purpose of intermediate nodes is only to transmit the message.

9. Give advantages and disadvantages of optical fiber.

Ans. **Advantages:**

- LED/laser diodes, light pulses
- High data rates even over long distances.

Disadvantages:

- Signal loss can occur.
- Expensive
- Immune to electromagnetic interference
- Direct wiring or passive star topologies known to work.

10. Explain network topologies.

Ans. It is the arrangement or layout of different connected networks. This can be of many types such as bus, ring, mesh, fully meshed and many more. In point-to-point topology, nodes are connected by direct/dedicated links. In shared topology, all the nodes share a common channel called broadcast channel and only one node can transmit at a time, otherwise it leads to collision in the network.

11. Explain network architecture issues.

Ans. We have three types of Network Architecture Issues.

(1) **High level architecture issues:** At the highest level, a distributed system comprises a set of nodes communicating through an interconnection network. Each node may itself be a multiprocessor comprising application system and N/w processor, a shared memory segment and I/O interface. The nodes of the system must be interconnected by a suitable N/w.

(2) **Low level architectural issues:** Low Level Architectural Issues involve Packet Processing, routing and error/flow control. In the distributed real time system, there are additional issues related to the support for meeting deadlines, time management and housekeeping. Since the support at these low level issues impedes the execution of application task nodes in a distributed real time system usually have a custom-designed processor for handling their chore.

(3) **I/O Architecture:** A real time computer can process data faster than it acquires it from sensors & operators. The nature of I/O devices in a real time environment, consisting of sensors and actuator, is quite different from the magnetic disk and taps that are the I/O devices commonly encountered in the general-purpose system.

12. Explain RTC protocols.

Ans. There are many protocols used in real time communication. These are:

(1) **Contention Based Protocol:** A contention based protocol and media access control (MAC) protocol is used in Ad hoc wireless networks. In Ad hoc wireless networks, mobile nodes exchange packets by sharing a common broadcast channel. The purpose of this network is to provide efficient bandwidth and guarantee of equal transmission of bandwidth to all nodes. This network provides limited bandwidth, and all the nodes are adjusted within this bandwidth. As shown in figure, both wired and wireless LAN share a common broadcast channel. The base station is the access point, from which all other systems receive the data.

(2) **Virtual Time Carrier Sensed Multiple Access (VTCSMA):** This protocol is used in bus and ring topologies. In this, all the nodes connected through a single channel are called broadcast channel. CSMA (Carrier Sense Multiple Access) is used to prevent collision.

Performance of the VTCSMA Algorithms

(*i*) It has a better loss rate than the CSMA Protocols.

(*ii*) The network should not be overloaded.

(3) **Window Protocol:** The window protocol is based on collision sensing like VTCSMA Protocol. As this protocol does not ensure of message transmission, so this protocol is only used for soft real communication.

(4) **Timed Token Protocol:** A token-based protocol is also known as timed token protocol. It is a MAC protocol. This protocol is widely used in various network standards such as the IEEE 802.4 token bus and the Fiber Distributed Data Interface (FDDI). This is the main protocol used in a real time communication system. It is a token passing protocol, in which each node must guarantee a share of the network bandwidth, because of this property, timed token-based protocol transfers synchronous based message. Synchronous messages are used in real time communication and have deadline constraints. However, sometimes this protocol can be used to transfer asynchronous messages. The IEEE 802.4 standard is Manufacturing Automation Protocol (MAP), which has been widely used in computer-integrated manufacturing and industrial applications. The medium access layer should be properly control to deliver packets in specific time. In the timed-token protocol, token manages and control the whole communication process of MAC layer, this token also passes among the various nodes in a network in a circular fashion.

(5) **Stop and go Multi hop Protocol:** This protocol is a static priority based method. This protocol can be work conserving or non-work conserving. Work conserving means, a link cannot be idle if it has packets to send and numbers of the packets are waiting for that link. Work conservation gives lower average end-to-end delay for packets. In contrast, in non-work conserving, a link can be idle if it has no packet to send and no packet is waiting for that link. Non-work conserving gives minimum jitter. In this, protocol, a new connection assigned a target link deadline.

(6) **The Polled Bus Protocol:** Polled bus protocol is a priority based protocol and is non-preemptive. Polling is performed on a set of tasks so that all tasks will meet its deadline. To do this poll number is assigned to each task, based on its deadline and task priority. The task having nearest deadline and higher priority will be assigned a high polled number so that it will execute first in the ready queue. Polling minimizes the probability of real time messages missing their deadlines. When a token bus is

used instead of a polling is bus, the chances of getting missing deadline are more. Therefore, it is preferred to use the polling bus in the network.

(7) Hierarchical Round Robin Protocol: This algorithm has also known as the processor-sharing algorithm. This protocol is mainly used for scheduling time-shared applications. When there are *n* tasks for execution, each task gets 1/*n*th share of the processor. An FIFO method is used to execute different tasks present in ready queue. Every task presents in ready queue gives a chance to execute. When there are *n* ready jobs in the queue, each job gets one time slice in *n*.

(8) Deadline Based Protocols: Real time systems respond to the input immediately. They have some specific time called timing constraints in which they have to give their outputs. Producing the output, after specific time degrade system performance, leads to catastrophic failure and sometimes output is useless for both system and user. They have to respond in order of milliseconds or in microseconds. Deadlines are necessary and must be fulfilled for the proper functioning (output) of the system.

6 Real Time Operating System

6.1 INTRODUCTION

A Real Time Operating System (RTOS) consists of two components as shown in Fig. 6.1. One is Real Time, and the other is operating system.

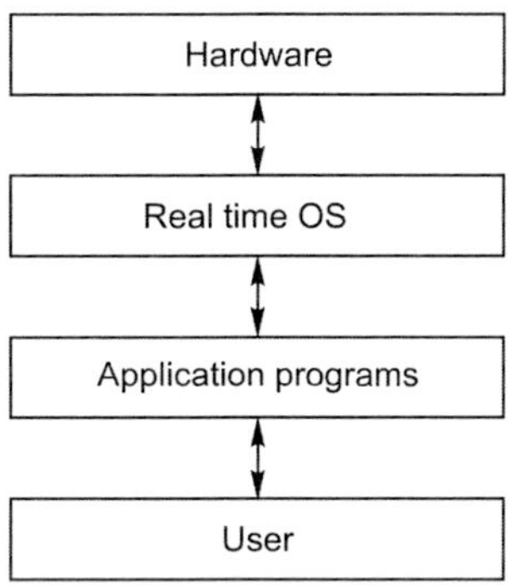

Fig. 6.1. Components of RTOS.

A real time operating system is specially designed for real time applications. Real time applications are concerned with timing constraints. All applications must be complete in time. Therefore, the operating system of a real time system is designed in such a way that it fulfils this need.

As a traditional operating system, real time operating system provides an interface between hardware and user (application programs). It is the combination of system call or function, having kernel, threads as formal operating system. As a conventional operating system, it has also the features of multitasking, synchronization, Interrupt and Event Handling, Input/Output, Inter-task Communication, Timers and Clocks and Memory Management. The kernel is the core of an operating system contains small, highly optimized set of libraries. Real time operating system not only gives the output but also provides output in time.

The basic structure of an RTOS is same as that of a conventional operating system, in addition, it handles real time data, gives output on time and allows real time task scheduling. Real time operating system does not increase execution speed; it gives precise output in time.

An RTOS is mainly used in embedded systems. Embedded systems with relatively simple and small hardware do not require an RTOS. Embedded systems with medium to large software applications need scheduling, and so they have RTOS.

6.2 RTOS CLASSIFICATION

RTOS before their execution knows the time in which execution of different tasks is completed. It is divided into following categories:

(*a*) **Hard Real Time OS:** These systems cannot miss their deadlines. They must be complete in a specific time. Missing a deadline leads to catastrophic failure.

(*b*) **Soft Real Time OS:** Deadline can be missing, but missing the deadline does not degrade system quality, the system has not failed or hanged.

(*c*) **Firm Real Time OS:** Deadline can be missing and missing a deadline can degrade system quality but the system has not failed or hanged.

Example 1: Soft real time system: TV live Broadcast, in which missing deadline is acceptable.

Example 2: Hard real time system: Air bags used in cars at the time of the accident. If airbags are not exaggerated at a specific time, it may lead to a serious condition for a driver.

6.3 REAL TIME OS FEATURES

RTOS features are shown in Fig. 6.2.

1. It gives output in time.
2. All the tasks meet their deadlines.
3. It gives minimum jitter.
4. Before the execution of the task, it can predict the time in which all the tasks will be complete. This feature is called deterministic.
5. Various scheduling algorithms are used to manage the tasks and meet their dead line.

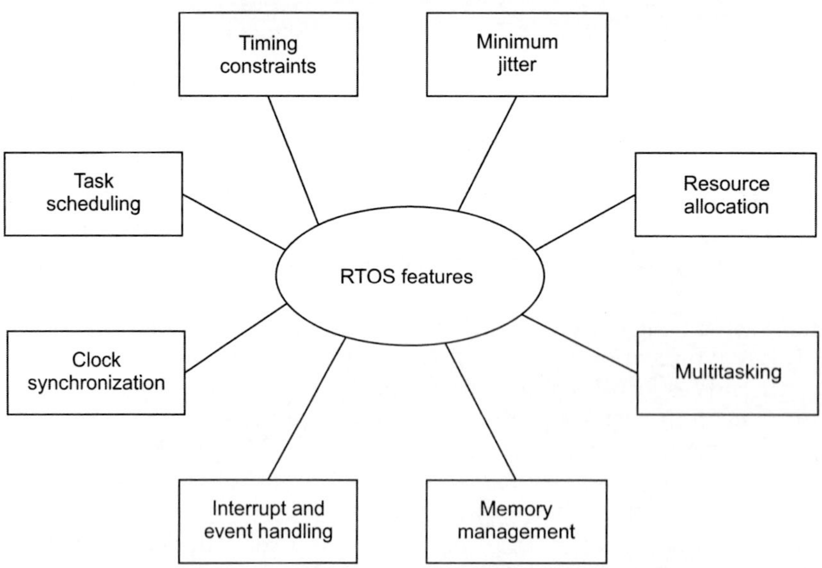

Fig. 6.2. RTOS features.

6. It has the features of multitasking, synchronization, Interrupt and Event Handling, Input/Output, Inter-task Communication, Timers and Clocks and Memory Management.
7. The kernel is the core of an operating system.
8. It is mainly used in an embedded system.
9. It does resource allocation.
10. It provides Multitasking and preemptive features: a task can preempt any other task to meet the deadlines.
11. RTOS has a large number of priority levels called priority inheritance & this prevents priority inversion.
12. It has short and predefined latencies such as interrupt latency; interrupt dispatches latency and task switching latency.

Real Time RTOS Example: POSIX COMPLIANCE

POSIX COMPLIANCE, aslo called POSIX 1003.1b (formerly 1003.4) is a known standard of IEEE Portable Operating System Interface for Computer Environments. This standard provides standard RTOS services in such a way that applications can easily be port across OSs.

POSIX 1003.1b covers these RTOS services:

1. *Asynchronous I/O capability:* With this application, process and I/O operations can be overlapped.
2. *Synchronous capability:* It returns interface procedure when the I/O operation is completed.
3. *Memory storage:* It stores those portions of the memory that are not recently referenced by secondary memory devices.
4. *Semaphores:* Resource access synchronized by multiple processes.
5. *Shared memory:* Provides a collective space of memory (both physical and virtual) two different independent processes.
6. *Task scheduling:* All the tasks are scheduled to meet required deadlines. For this, familiar scheduling methods could be used such as round robin and priority-based preemptive scheduling.
7. *Timers:* A clock used to get real time services. This clock improves predictability of task execution (called determinism).

6.4 RTOS ARCHITECTURE

Real time operating system has a kernel in simple applications.

However, as the complexity of the systems increases it has various other modules like device input/output, networking protocols, debugging etc. kernel is the core of operating system shown in Fig. 6.3.

1. **Kernel:** It is the core of the operating system, which has an abstraction layer between hardware and applications. It is of four types:
   (*a*) **Monolithic kernel:** This kernel exists in UNIX, LINUX and FREE BSD operating system. It does all the functions of operating systems such as memory management, task scheduling, synchronization, semaphores, provides a high abstraction between hardware etc. This kernel is faster than Microkernel.
   (*b*) **Microkernel:** This kernel exists in Mach, Mac OS X, AIX, BeOS, MINIX, and QNX etc. This kernel provides less abstraction between hardware and applications as it performs little features of operating systems such as managing memory protection,

Interprocess communication and the process management, it can't handle other functions like monolithic kernel. It is more stable than monolithic kernels as servers fail do not put any impact on its execution.

(*c*) **Hybrid kernel:** This kernel exists in Microsoft Windows NT, 2000 and XP. DragonFly BSD, etc. This kernel is an extension of microkernel with some properties of monolithic kernels.

(*d*) **Exo kernels:** This kernel gives privileges and revoking facility to the user. Its purpose is to check the authority. It has good control of hardware.

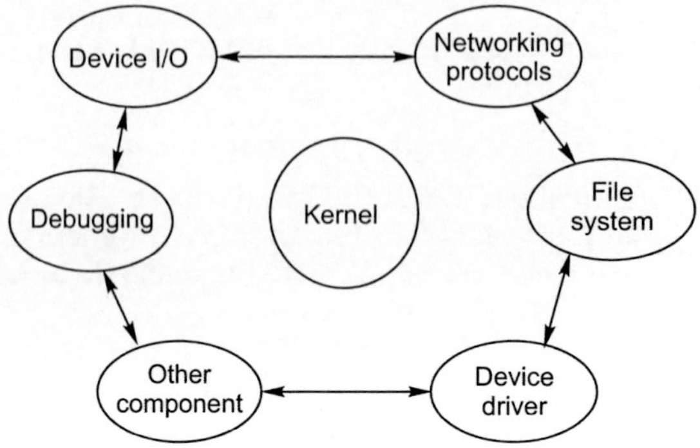

Fig. 6.3. RTOS architecture.

Common functions of kernel

The kernel performs six main functions shown in Fig.6.4. These are:

1. Task management
2. Timer Management
3. Memory management
4. I/O Device management
5. Interrupt and event handling
6. Synchronization and communication.

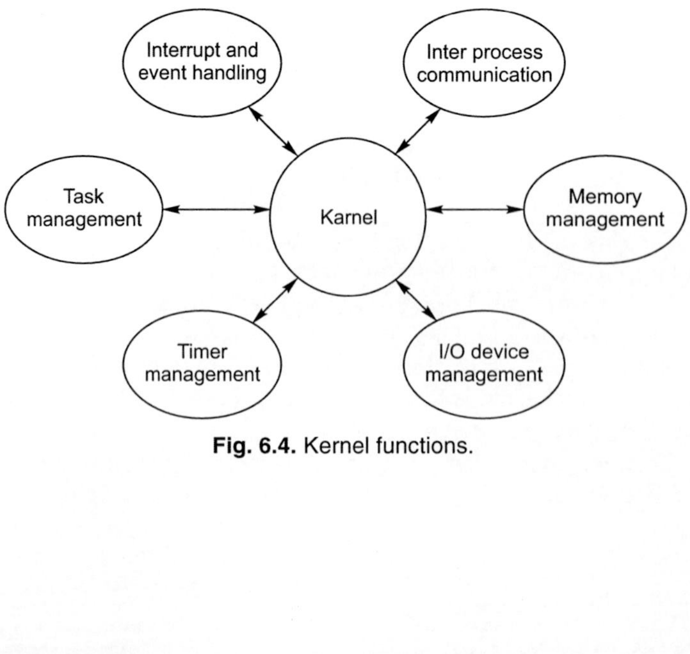

Fig. 6.4. Kernel functions.

2. **Task Management:** In this kernel plays a major role in managing the various tasks, so that all the tasks meet their specific deadlines. Each task has its own start time, release time, execution time and deadline as shown in Fig. 6.5.

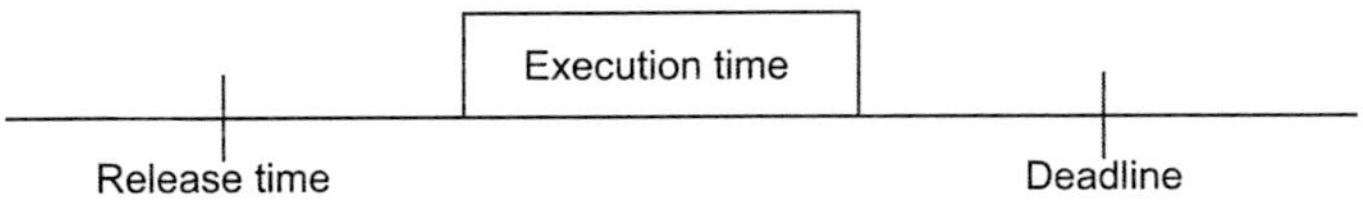

Fig. 6.5. Task time.

- Deadline: It is the task completion time.
- Execution time: It is the time taken by the task during its execution.
- Release time: Time at which a task is executed.

Task Stages: Each task has six stages shown in Figs. 6.6 and 6.7:

1. **Dormant stage:** It does not require computer time.
2. **Ready:** Task is in ready queue and is waiting for the processor.
3. **Active:** Task is executing.
4. **Suspended:** Because of the high priority task or any other task, the task is suspended for sometime.
5. **Pending:** Task is waiting for the resource.
6. **Ending:** Task completed.

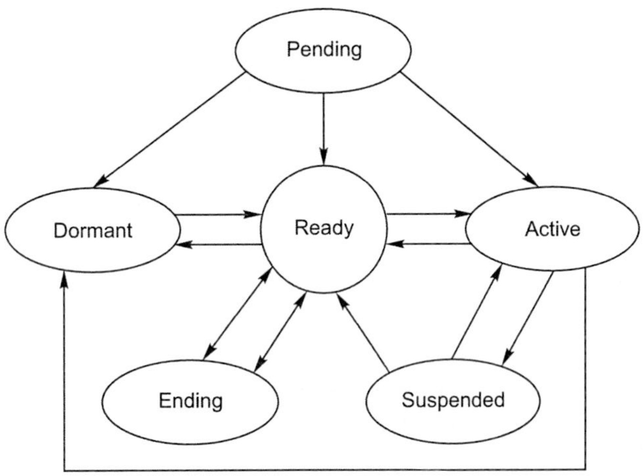

Fig. 6.6. Tasks states.

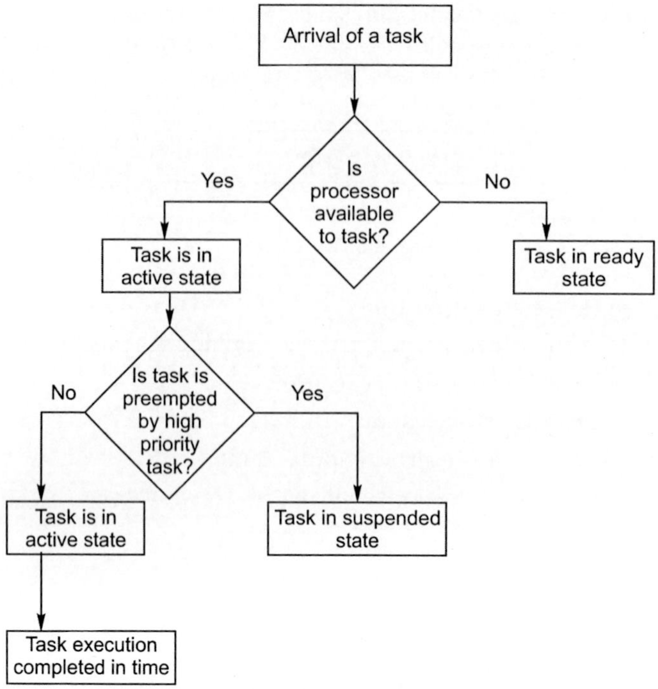

Fig. 6.7. Flow chart for task execution phase.

Task Components: A task has various components. These are:

(*a*) **Task Control Block (TCB):** TCB data structure is stored in RAM and it can only be access by the RTOS. The TCB data structure contains Task_ID, Task_STATE, TASK_PRIORITY, TASK_ROG_COUNTER, and TASK_STACK_POINTER.

(*b*) **Task stack:** It is stored in RAM and can be accessed by stack pointer.

(*c*) **Task routine:** It is a program code available in ROM.

3. Task Scheduling

All the tasks are scheduled in such a way that all the tasks meet their specific deadlines. The scheduler does the Scheduling. Various scheduling algorithms are used in a real time operating system. These are:

(*a*) **Round robin algorithm:** In this algorithm, each task gives a portion (slice) of the processor time as shown in Fig. 6.8.

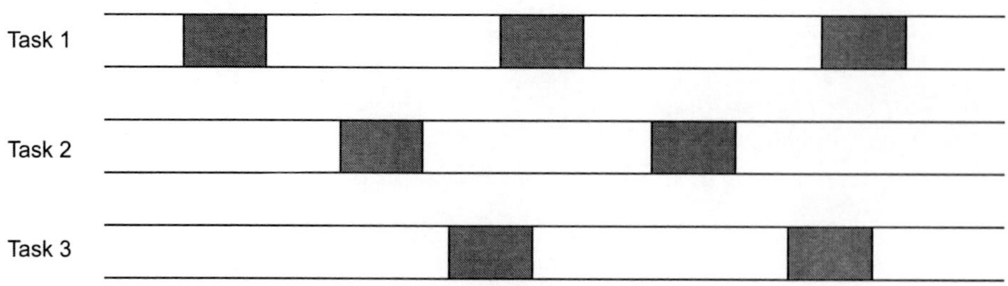

Fig. 6.8. RR scheduling.

(*b*) **Polled loop scheduling:** It will sequentially determine whether specific task requires time. It also handles interrupt as shown in Fig. 6.9.

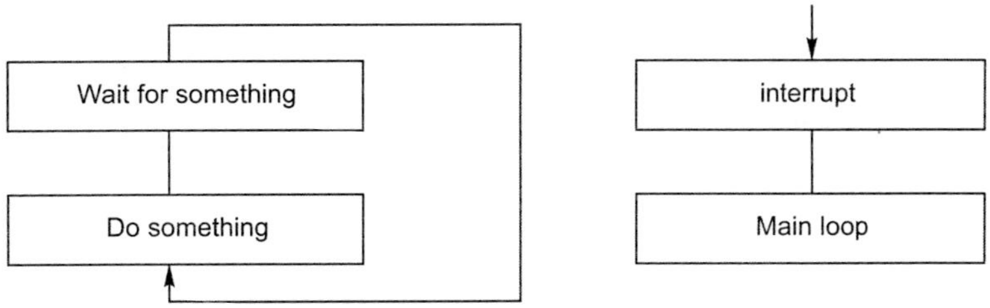

Fig. 6.9. Polled loop scheduling algorithm.

4. **Memory Management:** In RTOS, heap and stack data structure used to hold data.

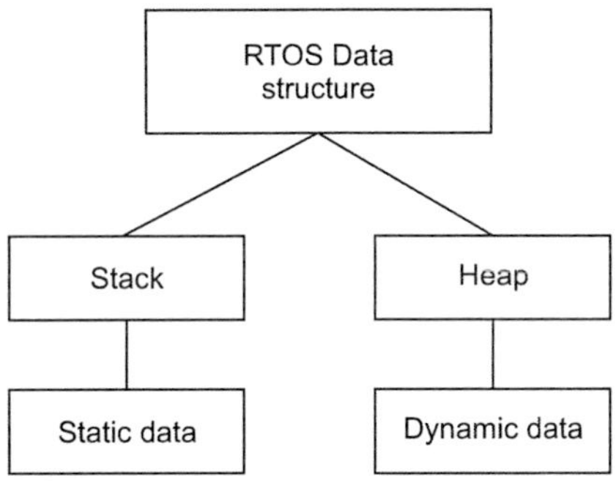

Fig. 6.10. RTOS memory structure.

Stack manages TCB, which is called stack management and program code, program data is managed by a heap called heap management. Stack management holds static data while heap management holds dynamic data shown in Fig.6.10.

5. **Timer Management:** A clock is used to check that all the tasks must be completed in deadline. Therefore, a timer keeps record of the occurrence of a delay in the system.
6. **Interrupt and Event Handling:** RTOS provides various functions for interrupt and event handling.
7. **Device I/O Management:** APIs do this.
8. **Synchronization and Communication:** Done so that all the tasks get processor time and needful resources, as there are a number of tasks executing concurrently. Semaphores do this.

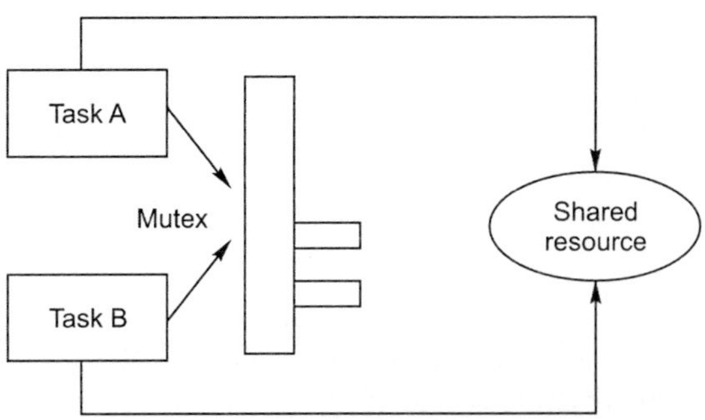

Fig. 6.11. Mutex semaphores.

Semaphores are of three types:

(*a*) Binary Semaphores

(*b*) Counting Semaphores

(*c*) Mutual Exclusion Semaphores also called Mutex shown in Fig.6.11.

6.5 COMMERCIAL MOST POPULAR RTOS

Table 6.1. Popular RTOS.

RTOS	Applications/Features
Windows CE	Used for Small footprint, mobile and connected devices. Supported by ARM, MIPS, SH4 and *x*86 architectures.
LynxOS	Complex, hard real time applications. POSIX-compatible, multiprocess, multithreaded OS. Supported by *x*86, ARM, PowerPC architectures.
VxWorks	Mostly used in the embedded industry. Used infamous NASA rover robots Spirit and Opportunity· Certified by several agencies and international standards for real time systems, reliability and security-critical applications.
Micrium μC/OS-II	Ported to more than a hundred architectures including *x*86, mainly used in microcontrollers with low resources. Certified by rigorous standards, such as RTCADO-178B.
QNX	Most traditional RTOS in the market. Microkernel architecture; completely compatible with the POSIX. Certified by FAADO-278 and MIL-STD-1553 standards.
RT Linux	Hard real time kernel. Good real time performance, but no certification.
Jbed	Developed for embedded systems and Internet applications under the Java platform. Allows an entire application including the device drivers to be written using Java.
Symbian	Designed for Smart phones. Supported by ARM, *x*86 architecture.
VRTX	Suitable for traditional board based embedded systems and SoC architectures, Supported by ARM, MIPS, PowerPC & other RISC architectures.

6.6 RTOS Vs. GENERAL OPERATING SYSTEM

1. An RTOS is mainly designed for high speed and real time applications while a conventional operating system is used in simple applications.
2. In RTOS, all the tasks meet their required deadlines, while in a conventional operating system, deadline does not occur.

3. In RTOS, output must be in time while in the conventional operating systems, it is not necessary.
4. In RTOS, latency is the main consideration in worst-case condition while the conventional operating system does not have any latency.
5. An RTOS is deterministic, which means that OS consumes only known and expected amounts of time.
6. In RTOS, scheduling is time based, which means that high-priority task will always be executed first otherwise financial or human loss can occur while conventional operating system scheduling is processed based in which each task is given processor time.
7. RTOS, all kernel operations are preemptable while it is not in conventional or general operating system.
8. RTOS has various methods to prevent priority inversion while conventional or general operating system does not have.
9. An RTOS is mainly used for embedded applications, while a conventional operating system is a desktop PC.
10. RTOS deals with real time data, so missing a deadline can lead to financial or human loss while a conventional operating system does not deal with real values.

SUMMARY

A Real Time Operating System (RTOS) consists of two components, one is Real Time and the other is Operating System. Real time operating system is specially designed for real time applications. Real time applications are concerned with timing constraints. All applications must be complete in time. Therefore, the operating system of real time system is designed in such a way that it fulfils this need. As a conventional operating system, real time operating system also provides an interface between hardware and user (application programs). It is also the combination of system calls or functions, having kernel, threads as conventional operating system.

EXERCISES

Fill in the Blanks

1. A system consists of ______ and the system's software supervises the running of the tasks.
2. ______ means information of the present program counter, stack pointer and other CPU registers. When the context of one task ______ and the context of other task ______ then that task runs.
3. RTOS controls a task which can be in one of the following states at any given instance ______ , ______ , ______ , ______ , waiting for a specific period, and waiting till some signal or message before some specific or undefined period.
4. Real time means ______ from the system's start and different actions takes place in the system at different instances of this time.
5. Real time constraint means ______ before which a task should start after an event(s). Real time constraint also means the ______ up to which it must respond to an event(s), and the time limit within which it must finish.
6. Real Time Operating System (RTOS) is ______ when the system requires ______ done at the ______ and in ______ space. RTOS is in between software layer between ______ and ______ and, ______ routines.

7. ______ controls the running of the tasks and interrupt-service routines using the hardware.
8. The task of ______ when ready, preempts (blocks) the low-priority task in order to function within the time constraints.
9. Task in ______ state of ready when it gets a signal for which it is waiting or gets a message for which it is waiting or time out when its waiting-period is over.
10. ______ assigned to the tasks in preemptive scheduling.
11. When the tasks run in cyclic schedule and when one completes, then other is signalled to start, then scheduling is called ______ .
12. The ______ generates a timeout at regular (preset) intervals. It is called ______ the ______ interrupts the RTOS at ______ . System clock ticks used for the ______ actions.
13. A task ______ *another task* but it can call the function(s) to implement certain action(s).
14. A task i waits for ______ when OS_wait function executes for a period = ______ .
15. A task i ______ a signal at time t_1. Then waiting task j takes the ______ and takes over the resources (CPU, memory, IOs, etc.) and starts at time t_2.
16. A task i ______ a semaphore (token) s_1 at time t_1. Then waiting task j takes the ______ and takes over the resources (CPU, memory, IOs, etc.) and starts at time t_2.
17. A task i ______ a ______ into mailbox M_1 at time t_1. Then waiting task j the ______ the message and takes over the resources (CPU, memory, IOs, etc.) and starts at time t_2.
18. A high priority task must be waiting for ______ , ______ , ______ , or ______ so that the lower priority task can run in preemptive scheduling.
19. RTX51 Tiny kernel requires only ______ bytes of program memory code space. When we do not need ______ , ______ , and ______ functions, we use it. Maximum number of defined tasks can be ______ . Maximum numbers of tasks, which can be active, are ______ at an instant. It requires maximum DATA space of ______ . Bytes in Internal RAM. It requires STACK space of ______ bytes per task.
20. RTX51 Full has the functions for preemptive scheduling. *RTX51 Full* has the following features.
    (*a*) Generates the timer ticks (for cyclic interrupts) using ______ .
    (*b*) Provides for ______ of a high priority task by switching from a lower priority task.
    (*c*) It has program codes of = ______ K bytes, data in internal RAM DATA = ______ bytes, stack in internal RAM (IDATA) = ______ bytes, and external memory XDATA = ______ bytes (minimum).
    (*d*) It has the functions to enable preemptive scheduling.

MULTIPLE CHOICE QUESTIONS

1. Identify which of these are real time application scenarios:
    (*a*) An online bus ticketing system
    (*b*) Printing of annual report of a company's annual report
    (*c*) Reconciling a day's transactions in an account book of a small company
    (*d*) An aircrafts' yaw control system
2. Identify the category of the following real time systems as "hard, soft or firm".
    (*a*) An online celebrity cricket bat auction
    (*b*) A patient monitoring system in an ICU
    (*c*) A library book reservation system
    (*d*) A bank credit card defaulters notice generation program

3. Which of the following describes the RTOS design philosophy best?
   (*a*) Maximize the throughput of the system
   (*b*) Maximize the processor utilization
   (*c*) Minimizing the response time
   (*d*) Response within certain stipulated time period
4. Which of the following are commercially claimed RTOSs?
   (*a*) Linux (*b*) Windows CE
   (c) Mindows NT (*d*) V*x* works
   (*e*) Sun Solaris
5. Scheduling of tasks is a very important consideration in an RTOS. Which of the following best describes the scheduling policy design?
   (*a*) The scheduler must follow a pre-emptive policy
   (*b*) The scheduler must not use pre-emptive policy option
   (*c*) The scheduler must not only use pre-emptive policy options with the priority considerations
   (*d*) The scheduler must not use pre-emptive policy option, but must employ priority consideration.
6. Keeping a task's schedulability in mind, which way a task may be scheduled:
   (*a*) The task has a predetermined time after which it may be scheduled.
   (*b*) The task has a predetermined time before which it may be scheduled.
   (*c*) The task has a predetermined time interval during which it must be scheduled any time.
   (*d*) The task state has a worst-case delay estimate before which it must be scheduled.
7. Describe which of these scheduling policies is most suited for controlling a set of periodic tasks.
   (*a*) FCFS
   (*b*) Least laxity first
   (*c*) Earliest deadline first
   (*d*) Rate monotonic policy schedule
8. Which of the following strategies can be employed for overcoming the priority inversion problem?
   (*a*) Abandon the notion of priorities altogether
   (*b*) Have only two priority levels
   (*c*) Allow for temporarily raising the priority of a lower level priority process
   (*d*) Use pre-emptive policies strictly based on priorities
9. Is it true that, in general, in an embedded system the application tasks have higher priority than system tasks?
   (*a*) Yes (*b*) No
   (*c*) May be (*d*) Sometimes
10. Where are the device drivers located in RTOSs with a microkernel?
   (*a*) In the kernel space
   (*b*) In the user space
   (*c*) In separately allocated space which is neither kernel space nor user space.
   (*d*) None of the above.

Case Study

1. RAPID PROTOTYPING ENGINE BASED ON MULTIPROCESSOR

Multiprocessors are very complex and need large data space (memory) for the execution. Designing of multiprocessor is very complex and to measure expected performance bit difficult. Handling real time data in case of multiprocessor is bit complex. To solve this problem, a new multiprocessor is designed, which uses emulation technique for data, rather than simulation. As emulation is much faster than simulation, so with this speed of data processing increase which leads to minimum delay. This is the rapid prototyping engine used for multiprocessor, is now currently in use. It runs on MIMD system with 8 processors. To estimate the program run times is very difficult, because of four reasons:

(*a*) *Source Code:* If source code is carefully optimized then only it takes less time in execution.

(*b*) *Compiler:* It maps source code to machine program. This mapping depends on the compiler.

(*c*) *Machine Architecture:* In this processor speed, I/O devices, number of registers and various other factors matter.

(*d*) *Operating System:* It does task scheduling, memory management and interrupt handling, which is having the major impact.

With this new rapid prototyping engine, this problem can be solving little bit. It is used in GFLOP multiprocessors, which is much better than RISC multiprocessors. This new rapid prototyping engine has 6.4 GB/sec system bus bandwidth, sixMB integrated L3 cache and 1.5 GHz core speed, the latest Itanium 2 processor.

Features of Rapid Prototyping Engine:

1. Processor Speed: 900 MHz
2. Package Type: FC-PGA2
3. Bus Speed: 100 MHz

4. L2 Cache Size: 128 K
5. Process: 0.18 micron.

2. DALI MAIN-MEMORY STORAGE MANAGER

It is designed for concurrency control, storage management and recovery. Its purpose is to provide consistent and safer data from disk residential database. Its speed of processing data is very high and its performance is very good.

Dali Main-Memory Storage Manager Designing:

(*a*) This provides direct access to the database. It uses memory mapped architecture in which database is mapped into virtual address space of the process and pointer given to access the data directly.

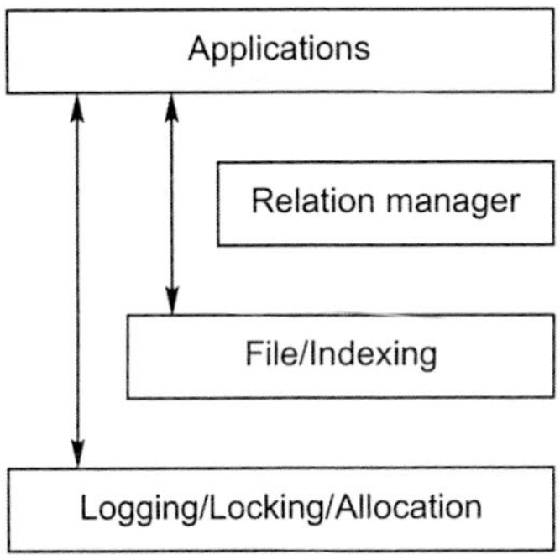

Fig. 1. Dali main-memory architecture.

(*b*) Shared memory is used for inter process communication instead of using server. All concurrency control and logging services gave by shared memory.

(*c*) This application is able to handle fault either hardware or software occur in the system.

(*d*) Logging features could be making inactive for non-consistent data.

(*e*) Lower levels can easily interact with the user to solve optimization.

Features of Dali

In this architecture, for storing user data, one or more database files are used and one-system database file stores all data related with database. All the layers are abstracted from each other. Every layer performs its own function, without knowing what the other layer does. For different regions of the database, different recovery methods are used.

1. It does multilevel recovery. It provides operation lock instead of giving exclusive/shared lock. This approach replaces the low-level physical undo log records with higher-level logical undo log records containing undo descriptions at the operation level.
2. It can handle the fault occurs in the system.
3. Solve the errors to provide consistent data.
4. The process called, as the *cleanup server* is responsible for cleanup of a dead process means the process crashes the system.

3. DCOM—A TECHNOLOGY TO SUPPORT REAL TIME EMBEDDED SYSTEM

Real time embedded system is growing large in these days and is widely used in practice. It is the current area and research is going on this field. It is designed to control normal life through web applications. Therefore, every device or application needs to connect remotely. For this there should be good connection between hardware and software and this is only possible with the help of middleware called DCOM (Distributed Component Object Model), which provides the interface between hardware and software. It is language independent and location transferable.

4. THE OLYMPUS ATTITUDE AND ORBITAL CONTROL SYSTEM

This system uses Ada and Deadline Monotonic Scheduling Algorithm and is implemented on M68020 based system.

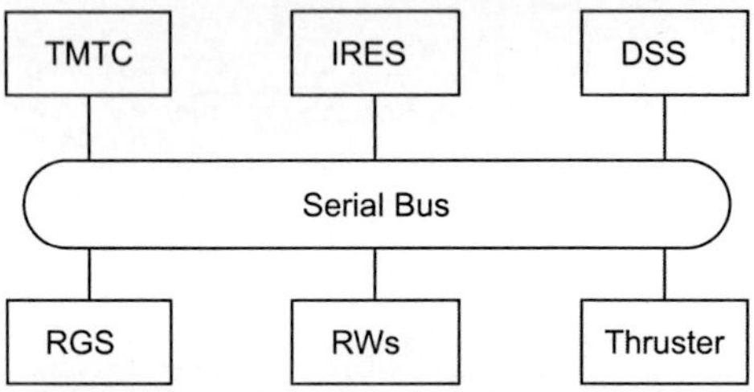

Fig. 2. Serial bus data transmission.

This software has been embedded in the Spacecraft Microcomputer Module (SMM). Serial bus is used to transmit the data. Communication done with following devices:

(*a*) A Telemetry and Tele command Subsystem (TMTC)
(*b*) An Infra Red Earth Sensor (IRES)
(*c*) Digital Sun Sensor (DSS)
(*d*) A Rate Gyro Sensor (RGS)
(*e*) Four Reaction Wheels (RWs)
(*f*) Thrusters

Relationship between control system and external devices

All the functions controlled by control system as shown in figure:

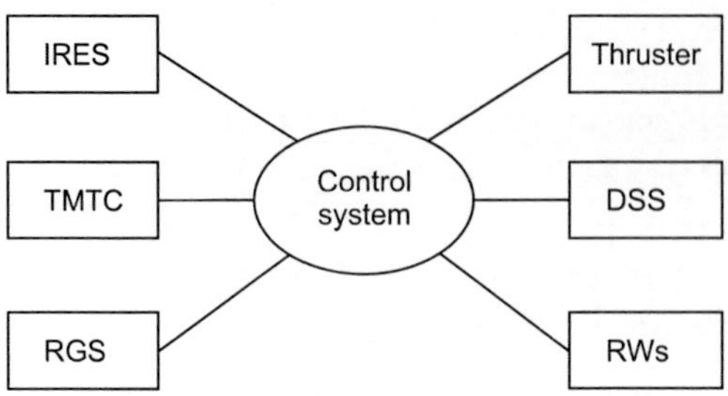

Fig. 3. A control system.

5. CENTRO REAL TIME INFORMATION

This system covers approximately 90 bus routes in the West Midlands area. This system does:

1. Passenger information
2. Trip planning
3. Load management.

Main Problems

In West Midlands area, approximately 2.3 million people live. People of this area have high frequency in Public Transport, but bus does not support this. Bus services in this area during the daytime are every four minutes, which is very high and should be minimized. This leads is poor bus service and traffic congestion. Bus should follow many routes for time reliability.

What actually scheme is:

(*a*) In CENTRO real time information, there are total 650 buses, each bus having automatic vehicle apparatus.

(*b*) There are 750 stop displays.

(*c*) 23 1 9-line displays used to show the information related to buses travelling.

(*d*) There are total 2000 stops, which have real time information of buses through SMS.

(*e*) A map-based website is available, which gives the latest information to users about the real time predictions of their stops.

Fig. 4. CENTRO real time information.

Through satellite bus, position is regularly calculated. After every 20 sec, this information is passed to central computer using GPRS. On bus, computers continuously calculate their position by looking at satellites. Then central computer calculates from how much distance each bus is from upcoming stops on the route and predict the time at which bus will reach to the upcoming stop. Complex algorithms are used to formulize all of this. Every 20 seconds this information is fed back to a central computer using the GPRS data communications network. The central computer then calculates how far each bus is from upcoming stops on route and estimates how long they will take to get there.

Fig. 5. Bus positioning locator.

Objective of this scheme

Objective of this system is:

- **Improving financial renewal** – as information based on real data and this information delivered directly to business and office centres via a website helps employers a lot.
- **Improving social presence** encourages those people who are travelling first time.
- **Encouraging customers** – real time information provides travel patterns which help and encourage existing customers.
- **Improving safety and health** – improves the health and safety of the people.
- **Improving integration** – provides travelling information.

Costs

Capital costs: approximately £10 million

Revenue costs: approximately £400,000 / annum.

6. MARUTI UDYOG LIMITED

Maruti Udyog was established in February 1981 through an Act of Parliament, to meet the personal demand of each person. It has grown more because of less availability of public transports. Its objective was to produce such cars which could easily cope with Indian population. Its purpose was to give a modern look to the automobile industry. Initially Suzuki gets hold of 26% of the equity and offers latest technology of Japan.

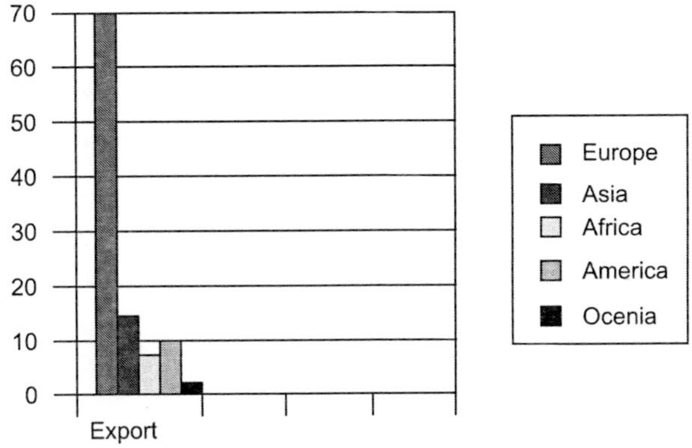

Further, in 1987, this hold increased to 40% and in 1992, it was 50%. In 2005, Maruti productions for producing cars were highest in Asia, outside Japan and Korea. It had then produced over 5 million vehicles. In other words, it can be said that Maruti was number one joint venture before 2000-01. In 2000-01, although Maruti made operating profits of ` 92.5 billion, but its demand decreased a lot, because less cost of new models. Initially car-manufacturing companies get license for manufacturing, but after 1990s, multinational companies started to invest their money in car manufacturing industry. With this, car-manufacturing industry does not require license, makes their work easy.

Maruti exported from India to abroad a lot. India is becoming a central hub for this.

Maruti Competitors

1. Hyundai Motor India Limited

This company is the second largest growing car manufacturing company in India. This company produced santro under the title a car that has changed the life of youth, a car for youngster. This name is given because company thought that instead of giving the name a car for family (as given by Maruti) this name was much better, as the most buyers of the company were youngsters. Company had introduced the cars at the rate of 3,26,999 (XK) and ` 3,45,999 (XL) and new non-AC car of the Santro at ` 2.79 lakh.

2. Tata Motors

This is the India's first largest fully integrated company collaborated with Germany. Tata motors launched first car named as Tata Indica in 1999. This car provided more space, more comfort, more style, more power and more options. Indica came in the range of ` 2.56 lakh to ` 3.88 lakh with 4 models.

Current Pricing scheme of MUL

Maruti car price is ` 1,87,000, which is the lowest offer on road. Its motive is to give the car to each person, so that India get a modern look in which each person has his/her own car. Maruti has done 70% business from its repeated customers who already have Maruti (they buy a new Maruti model again).

Table 1. Different brands of maruti.

S. No.	BRAND	VARIANTS	PRICE IN DELHI (`)
1.	GRAND VITARA	XL7	16,97,000.00
2.	MARUTI BALENO	LXi	5,72,000.00
		VXi	6,42,000.00
3.	MARUTI ESTEEM	LX	4,66,000.00
		VX	5,39,000.00
4.	MARUTI VERSA	DX	4,19,000.00
		DX2	4,58,000.00
5.	MARUTI SWIFT	LXi	3,95,000.00
		VXi	4,05,000.00
		ZXi	4,85,000.00
6.	MARUTI WAGON-R	LX	3,35,000.00
		LXi	3,62,000.00
		AX	4,63,000.00
		VXi	3,87,000.00
		VXi ABS	4,20,000.00
7.	MARUTI GYPSY	ST	5,06,000.00
		HT	5,29,000.00
8.	MARUTI ZEN	D	3,58,000.00
		LX	3,41,000.00
		LXi	3,68,000.00
		VXi	3,93,000.00
9.	MARUTI OMNI	CARGO	2,05,000.00
		CARGO LPG	1,83,000.00
		5 SEATER	2,27,000.00
		8 SEATER	2,21,000.00
		XL 5 SEATER	2,19,000.00
		XL 8 SEATER	2,31,000.00
10.	MARUTI ALTO	STANDARD	2,38,000.00
	MARUTI ALTO	LX	2,74,000.00
		LXi	2,94,000.00
11.	MARUTI 800	STD. MPFI	2,14,000.00
		A/C MPFI	2,37,000.00

Bibliography

1. A. Burkle, M. Gaub, T. Langle, H. Worn *"An Architecture and Communication Protocol for Interaction of Industrial Robots and Vision Systems".* Proceedings of ICAR 2003 The 11th International Conference on Advanced Robotics Coimbra, Portugal, June 30–July 3, 2003.
2. Blerta Bishaj " *MAC protocols, contention-based with reservation and scheduling"* 2006 IEEE paper.
3. Choi Sunghyun and G. Shin Kang *"A Unified Wireless LAN Architecture for Real Time and Non Real Time Communication Services"* IEEE/ACM TRANSACTIONS ON NETWORKING, VOL. 8, NO. 1, FEBRUARY 2000.
4. Gianluca Franchino, Giorgio C. Buttazzo and Tullio Facchinetti *"Token Passing Techniques for Hard Real Time Communication"* IEEE paper 1999.
5. Hector Garcia Molina and Kenneth Salem *"Main memory data base systems: An overview"* IEEE transactions on knowledge and dat engineering Vol 4 No. 6 December 1992.
6. James F. Kurose et.al *"Real time communication in packet switched network"* 1994 IEEE paper. Proceedings of the IEEE vol. 82, No.1, Jan. 1994.
7. Liliana Cucu, Nicolas Pernet and Yves Sorel *"Periodic real time scheduling: from deadline-based model to latency-based model"* 2005 IEEE Paper.
8. Risat Mahmud Pathan *"Scheduling Algorithms For Fault-Tolerant Real Time Systems"* IEEE paper 2010.
9. Sang H. Son and Juhnyoung Lee *"A New Approach to Real Time Transaction Scheduling"* 1992 IEEE paper.
10. Stankovic John A. and Sang Hyuk Son *"Misconceptions About Real Time Databases"* University of Virginia, Charlottesville Jorgen Hansson and University of Skovde, Sweden 1999 IEEE paper.
11. Victory Bradely Lortz *"An object oriented real time data base system for multiprocessors"* 1994 paper.

Reading Books

1. Kam-yiu Lam and Tei-Wei Kuo, *"Real Time Database Systems: Architecture and Techniques",* Kluwer Academic Publishers, 2000.
2. Krishna and Kang, *"Real TimeSystems,"* McGRAW-HILL, 1997.

Abbreviations

A

ADA		
API	:	Application Programming Interface
ATM	:	Asynchronous Transfer Mode

B

BOCC	:	Backward Optimistic Concurrency Control
BEB	:	Binary Exponential Back-off

C

CR	:	Capacity Reliability
CSMA/CD	:	Carrier Sense Multiple Access with Collision Detection
CTS	:	Clear to Send
CTS/BI	:	Clear To Send / Busy Indication
CA	:	Computational Availability
CPU	:	Computer Processing Unit
CBR	:	Constant Bit Rate
CORBA		
CAN	:	Control Area Network

D

DMA	:	Deadline Monotonic Algorithm
DRDB	:	Disk Residential Databases
D-PRAMA	:	Distributed Packet Reservation Multiple Access

E

EDF	:	Earliest Deadline First

F

FTRM : Fault Tolerance Rate Monotonic
FC : Feasibility Condition
FDDI : Fiber Distributed Data Interface
FRTS : Firm Real Time System
FCFS : First Come First Served
FIFO : First In First Out
FAB : Focused Addressing and Bidding Algorithm
FOCC : Forward Optimistic Concurrency Control
FDD : Frequency Division Duplexing

H

HRTS : Hard Real Time System
HRR : Hierarchical Round Robin Protocol

I

IEEE
IP : Internet Protocol
ISP : Internet Service Provider

L

Lc : Late counter
LSB : Least Significant Bit
LISP
LED : Light Emitting Diode
LAN : Local Area Network

M

MMDB : Main Memory Databases
MAN : Metropolitan Area Network
MAP : Manufacturing Automation Protocol
MAC : Medium Access Control
MSB : Most Significant Bit
MACA : Multiple Access Collision Avoidance
MDARTS : Multiprocessor Database for Hard Real Time Systems
MOS : Myopic Offline Scheduling Algorithm
MTBF, MTDF, MTTF, and MTTR

N

NGC

O

OCC : Optimistic Concurrency Control

P

2PL : 2 Phase Locking
PCP : Priority-Ceiling Protocol
PCB : Process Control Block
Prolog

Q

QoS : Quality of Service

R

RMA : Rate Monotonic Algorithm
RTC : Real Time Clock/ Communication
RTDBMS : Real Time DBMS
RTOS : Real Time Operating System
RTS : Real Time System
RPC : Remote Procedure Call
RFB : Request for Bids
RTS/BI : Request To Send / Busy Indication
RTS : Request to Send
RR : Round Robin

S

SMS : Service Management Systems
SRTS : Soft Real Time System
SGMP : Stop and Go Multihop Protocol
SC : Sufficient Condition

T

TCB : Task Control Block
TTRT : Target Token Rotation Time
TDD : Time Division Duplexing
TDMA : Time Division Multiplexing
TTP : Timed Token Protocol
TO : Time Stamp Odering
THT : Token holding Timer
TRT : Token Rotation Timer

V

VBR : Variable Bit Rate
VME
VPN : Virtual Private Network
VTCSMA : Virtual Time Carrier Sensed Multiple Access

W

WAN : Wide Area Network
WC : Work Conserving
WCET : Worst Case Execution Time
WCRT : Worst Case Response Time

Glossary of Terms

A

Abnormal end: A task or a job terminated because of occurrence of some error and recovery facility is not able to recover it. See abnormal termination.

Abnormal termination: Because of system failure, a task not able to compete its operation. Synonymous with abnormal end.

Access: Access the data from memory or disk.

Access authority: An authority that relates to a request for a type of access to protected resources.

Access control: For the sake of security, users give authority for accessing the data.

Access methods: It is the method of moving data between main memory and I/O devices.

ACID properties: Transaction properties are atomicity, consistency, isolation and durability.

ACK: Acknowledgement a sender receives from receiver.

Action: It is the smallest decomposition of a response. This action can use zero and one or more resources.

Adjacent node: Anode that connects to other node by a path, and there is no any other node exist in this path.

Administrator: A person gives authority to other users. This person does various administrative work such as access authorization and content management.

Advanced Peer-to-Peer Networking (APPN): Provides automatic resource registration, directory look up, ease of connection, reconfiguration and many more features.

Allocate: Assign the resources to a task.

Alphanumeric character: A letter or a number or combination of both.

American Standard Code for Information Interchange (ASCII): A standard code used for information exchange among data processing systems, data communication systems and associated equipment. ASCII uses a coded character set consisting of 7-bit coded characters.

Aperiodic event: Sequences of these events are not periodic.

Aperiodic tasks: These tasks are event-driven and generated randomly. Aperiodic tasks tend to have soft deadlines.

Application Programming Interface (API): It is the set of programming language. It provides the interface for different applications to communicate with each other. This programming interface accesses the services from operating system.

ARPANET: A network established by the United States Department of Defense Advanced Research Projects Agency (now the Defense Advanced Research Projects Agency).

Assembler: A computer program converts assembly language into machine language.

Asynchronous processing: No nodes synchronized with the same clock pulse. They requested to behave separately.

ATM: (1) Asynchronous Transfer Mode. (2) Automatic teller Machine.

Asynchronous Transfer Mode (ATM): This transfer mode organized the information into cells.

Atomicity: Operation on each transaction is atomic (means single or indivisible). Sometimes none of the operations is performed on the transactions.

Audit: The test performed to check data security methods and data accuracy methods. It checks the effectiveness of data processing.

Authentication: Check whether the person is an authorized user or not. The user has an authority gain access to the data or not.

Authority: The right to access objects, functions and resources.

Authorization: The process of granting a user either complete or restricted access to an object, function and resource.

Authorization checking: Action to check the user is an authorized user or not.

Auxiliary storage: Secondary storage stores the data.

Automation: It is an automatically performed operation in response to some events.

Availability: The given resource is available or not.

Average-case: Average response time of a task is within an interval. This time is obtained via simulation. It may be the case that for a particular task, average repose-time and worst-case response time differ from each other. In case of hard real time system, worst-case response time must be within specific time interval.

B

Background: It is the environment in multiprogramming in which low-priority tasks are executed. Contrast with foreground.

Background task: It is a low-priority task or non-interactive task. Contrast with foreground task.

Backup: When data is lost because of system crash, then data can be updated through backup. It is the device, system and file which provides the data in case of loss.

Backup host: A device, system and file provide the data in case of loss to all other systems. This loss can take place because of accidental failure or permanent failure.

Bandwidth: It is the capacity of a communications line, normally expressed in bits per second (bps). Data rate transfer is in K bits, K bytes, M bits, and M bytes per second. In Asynchronous Transfer Mode (ATM), the capacity of a virtual channel, expressed in terms of Peak Cell Rate (PCR), Sustainable Cell Rate (SCR) and Maximum Burst Size (MBS).

Batch: Same tasks grouped together and processed together for easy functioning.

Batch job: A predefined group contains all the similar jobs needs to process for easy function of the system.

Batch processing: Similar types of tasks processed together.

Binary data: Data is in the form of 0 and 1 (numeric values). The data is readable by machine. Various compilers used to convert data in binary form so that machine can easily read it.

Block: (1) A set of consecutive pages on disk. (2) A unit of data storage on a device. (3) A set of contiguous pages in a buffer pool. (4) A string of data elements that is recorded or transmitted as a unit. (5) A sequence of text, commands, or records that are read, written, or processed as a unit.

Blocking: A higher-priority task has been delayed because of a lower-priority task ((known as priority inversion), this creates blocking state and makes implementation of distributed and shared memory difficult.

Block size: The number of data elements in a block.

Blocking time: In this time, a higher-priority task is delayed because of a lower-priority task.

Bridge: Connects multiple LANs locally or remotely together.

Broadcast: (1) Same data transmitted to all destinations. (2) Instantaneous data transmitted to more than one destination.

Broadcast search: A request made, when receiver is unknown to the sender.

Browser: It is a software package used for locating, requesting and displaying web pages. Examples include Netscape Navigator, Mozilla, and Internet Explore, etc.

Buffer: Carry input or output data temporarily.

Buffer pool: It is the memory portion in which data pages are read and modified.

Bursty arrivals: Several events have occurred arbitrarily together.

Bus: Transfer the data between different devices placed between two ends.

C

C language: A high-level language used to develop various software applications. Portable in nature and can be used on different machines with minor changes.

Cabinet: Organized long, different and several cables, patch ports, adapters and couplers together. It connects cables with processors and controllers.

Cache: A small memory, very much faster than main memory, holds the data used for execution. Memory is near to processor and used by processor mostly.

Capacity Reliability (CR): Capacity of the system, even work in high load conditions called worst case.

Carrier Sense Multiple Access with Collision Detection (CSMA/CD): Detects the collision before sending the data. If channel is idle then only it sends the data, otherwise it will wait. Used in MAC layer.

Catastrophic failure: This leads to financial or human loss.

Case-sensitive: Makes distinction between uppercase and lowercase letters.

Central storage: It stores real time data and mainly processes by processor.

Channel: It is the path for information communication. This channel is common in case of broadcast communication. The channel is called as path or way through which information is transmitted.

Channel interface: Connects a channel to its host.

Channel path: Interconnection between a channel and its associated control units.

Channel path identifier: The numbers through which a channel can be identified. Each channel has its number written in routing table.

Channel-to-Channel (CTC): It is the communication among Channel-to-Channel Adapters (CTCA).

Channel-to-Channel Adapter (CTCA): An input/output device can communicate among one system to another system through set of programs.

Character: A letter, digit, or other symbol called representation of data.

Checkpoint: It is a place where recording of data and check is made for restart purposes.

Checkpoint data set: A data set in which information is recorded for restart purposes.

Checkpoint write: Any write to the checkpoint data set. This write is to update the data set.

Circuit switching: A connection establishes before transmitting the data. Follow a handshake process. Intermediate nodes also contain the message is transferred.

Client: A user is using the system or resources. This client depends on other system or server for its function. It accesses data, services, programs, or resources from server.

Client-server: Client makes the request and server responses to that request. Server can give repose to client through local data access or remote data access.

Clock synchronization algorithm: Uses locked locks for hardware synchronization.

Collision: Number of sender sending data through same path at the same time. Various protocols are used to resolve collision.

Command: It is a request to perform an operation.

Commit: Save the changes, a user has made. It is mostly closed with commit command. Committed data stored in log files for recovery and in memory for user display.

Commit Phase (CP): When a transaction commits, all the changes made by that transaction will be stored permanently in the database. To maintain the consistency of the database it is a mandatory step.

Communication controller: Controls the whole communication process.

Communication line: A path on which information flows, also called telecommunication line.

Communication protocols: Have inter-processor communication that has the predictable delays and is controllable.

Component: A functional part of an operating system that performs various functions, for example, the scheduler or supervisor.

Computational availability: This is the expected value of the system computation capacity at any given time.

Connection: In data communications, a path is established for transferring the information between different users, located at different places.

Connectionless protocol: Like UDP, which does not need any connection establishment phase before transmission.

Connection-oriented protocol: Like TCP needs first to establish a connection before sending the data.

Connectivity: The capability of a system or device to attach to other systems or devices without modification.

Consistency: Each transaction must be able to view consistent database regardless of the failure. Data must be consistent.

Consistent copy: A copy has consistent view, means backup or log files data has maintained the consistency by providing entire data set from a single instant in time.

Console: An input/output device does the communication between different computers.

Control block: A block or storage area contains control information.

Controller area network: These networks are smaller than LAN and mainly used to connect the different components of embedded controllers. In general, a CAN behaves like a local bus in a computer. In an automotive system the different components such as engine, brakes, etc., are connected and controlled through a CAN.

Control Unit (CU): A device that controls whole processing.

Critical section: It is the period a real time task is holding a shared resource.

Critical tasks: The task needs to be complete within specific time without missing deadline. For example, Aircraft Control System.

Cryptographic key: This parameter transforms information between plaintext and cipher text.

D

Daemon: In UNIX® systems, a long-lived process that runs unattended to perform continuous or periodic system-wide functions, such as network control. Some daemons triggered automatically to perform their task; others operate periodically. An example is the cron daemon, which periodically performs the tasks listed in the crontab file. The z/OS equivalent is a started task.

Database: A collection of different independent data items stored together to perform various operations.

Database Administrator (DBA): A person who is responsible for the design, development, operation, security, maintenance, and use of a database or database management system.

Database Management System (DBMS): A software system that controls the creation, organization, and modification of a database and the access to the data that is stored in it.

Data integrity: Data must be consistent even in the presence of system crash, data lost.

Data set: The recodes on which various operations are performed.

Data set backup: Backup the data, protecting the data when data lost occurs.

Data-sharing: Data is shared among different users. This sharing can be locally or remotely. There are various sharing policies, such as priority inheritance protocol, priority ceiling protocol, etc.

Deadlock: When a lower priority task has delayed the execution of higher priority task by getting the resources and putting high portion task in waiting state, then a deadlock occurs. This is an unavoidable condition. Various algorithms are used to resolve this problem.

Deadline: A task must be complete before its specific time; this time is known as task deadline. In case of hard real time system, a task must be completed before its deadline. In soft real time system, task-missing deadline is tolerable but it leads to degrade system performance and sometimes-catastrophic failure leads to financial or human loss.

Deadline monotonic algorithm: A static based algorithm, DMA assigns the priority to the tasks based on their shorter deadlines while in RMA priority assigned occurrence based. DMA is more capable than RMA. RMA and DMA give same result, when deadline of a task is proportional to its period.

Dedicated: It is a direct path used for transmitting the data between sender and receiver.

Default: A value used when there is no any other alternative exists.

Delay: It is also known as latency is time taken to deliver a packet.

Desktop computer: It is also known as traditional office computer or personal computer. This has only main devices such as central processing unit, disk drives, the monitor, a keyboard and a mouse.

Desktop publishing: Creating graphics, words and images of different size and styles through desktop or personal computer by copying from newspapers and magazines.

Destination: Receiving node to which actually information passed.

Destination node: The node receives the information from sender.

Deterministic: A system in which it is possible to determine system exactly what is or will be executing on the processor during system execution.

Device: A computer peripheral has to perform certain functions.

Device number: A four-hexadecimal-character identifier

Domain: A domain is the web address (URL) that customers use to find your Web Store.

DNS server: DNS stands for Domain Name Server. These servers have fully qualified domain with the proper IP address.

Durability: When a transaction is committed, all of its changes must be stored permanently in the database regardless of failure.

Dynamic-priority: A priority when assigned to a task changes during run time. In dynamic priority, different jobs of a task may have different priorities relative to other tasks in the system. For example, Earliest Deadline First (EDF) scheduling algorithm assigns dynamic priorities to tasks such that a task whose absolute deadline is the nearest has the highest priority.

E

Earliest deadline: A dynamic-priority assignment policy, the highest priority assigned to the task with the most coming up deadline.

Earliest Deadline First (EDF) algorithm: Called as least time to go algorithm. It is a dynamic scheduling algorithm and mostly used in real time systems. It places tasks in a priority queue. Whenever a task finishes its execution, the queue searches for the task closest to its deadline and closest deadline task will execute first.

EDI: Electronic data interchange, with this companies place their orders, give offers on various projects, and makes payments on the internet or private networks.

Encapsulation: Encapsulates the data; a packet would contain control information from the physical layer, followed by control information from the network layer, followed by the application protocol data.

Encrypt: Encode data so that other person will not be able to check the data, only authorized person can see the data.

End node: It can also be termed as destination node. This end node can have direct path from the source node or can have various intermediate nodes in between.

End Phase: After the commit phase, a transaction will complete by releasing all the locks that it has acquired. With the end phase, all changes made by the transactions will also be no visible to other transactions.

Error: When an error occurs in the system, the procedure rules of the system are violated. System errors are inner instructions. This error produces incorrect result in the system.

Ethernet: A packet-based network technology used in local area networks (LANs). This provides multiple accesses of the users and can handle conflict by using Carrier Sense Multiple Access with Collision Detection (CSMA/CD). Ethernet standardized in the IEEE 802.3 specifications.

Event: An action performed to do some task. An action generated by trigger. This can also cause by interrupt.

Executable: A task is in a ready state and needs to be loaded for execution.

Executable program: A program is in a ready state and needs to be loaded for execution.

Execution time: Amount of time taken to execute the task by processor.

Extended Binary-Coded Decimal Interchange Code (EBCDIC): An encoding scheme that represents character data.

F

Failed: A system is not able to achieve its tasks in specific deadlines.

Failure: A system is said to be failed or in a failure state, if a system or its components does not perform well and do not give require output within specific time. When a system comes across the fault, then failure occurs.

Fault: It is an external instruction. It produces an error in system. A fault in the system causes system failure. Some faults of the system are tolerable and some are not. When fault cause error in the system, then that fault managed.

Fetch: The Access the data to perform various functions.

Fiber distributed data interface: An American National Standards Institute (ANSI) standard for 100-Mbps LAN using fiber optic cables.

Fiber optic cable: A fiber or bundle of fibers in a structure built to meet optic, mechanical, and environmental specifications.

File Transfer Protocol (FTP): In TCP/IP, used to transfer the files.

Firm Real time system: The systems are like soft real time system but late delivery of service is not tolerable. E.g. Video and Audio Conferencing. Produces outdated output, if task does not follow deadline. Examples are forecast systems.

Fixed-priority: A priority when assigned to a task never changes during run time. In a task set, all the tasks will have the same priority relative to any other task set. For example, RM scheduling algorithm assigns static priorities to tasks such that shorter the period of the task higher is the priority.

Foreground: The environment in multiprogramming in which high priority tasks are executed. Contrast with background.

Foreign key: Key makes a connection between different tables. The key must have the same number of columns, with the same descriptions, as the primary key of the parent table.

Foreground task: A high-priority task or a real time task. Contrast with background task.

Frame: Contains header, trailer, data, address will pass from sender to receiver.

Frame relay. A protocol for routing frames for managing the route or virtual connection on the network.

Function: A function can perform its function in zero simulation time. Function execution does not follow any deadline. For the execution of a function, at least one argument is passed.

Functional consistency: Defines over the values stored in data objects.

G

Gateway: A device used to connect different networks. These different networks can have different communication protocols, different security policies. Gateway acts as translator or connector.

H

Half-duplex: In half-duplex, RTC, real time data or live data can be transmitting in both directions on a single carrier but not at the same time.

Handshake: As in circuit switching, connection is established before sending the data.

Hard real time system: A system in which task must be completed within specific time or deadline. It is compulsory to produce the output within specified tome or deadlines. For example, flight control systems such as Aircraft and Nuclear Power Plant.

Hardware: Peripheral devices, electronic devices, computer devices also called as Physical equipment such as mechanical, magnetic, electrical, or electronic devices. Contrast with software.

Hub: Hub is the central node through which various devices are connected together. It is used in star or ring topology.

I

I/O: Input/output device takes the input from the keyboard and gives the output on the screen. Printer and monitors are output devices while keyboard and scanner are software devices.

I/O cage: It is the physical area used for making various connections by the processors.

Initiator/terminator: Scheduling algorithm selects the ready task, a task needs to execute assigned resources to the tasks and place them under task control and at the completion of the task and supplies output at output unit.

Internet: It is the worldwide collection of interconnected networks that use the Internet suite of protocols and permit public access.

Internet protocol address: The Internet Protocol address is the standard way of identifying a computer connected to the Internet. The IP address consists of four numbers separated by periods - each number is less than 256.

Interrupt: An error or emergency occurrs in the system, which causes system to stop for sometimes and moves the control operation to the emergency side.

Intranet: A private network used within the organization.

Intrusion detection service: Software attacks on the computer attached in the network to access their confidential information.

Input jitter: Variation in delay at sender side while sending data to the receiver.

Isolation: Multiple transactions can execute concurrently without the interference of any other transaction.

ISP: A firm gives access to the Internet, including email and web browsing. ISPs often offer connections by dialing a telephone number through your computer's modem.

J

Jitter: It is variance of the latency. This can be of two types. First is fixed minimum propagation delay due to speed of light and second is variation due to waiting on path.

Job class: This class arranged in specific classes of jobs, according to similarity of their tasks.

Job priority: A value assigned to a job that is relative important for other system resources.

K

Kernel: It is an operating system part performs various basic functions such as hardware allocation.

Kernelized: Tasks executed in non-preemptive fashion also called as kernel priority. This mainly used to resolve the problem of priority inversion.

L

Local Area Network (LAN): It is within a building or a campus and usually privately owned. A LAN used to connect a number of computers within an organization to hardware and software resources. In hardware resources scanner, printer and fax machines can be share and in software files, folders and other data can be share. LAN typically operates at data rates exceeding 10 Mbps and present day LAN (like Gigabit Ethernet) operate at 1 Gbps. LAN is usually implemented using broadcast networks.

Lock Phase (LP): A transaction gets the required read/write lock.

Logical resource: A system shared among multiple tasks. A logical resource bounded to a physical resource like a processor.

M

MAC: Media access control (MAC).

MAC address: A standardized data link layer address used by each port or device connected via Local Area Network (LAN). Other devices use this address to locate specific ports in the network and to create and update routing tables and data structures. MAC addresses are 6 bytes long and controlled by the IEEE.

Machine readable: Data read by machine like binary form.

Main task: In a multitasking environment, it is main task which has to be executed first prior to other tasks.

Mainframe: A computer placed in computer center having extensive capabilities and resources; from this computer other computers share resources and other facilities.

Media access control: In LANs, MAC is the sub layer of the data link layer. This layer detects collision and provides various collision free protocols. This layer gets the services from physical layer and gives to the Logical Link Control (LLC) sub layer.

Message queue: When the processor is busy, then coming message placed in *q* queue called waiting queue.

Message text: The part of a message contains actual information a sender wants to send.

Metropolitan Area Network (MAN): A network formed by the interconnection of two or more networks may operate at higher speed than those networks.

Multiprocessor Database Architecture for Real Time Systems: MDARTS avoids client server overhead. In this, transactions execute into application tasks. It eliminates extra overhead and focuses on basic data management services such as concurrent access, serializability, and multiprocessor transaction support.

N

Network: A number of computers are connected together to exchange their information.

Network Accessible Unit (NAU): A Logical Unit (LU), Physical Unit (PU), Control Point (CP), or System Services Control Point (SSCP). It is the origin or the destination of information transmitted by the path control network.

Network administrator: A person manages the use and maintenance of a network.

Network controller: A controller manages the network operations through converting protocols, which manage the way data sent and received.

Non-Critical Tasks: These are like soft real time system in which deadline can be missing, but it leads to performance degrading.

Non-preemptive Tasks: The task cannot preempt by any other tasks. In addition, a higher priority task cannot preempt lower priority task, although higher priority tasks miss its deadlines.

Non-real time system does not follow these conditions; they do not have any timing constraints and can response to output at anytime.

O

Offline tasks: These tasks are already known to the processor, their deadline, execution time, start time, etc. Processor knows everything before their execution.

Offline scheduling also said to be static scheduling. In offline scheduling in advance (before executing the task set), we know whether the given task set is schedulable or not. To check the feasibility condition, it requires the various static task parameters like period, execution time, and deadlines of different tasks in a given task set.

Offset: Number of measuring units from an arbitrary starting point in a record, area, or control block, to some other point.

Online tasks: Processor does not know about these tasks. Processor does not know their deadline, execution time, start time. Anytime a new task can arrive with shorter deadline.

Online scheduling also called as dynamic scheduling. Offline scheduling is only used when before executing the task, we will be able to know whether the given task is schedulable or not. If all task parameters are *not* known before the task execution, then schedulability analysis is not possible to predict. Online scheduling is mainly used when a new task arrives in the system with new period, deadline and timing constraints.

On-time real time system: It is like hard real time system, produce their output in specific time without missing their deadlines.

Operator commands: Used to perform various operations such as access information, alter and update information.

Operator message: It is the message given by operating system directing to the operator for performing specific functions.

Operations log: A central record of communications and system problems.

Operating system: Act as the interface between user and computer. It provides various services such as hardware allocation, I/O control, and data management.

Optimistic concurrency control: Assumes that although data conflicts are possible, but they occur very rare.

Output jitter: It is the variation in delay at receiving side.

P

Packet: Contains data and control information, passed from sender to receiver.

Packet mode operation: See packet switching.

Packet switching: Message transmitted from sender to receiver, this message cannot be stored in intermediate nodes.

Page: It is a fixed-length block of instructions, data, or both which can be transfer between main storage and external storage.

Page fault: When a page not found in main storage then page fault occurs.

Password: It is a unique string of characters known to a computer system and to a user, who must specify the character string to gain access to a system and to the information stored within it.

Peer network: A network in which each resource is capable of doing its functions own.

Period: The tasks occur at regular intervals of time. These tasks follow hard deadlines and their time occurs in worst-case execution.

Periodic event: An event occurs in constant time intervals.

Periodic tasks: The tasks occur at regular intervals of time. These tasks follow hard deadlines and their time occurs in worst-case execution.

Pessimistic locking: Mainly used in resolving the problem of data conflicts, when there are number of updates has to be perform then this technique used. If number of users wants to update the same record at the same time then preferably this technique is used.

Precedence graph: It is the graph in which tasks execute in an order. A precedence graph is a directed *acyclic* graph whose nodes correspond to individual statements.

Preemption: A higher priority task can take control from a lower priority task.

Preemptive tasks: The task preempted by other tasks. The tasks having nearest deadline (task deadline time is near to occur) is assigned a higher priority task and other is assigned lower priority task. Only a higher priority task can preempt lower priority task. The tasks which is having high priority will be executed first other will be later on.

Priority: A data sharing policy in which a higher priority task executed first.

Priority ceiling: It related with logical resource and that resource use high priority action.

Priority inversion: A higher priority task has been delayed because of a lower priority task (known as priority inversion), this creates blocking state and makes implementation of distributed and shared memory difficult.

Procedure: It is a set of self-contained High-Level Language (HLL) statements performs a particular task and returns to the caller.

Processor: The physical processor, or machine, has a serial number, a set of channels, and a logical processor associated with it. The logical processor has a number of channel path IDs, or CHPIDs, which are the logical equivalent of channels. The logical processor divided into a number of logical partitions.

R

Rate-monotonic algorithm: It is static priority algorithm and mostly used in practical applications. It is very simple algorithm and it is very easy to implement it. It is widely used in Industry. RMA assigns priorities to the various tasks based on their rates of occurrence. A task assigned lower priority according to its lower occurrence rate. A task assigned higher priority according to its higher occurrence rate.

Read access: Permission to read information.

Reader: A program reads the data from an input device or data base file.

Real address: In virtual storage systems, the address of a location stored in central storage.

Real storage: Synonymous with central storage.

Real time operating systems specially used for real time applications. They produce the result in specific time following the timing constraints. In embedded system, there is no operating system.

Real time system: Real time systems respond to the input immediately. They have some specific time called timing constraints in which they have to give their outputs. Producing the output, after specific time degrade system performance, leads to catastrophic failure and sometimes output is useless for both system and user. They have to response in order of milliseconds or in microsecond.

Reason code: A return code explains the reason of failure.

Record: A group of related data items treated as a unit.

Record data: The data sets accessed record by record.

Recoverability: System is able to recover the data, in case of failure.

Recovery: Processes of recover the data in case of system failure, crash and any other emergency conditions.

Recovery system: A system that is capable to recover the data by storing back up of the data.

Redundancy: Contains duplicate data. Various algorithms used to avoid duplicity to save the space of the memory.

Register: An internal computer component capable of storing a specified amount of data and accepting or transferring this data rapidly.

Release time: The release time of job is the time at which the job becomes available for execution. The job can be scheduled and executed at anytime at or after its release time whenever its data and control dependency conditions met.

Reliability: It is the probability the system will not fail in an interval.

Remote copy: A copy stored in remote location to access the data in case of failure.

Resource: A *physical* unit such as processor, bus, channel, and router used to transfer the information. A resource can have resource allocation policy and data-sharing policy.

Response: Output given by the system, time have great impact in this. A real time system must produce its output immediately known as response of the system.

Rollback: Process of restoring data changed by user at its last commit.

Routing protocol: A technique used by a router to find other routers and to remain up to date about the best way to get to reachable networks.

Routing table: A collection of routes used to direct datagram forwarding or to establish a connection. The information passed among routers to identify network topology and destination feasibility.

Routing A Path where information is passing.

Runtime environment: It is the environment in which program executes.

S

Save area: Area of main storage in which data saved.

Scalability: The ability of a system to expand as resources, such as processors, memory, or storage, added.

Scan attack: An attack in which a host on the network is trying to determine what ports are open on the target host. The host doing the scan may later be the same host that does a more virulent attack.

Serializability: All the transactions must execute in particular order so that all transactions will meet specific deadlines. Purpose of serialization is also to resolve data conflicts occurs between concurrent transactions. Serializability maintains the serialization of different transactions.

Server: Gives services to the client. Client makes a request and server response on that request. A server can never be idle while a client can be. Server are file server, mail server printer server etc. server gives response to the client by accessing the data locally or remotely from other server. Contrast with client.

Session: Before sending data to receiver, a connection established, this is session creation, as appear in TCP/IP networks. It is time in which sender and receiver communicate with each other. When a user login any website such as yahoo, Gmail, then a session creates and when user log out of the system, then session will be terminate itself.

Soft real time system: Response to input immediate within specific time, but in some cases systems will still function correctly although system has occasionally missed their deadlines. Missing deadlines degrade the system performance. For example, online transaction systems, airline reservation systems etc.

Sporadic tasks: It is an aperiodic task with known minimum inter-arrival time. Sporadic tasks are aperiodic in nature, but they have hard deadlines. These tasks used to handle emergency conditions and exceptional situations.

Star topology: In this, various nodes in a network connected to a central node called hub through which they communicate with each other.

Subnet work: This group of nodes has same characteristics such as Network ID.

T

Task: Tasks can be executed both in zero simulation and in non-zero simulation time. Task execution must follow specific deadline. A task can have zero or more arguments. A task can enable a function or other tasks. A Task cannot return a value. A task is a program or a code block, which after execution gives some result. Task is the basic component of scheduling. Examples of task are reading sensor data, data processing and transmission of sensor data etc.

Temporal consistency: It is related with time.

Thrashing: When load increases in the system, then system performance degrades.

Throughput: Throughput is the average number of instructions per unit time that a system can process.

Timing constraints: A timing constraint of a job is specified in terms of its release time and relative or absolute deadlines.

Token ring network: All the nodes are connected in the form of ring. In this, a token is used to transfer the data, as connection if from one computer to another.

Transaction: Maintaining the consistency of the database by applying various read and write operations on the database called ***transaction.*** Each transaction must get consistent view of the database.

Transmission control protocol: Establishes handshake process before sending the data. Connection is established after that data is sent.

Transmission priority: Each transmission is assigned a priority according to its deadline. The shorter the deadline, the higher priority is assigned to the transmission, means this transmission will be executed first.

Transaction start phase: Transaction is in a ready state or active state.

Transient overload: Some tasks of the system are not able to complete their execution in specific time especially the time, which was planned during their design time. This is called transient overload.

Tree topology: A parent node has child nodes and these child nodes can have sub child nodes as in a tree.

Trigger: Execute the task to perform various functions. Mainly triggers execute on sequence events. These triggers executed in particular time.

Twisted pair: Twisting cables provide less interference line an antenna used for transmission up to long distances.

U

Uniprocessor: Uses a single processor to execute a set of tasks. Before executing the task, task feasibility condition is checked, then scheduling algorithm feasibility is checked to see whether all the tasks in a given task set meet their required deadline. Its examples are RM and EDF algorithm.

Unit of Recovery (UR): A set of changes on one node has been committed and stored in log files for the purpose of recovery in case of failure.

UNIX operating system: An operating system provides multiprogramming in a multiuser environment. Bell Laboratories developed this. Unix operating system was initially used in minicomputers, then in mainframes and now in microcomputers.

Utilization: A processor is fully utilized, when a processor cannot handle the increase in the computation time of any of the tasks in a task set, because increase in computation time in task set makes the task set unschedulable. Utilization of one task is ratio between WCET and its period. Total utilization is the sum of all tasks utilization of a task set.

W

WCET: WCET (Worst Case Execution Time) is the maximum time that a task can take to complete the execution of the task. WCET is important for schedulability analysis in hard real time systems. It is a software development metrics.

Wait state: Synonymous with waiting time.

Waiting time: Task is waiting in queue for execution because of some conditions or circumstances.

Workload: A group of work needs to be managed and reported as a unit.

PTU Question Papers

REAL TIME SYSTEM (CS - 324) (APRIL 2012)

B. Tech (Sem. - 6th)

Paper ID [CS324]

(Please Hit this Paper ID in OMR Sheet)

Time: 03 Hours Maximum Marks: 60

Instruction to Candidates:

1. Section—A is Compulsory.
2. Attempt any Four questions from Section–B.
3. Attempt any Two questions from Section–C.

Section–A (10 × 2 = 20)

1. (*a*) What is cache? List the different 5 types of cache.
   (*b*) Define 'Virtual memory and the advantage of virtual memory'.
   (*c*) What is precedence graph, explain with example?
   (*d*) What is sproadic task? Explain.
   (*e*) What is 2 stage pipelines?
   (*f*) List the various performance measure of real time system.
   (*g*) What are periodic and aperiodic tasks?
   (*h*) How a real time system is different from other computer based systems?
   (*i*) What is software reliability?
   (*j*) What is rectangular mesh? Explain with example.

Section–B (4 × 5 = 20)

2. What are Hypercube networks? Explain all its types.
3. State the difference between preemptive and non-preemptive scheduling with example.
4. Write short note on main memory databases.
5. Explain optimistic concurrency control.
6. Explain the architecture of a real time system. How can you classify the tasks for the real time systems?

Section–C (2 × 10 = 20)

7. List all the disk scheduling algorithms and explain any two (with diagram).
8. Find the computational complexity of IRIS5.
9. Write the algorithm procedures for expand window and send protocol.

REAL TIME SYSTEM (CS - 324) (MAY 2011)

B. Tech (Sem. – 6th)

Paper ID [CS324]

(Please Hit this Paper ID in OMR Sheet)

Time: 03 Hours Maximum Marks: 60

Instruction to Candidates:

1. Section–A is Compulsory.
2. Attempt any Four questions from Section–B.
3. Attempt any Two questions from Section–C.

Section–A **(10 × 2 = 20)**

1. (*a*) Hard real time.
   (*b*) High performance computing.
   (*c*) Real time operating system.
   (*d*) Application of real time systems.
   (*e*) Sot Real time systems.
   (*f*) Shortest job first.
   (*g*) Round robin mechanism.
   (*h*) Define deadlock.
   (*i*) Deadline based protocols.
   (*j*) Performance measures for real time systems.

Section–B **(4 × 5 = 20)**

2. What you understand by fault tolerant scheduling. Explain with example.
3. Differentiate between real time and general purpose databases.
4. What are different concurrency control mechanisms for real time databases? Write in detail.
5. Discuss different architectural issues in real time communication.
6. Write Earliest Deadline First (EDF) algorithm for scheduling purposes.

Section–C **(2 × 10 = 20)**

7. Explain the following protocols used in real time communication:
   (*a*) Polled bus protocol.
   (*b*) Stop and Go multihop protocol.
8. How the scheduling of real time systems differ from general traditional scheduling? Illustrate taking an example.
9. Write note on the following:
   (*a*) Task classes.
   (*b*) Main Memory databases.
   (*c*) Token based protocols.
   (*d*) Contention based protocols.

REAL TIME SYSTEM (CS - 324) (DEC 2011)

B. Tech (Sem. – 6th)

Paper ID [CS324]

(Please Hit this Paper ID in OMR Sheet)

Time: 03 Hours | Maximum Marks: 60

Instruction to Candidates:

1. Section–A is Compulsory.
2. Attempt any Four questions from Section–B.
3. Attempt any Two questions from Section–C.

Section–A (10 × 2 = 20)

1. (*a*) Classify real time applications based on their timing attributes.

(*b*) Explain, at least three uni-processor scheduling algorithms in brief.

(*c*) How fault tolerance is managed by properly using redundancy?

(*d*) Why does it become difficult to predict the response time of transactions?

(*e*) Explain briefly what do you understand by rollback and recovery.

(*f*) How can fault-tolerant communication be achieved in the presence of link and node failures?

(*g*) Explain how absolute and relative consistency differs.

(*h*) What is hierarchical round robin protocol?

(*i*) How are contention cased protocols different from random access protocols?

(*j*) What is EDF algorithm used for?

Section–B (4 × 5 = 20)

2. Suppose that a system is in an unsafe state. Show that it is possible for the processes to complete their execution without entering a deadlock state.
3. Why can't hard real time systems use rollback for error detection/recovery?
4. Explain Time token protocol in detail with a flow chart.
5. Why is the polling latency typically faster than the interrupt latency?
6. Specify the necessity of distinguishing the step system integration involved in real time system design process.

Section–C (2 × 10 = 20)

7. What are the benefits of using a general purpose processor in the case of designing a real time system? In this context, describe the benefits of using a standard single purpose processor instead of using a general purpose one.
8. What do you mean by real time system design process? Why is it important? Specify the requirements involved in real time system design process.
9. By giving state diagram of the fault classes, explain the causes for different types of faults and their remedies. What are the various methods of concurrency control? Which of these may lead to deadlock and why?

REAL TIME SYSTEM (CS - 324) (MAY 2010)

B. Tech (Sem. – 6th)

Paper ID [CS324]

(Please Hit this Paper ID in OMR Sheet)

Time: 03 Hours   Maximum Marks: 60

Instruction to Candidates:

1. Section–A is Compulsory.
2. Attempt any Four questions from Section–B.
3. Attempt any Two questions from Section–C.

Section–A (10 × 2 = 20)

1. (*a*) Define real time systems.
   (*b*) Correlate cost functions with real time systems.
   (*c*) Write two advantages of rate monotonic scheduling.
   (*d*) What are task assignments?
   (*e*) Define token based protocol.
   (*f*) Discuss multihop protocol.
   (*g*) What is the role of interrupts in real time systems?
   (*h*) What are performance measures in real time systems?
   (*i*) What is scheduling analysis?
   (*j*) What are real time languages?

Section–B (4 × 5 = 20)

2. Explain main memory database.
3. What are characteristics of real time systems?
4. Discuss fault tolerant scheduling in detail.
5. What are designing issues in real time systems?
6. What are disadvantages of polled bus protocol?

Section–C (2 × 10 = 20)

7. Compare real time systems with traditional systems in terms of task assignment and scheduling.
8. How concurrency control is done in real time databases?
9. Discuss hierarchical round robin protocol by taking suitable example.

REAL TIME SYSTEM (CS - 324) (DEC 2010)

B. Tech (Sem. – 6th)

Paper ID [CS324]

(Please Hit this Paper ID in OMR Sheet)

Time: 03 Hours Maximum Marks: 60

Instruction to Candidates:

1. Section–A is Compulsory.
2. Attempt any Four questions from Section–B.
3. Attempt any Two questions from Section–C.

Section–A (10 × 2 = 20)

1. (*a*) What are applications of real time system?
   (*b*) Differentiate between real time database and general purpose database.
   (*c*) What is the role of fuzzy logic in real time system?
   (*d*) What is the difference between tightly coupled and hierarchical system?
   (*e*) Discuss important issues in design of real time system.
   (*f*) What is the concept of deadline based protocols?
   (*g*) How hardware real time scheduler is different from other real time schedulers?
   (*h*) Discuss multihop protocol.
   (*i*) What are the advantages of integration of real time and knowledge-based systems?
   (*j*) Define hard real time systems.

Section–B (4 × 5 = 20)

2. Explain the concept of periodic and aperiodic tasks with the help of suitable examples.
3. How the performance of a real time system can be evaluated? Discuss the different properties that evaluating parameter should have.
4. Explain the architecture of a real time system. How can you classify the tasks for the real time systems?
5. Explain which type of real-time kernel would be most appropriate for the following systems and why: an air traffic control system, a batch update system, a video arcade system.
6. Discuss fault tolerant scheduling. What are its different advantages over other scheduling algorithms?

Section–C (2 × 10 = 20)

7. Discuss in detail the token-based protocol for communication in real time systems.
8. What is the advantage of executing concurrent transactions? Discuss in detail the different concurrency control approaches used for real time system.
9. Discuss different protocols used for real time communication.

REAL TIME SYSTEM (CS - 324) (MAY 2009)

B. Tech (Sem. – 6th)

Paper ID [CS324]

(Please Hit this Paper ID in OMR Sheet)

Time: 03 Hours Maximum Marks: 60

Instruction to Candidates:

1. Section–A is Compulsory.
2. Attempt any Four questions from Section–B.
3. Attempt any Two questions from Section–C.

Section–A **(10 × 2 = 20)**

1. (*a*) Name the architectural requirements for tightly coupled real time systems.
   (*b*) List the important features of ADA useful for real time programming.
   (*c*) How alpha testing is different from beta testing?
   (*d*) Define the term hard real systems.
   (*e*) What is the role of deterministic scheduling?
   (*f*) What is software reliability?
   (*g*) List the advantages of mutihop protocol.
   (*h*) What are main memory databases?
   (*i*) What is the role of neural networks in real time systems?
   (*j*) How a network topology is important for real time communication?

Section–B **(4 × 5 = 20)**

2. Discuss the different architectural issues in designing a real time system.
3. What are purpose of a general purpose database and compare it with real time database?
4. What are advantages and disadvantages of fault tolerant scheduling over other scheduling algorithms?
5. What are periodic and aperiodic tasks? Explain with the help of suitable examples.
6. How the performance of a real time system can be evaluated? Discuss the different properties that evaluating parameter should have.

Section–C **(2 × 10 = 20)**

7. Explain the Rate-Monotonic scheduling algorithm in detail.
8. Explain the difference between contention based protocol and token based protocol.
9. What different procedures are available to control the concurrent transactions in real time systems?

REAL TIME SYSTEM (CS - 324) (DEC 2009)

B. Tech (Sem. – 6th)

Paper ID [CS324]

(Please Hit this Paper ID in OMR Sheet)

Time: 03 Hours | Maximum Marks: 60

Instruction to Candidates:

1. Section–A is Compulsory.
2. Attempt any Four questions from Section–B.
3. Attempt any Two questions from Section–C.

Section–A **(10 × 2 = 20)**

1. (*a*) Define the term hard real systems.
   (*b*) What is the role of deterministic scheduling?
   (*c*) What is the difference between reliable software and software reliability?
   (*d*) What is the role of neural networks in real time systems?
   (*e*) List the advantages of multihop protocol.
   (*f*) What are main memory databases?
   (*g*) How a network topology is important for real time communication?
   (*h*) Give the applications of real time systems.
   (*i*) What is the concept of deadlines based protocols?
   (*j*) How microprocessor based real time scheduler is different from real time schedulers?

Section–B **(4 × 5 = 20)**

2. Explain the architecture of a real time system. How can you classify the tasks for the real time systems?
3. Differentiate between general purpose database and real time database.
4. Write the advantages of fault tolerant scheduling algorithm over other algorithms. Explain this algorithm in detail.
5. Explain the concept of periodic and aperiodic tasks with the help of suitable examples.
6. Write the algorithm for hierarchal round robin protocol.

Section–C **(2 × 10 = 20)**

7. Explain EDF Algorithm in detail.
8. Write and compare between contention based protocol and token-based protocol.
9. How the execution of concurrent transactions can be controlled in real time systems?

REAL TIME SYSTEM (CS - 324) (MAY 2008)

B. Tech (Sem. – 6th)

Paper ID [CS324]

(Please Hit this Paper ID in OMR Sheet)

Time: 03 Hours Maximum Marks: 60

Instruction to Candidates:

1. Section–A is Compulsory.
2. Attempt any Four questions from Section–B.
3. Attempt any Two questions from Section–C.

Section–A **(10 × 2 = 20)**

1. (*a*) How a real time system is different from other computer based systems?

(*b*) "Round Robin Scheduling does not work for the real time applications", comment on the statement.

(*c*) How hard deadlines are performance measures for the real time systems?

(*d*) What is the difference between static priority and dynamic priority algorithms? Give example for each.

(*e*) What do you mean by a Bin Packing algorithm for scheduling?

(*f*) How real time databases are different from the general purpose databases?

(*g*) What do you mean by optimistic concurrency control for real time systems?

(*h*) How a network topology is important for real time communication?

(*i*) What is the principle of Stop and Go Multihop protocol?

(*j*) Give the applications of real time systems.

Section–B **(4 × 5 = 20)**

2. Explain the architecture of a real time system. How can you classify the tasks for the real time systems?

3. What are the performance measures for real time systems? Discuss the properties that the different performance measures should have.

4. Discuss fault tolerant scheduling. What are its different advantages over other scheduling algorithms?

5. Write short note on main memory databases.

6. Discuss the different architectural issues in designing a real time system.

Section–C **(2 × 10 = 20)**

7. Explain Earliest Deadline First (EDF) algorithm in detail.

8. How the execution of concurrent transactions can be controlled in real time systems? Discuss with the help of suitable examples.

9. Discuss in detail the token-based protocol for communication in real time systems.

REAL TIME SYSTEM (CS - 324) (DEC 2008)

B. Tech (Sem. - 6th)

Paper ID [CS324]

(Please Hit this Paper ID in OMR Sheet)

Time: 03 Hours Maximum Marks: 60

Instruction to Candidates:

1. Section–A is Compulsory.
2. Attempt any Four questions from Section–B.
3. Attempt any Two questions from Section–C.

Section–A **(10 × 2 = 20)**

1. (*a*) How can you classify the tasks for a real time system?
   (*b*) How performability is a performance measure for real time systems?
   (*c*) What is the difference between static priority and dynamic priority algorithms? Give example for each.
   (*d*) What do you mean by response time predictability?
   (*e*) What do you mean by pessimistic concurrency control?
   (*f*) How network topology is important for real time communication?
   (*g*) What is the concept for deadline based protocol?
   (*h*) What is MOS?
   (*i*) Give the applications of real time systems.

Section–B **(4 × 5 = 20)**

2. Explain the architecture of a real time system. How can you classify the tasks for the real time systems?
3. How the performance of a real time system can be evaluated? Discuss the different properties that evaluating parameters should have.
4. Write the advantages of fault tolerant scheduling algorithm over other algorithms. Explain this algorithm in detail.
5. Write short note on databases for hard real time systems
6. Discuss the different architectural issues in designing a real time system.

Section–C **(2 × 10 = 20)**

7. Explain Rate Monotonic Algorithm (RM) algorithm in detail.
8. What is the advantage of executing concurrent transactions? Discuss in detail the different concurrency control approaches used for real time systems.
9. Discuss different communication protocol used in real time systems.

REAL TIME SYSTEM (CS - 324) (MAY 2007)

B. Tech (Sem. – 6th)

Paper ID [CS324]

(Please Hit this Paper ID in OMR Sheet)

Time: 03 Hours Maximum Marks: 60

Instruction to Candidates:

1. Section–A is Compulsory.
2. Attempt any Four questions from Section–B.
3. Attempt any Two questions from Section–C.

Section–A (10 × 2 = 20)

1. (*a*) What are important characteristics of real time systems?
   (*b*) Define the term hard real systems.
   (*c*) How microprocessor based real time scheduler is different from real time schedulers?
   (*d*) What is the role of deterministic scheduling?
   (*e*) List the important features of ADA useful for real time programming.
   (*f*) Name the architectural requirements for tightly coupled real time systems.
   (*g*) What is the difference between reliable software and software reliability?
   (*h*) Give the advantages of integration of real time and knowledge based systems.
   (*i*) How alpha testing is different from beta testing?
   (*j*) What is the role of neural networks in real time systems?

Section–B (4 × 5 = 20)

2. Explain the concept of periodic and aperiodic tasks with the help of suitable examples.
3. Give an overview of value based schedulers.
4. Write Euclid's algorithm in ADA using recursion.
5. Give the design procedure for an interrupt drive GEM.
6. Discuss the role of fuzzy logic in detail in real time knowledge based system.

Section–C (2 × 10 = 20)

7. Design a real time system, which models the operation of an automobile. The Simulator consists of the following sub-systems.
   (*a*) Steering
   (*b*) Breaking
   (*c*) Acceleration
   (*d*) Dashboard display
8. (*a*) Give an overview of TMR systems.
   (*b*) Explain which type of real time kernel would be most appropriate for the following systems and why? Navigation system, Airline reservation system, Nuclear power station.
9. (*a*) What do you mean by the term arbitration scheme?
   (*b*) Write the ring buffer read and write procedure in ADA.

REAL TIME SYSTEM (CS - 324) (DEC 2007)

B. Tech (Sem. – 6th)

Paper ID [CS324]

(Please Hit this Paper ID in OMR Sheet)

Time: 03 Hours Maximum Marks: 60

Instruction to Candidates:

1. Section–A is Compulsory.
2. Attempt any Four questions from Section–B.
3. Attempt any Two questions from Section–C.

Section–A (10 × 2 = 20)

1. (*a*) Write about interrupt handling process in a multiple interrupt system.

(*b*) Can you describe a computer system that is completely a Real Time System?

(*c*) Differentiate between direct mode addressing & indirect mode addressing.

(*d*) Which is the traditional performance measures used for real time systems?

(*e*) How much scheduling is important in Real Time Systems?

(*f*) What are main memory databases?

(*g*) List the advantages of multihop protocol.

(*h*) What are the hard deadlines mentioned for real time systems?

(*i*) Mention concurrency control issues related to real time databases.

(*j*) Write the disadvantages of pooled bus protocol.

Section–B (4 × 5 = 20)

2. What system considerations are required in designing real time system?

3. Write using example Compare, Jump & Subroutine instructions.

4. Which language provide for some sort of GOTO statement? Does the GOTO statement affect real time performance? How?

5. Differentiate between classical uniprocessor scheduling and fault tolerant scheduling.

6. Differentiate between general purpose database and Real Time database.

Section–C (2 × 10 = 20)

7. Write and compare between contention based protocol and token-based protocol.

8. What are the architectural issues must be considered in designing the communication protocols for real time system?

9. Write the algorithm for hierarchal round robin protocol.

REAL TIME SYSTEM (CS - 324) (MAY 2005)

B. Tech (Sem. – 6th)

Paper ID [CS324]

(Please Hit this Paper ID in OMR Sheet)

Time: 03 Hours Maximum Marks: 60

Instruction to Candidates:

1. Section–A is Compulsory.
2. Attempt any Four questions from Section–B.
3. Attempt any Two questions from Section–C.

Section–A (10 × 2 = 20)

1. (*a*) How a real time system is different from other computer based systems?

(*b*) "Round Robin Scheduling does not work for the real time applications", comment on the statement.

(*c*) How hard deadlines are performance measures for the real time systems?

(*d*) What is the difference between static priority and dynamic priority algorithms? Give example for each.

(*e*) What do you mean by a Bin Packing algorithm for scheduling?

(*f*) How real time databases are different from the general purpose databases?

(*g*) What do you mean by optimistic concurrency control for real time systems?

(*h*) How a network topology is important for real time communication?

(*i*) What is the principle of Stop and Go Multihop protocol?

(*j*) Give the applications of real time systems.

Section–B (4 × 5 = 20)

2. Explain the architecture of a real time system. How can you classify the tasks for the real time systems?

3. What are the performance measures for real time systems? Discuss the properties that the different performance measures should have.

4. Discuss fault tolerant scheduling. What are its different advantages over other scheduling algorithms?

5. Write short note on main memory databases.

6. Discuss the different architectural issues in designing a real time system.

Section–C (2 × 10 = 20)

7. Explain Earliest Deadline First (EDF) algorithm in detail.

8. How the execution of concurrent transactions can be controlled in real time systems? Discuss with the help of suitable examples.

9. Discuss in detail the token-based protocol for communication in real time systems.

REAL TIME SYSTEM (CS - 324) (DEC 2005)

B. Tech (Sem. – 6th)

Paper ID [CS324]

(Please Hit this Paper ID in OMR Sheet)

Time: 03 Hours Maximum Marks: 60

Instruction to Candidates:

1. Section–A is Compulsory.
2. Attempt any Four questions from Section–B.
3. Attempt any Two questions from Section–C.

Section–A **(10 × 2 = 20)**

1. (*a*) Write about interrupt handling process in a multiple interrupt system.
   (*b*) Can you describe a computer system that is completely a real time system?
   (*c*) Differentiate between direct mode addressing and indirect mode addressing.
   (*d*) Which is the traditional performance measures used for real time systems?
   (*e*) How much scheduling is important in real time systems?
   (*f*) What are main memory databases?
   (*g*) List the advantages of multihop protocol.
   (*h*) What are the hard deadlines mentioned for real time systems?
   (*i*) Mention concurrency control issues related to real time databases.
   (*j*) Write the disadvantages of pooled bus protocol.

Section–B **(4 × 5 = 20)**

2. What system considerations are required in designing real time system?
3. Write using example Compare, Jump and Subroutine instructions.
4. Which language provide for some sort of GOTO statement? Does the GOTO statement affect Real Time performance? How?
5. Differentiate between classical uniprocessor scheduling and fault tolerant scheduling.
6. Differentiate between general purpose database and real time database.

Section–C **(2 × 10 = 20)**

7. Write and compare between contentions based protocol and token-based protocol.
8. What are the architectural issues must be considered in designing the communication protocols for real time system?
9. Write the algorithm for hierarchal round robin protocol.

Index